GREAT SCOT

GREAT SCOT

THE JAMES SCOTLAND SYMON STORY

DAVID LEGGAT

BLACK & WHITE PUBLISHING

First published 2012
by Black & White Publishing Ltd
29 Ocean Drive, Edinburgh EH6 6JL

1 3 5 7 9 10 8 6 4 2   12 13 14 15

ISBN: 978 1 84502 473 4

Typeset by Ellipsis Digital Ltd, Glasgow
Printed and bound by ScandBook, AB, Sweden

For my dad, Andrew Leggat (1922–1970),
and my grandad, David Buchanan (1903–1987).
The two finest men I have ever known.

CONTENTS

ACKNOWLEDGEMENTS

The list of people who have helped in both a practical way and with words of encouragement is almost endless. I'd like to start with a moment to remember those who are no longer with us and whose interviews in the past have been invaluable, particularly Bobby Shearer, with whom I spent many a happy hour. Willie Waddell, one of my dad's great heroes, belied his gruff image, especially during one interview when he was kindness personified. Bob McPhail, a great favourite of my grandad's, was a treat to talk to too. All three were great Rangers men.

Jim Baxter was the man I idolised when growing up and the many long afternoons and evenings I spent with him gave me a grasp of what that era inside Ibrox was like. Alex Willoughby, a great Ranger despite the many disappointments he suffered under Scot Symon, was another sadly taken far too early, whose friendship with me allowed me to put much into context. To them, all the others who have gone, whose stories I have called on, I pause in memory.

In the here and now, Scotland's oldest working sports writer, Rodger Baillie, now in his seventies, was invaluable in helping to paint a picture of Scot Symon the man, as well as the manager.

Brian Scott, another of the 'old' hacks brigade, who writes the

ix

superb Scott on Saturday column in the *Scottish Daily Mail*, provided some top-class memories too.

Colin Jackson's memories of Berwick were an important and missing piece of that particular jigsaw and how the defeat came about.

Stephen Halliday of *The Scotsman*, who I've known since he was a teenager, and who is still stick thin, though now topped by a grey instead of a black thatch, was always willing to listen to my ramblings when I needed to talk over what I wanted to do. While another reporter the Scottish media is fortunate to have and another who I have known since he was just a big skinny laddie, the *Daily Record*'s Gary Ralston, negotiated internet research on my behalf, which would have had me tearing my last remaining strands of hair out. As did freelance Mark Walker, whose research confirmed my memories of the day Scot Symon was sacked.

For statistics, the many books written by the publisher of the Rangers historian, Robert McElroy, were invaluable. He is the author of many books about many aspects of the Ibrox club and he had his dinner interrupted more than once by phone calls from me begging extra details, requests he was pleased to answer generously.

Robert Reid, Mr Partick Thistle, whose association with the Firhill club where Symon spent the last years of his career goes back more than sixty years, gave me his time, his records and his recollections of Symon in a generous-spirited way. Just as I predicted he would.

Also, particular thanks to the last major signing made by Scot Symon, Sir Alex Ferguson. Despite his heavy schedule at Manchester United, Sir Alex took time to help me with many of his recollections and views about Symon. Thanks also to well-known Glasgow entertainment enterprenuer James Mortimer, who paved the way to Fergie for me.

To them all, a hearty and heartfelt thanks. And, of course, to anyone I have missed, an apology coupled with a collective thank you.

But I'd like to add a particular thank you to Alex Gordon. Big Alex was my sports editor on the *Sunday Mail* in the days when it sold almost a million every week. He was the best sports editor I have ever worked for. As ever, his keen subbing eye and even keener eye for detail and syntax saved me from myself – more than once.

Alex, though, is only one half of the Gordon partnership. His long-suffering wife, Gerda, an IT wizard, ensured that everything I wrote and big Alex subbed, was well backed up, thus releasing two codgers from worrying that the Scot Symon biography would fly off into the ether and land in the inbox of some startled sub editor on the back of beyond Bugle.

If there are faults in what follows, they are mine.

1

THE BEGINNING OF THE END

WHEN, on Saturday, 26 April 1964, he watched his captain Bobby Shearer, raised shoulder high, brandishing the Scottish Cup for the third successive season to complete the clean sweep of Cup, League Cup and title – the Treble – there is no record of what Scot Symon was thinking. That day, ten years after he had returned to Rangers as manager to succeed Bill Struth, was the crowning glory of his decade in charge. But, given the success that he had managed Rangers to in the previous three seasons and the age of the team he had shaped, there was little to suggest the period of dominance Symon's Rangers were enjoying would not last for many years.

However, despite Symon's natural reticence, robbing posterity of what he thought, one of the men who was closest to Symon at that time, Bobby Shearer, revealed his own thoughts on what lay ahead. Shearer was only thirty-two, yet the Scottish Cup final of 1964, when he skippered Rangers to a 3-1 win over Dundee, was to be his last shot at glory. He played only four more matches. Many years later when I interviewed him, Shearer recalled his thoughts after the dust had settled on season 1963-64, and he freely admitted that he did not see what was coming for himself or for Rangers. Shearer recalled, 'We were not an old team and there was no reason that I could see that the side would break up. Jimmy Millar hadn't had his thirtieth birthday, and Ralph Brand was only twenty-seven. John Greig was a young man and so were Ronnie McKinnon. Willie Henderson and Davie Wilson. Jim Baxter was only twenty-four. All of them were at their peak. There was competition, too, from youngsters Alex Willoughby and Jim Forrest, while Eric Caldow was expected back the next season after being out for a year recovering from a broken leg.

'I remember talking to Ralphy at the Cup-winning party and we both agreed that the team was better than ever. We had won the League and Cup double the year before and there was no doubt in anybody's mind that we had actually improved. In fact, one of the things in our mind was that maybe we could do something in the European Cup the following season.

'That wasn't just nonsense either. It was realistic. As far as Scotland was concerned, there was nobody to touch us. Dundee had had their moment a couple of years earlier, but their championship team had broken up. Hearts didn't have as good a team as they had four years earlier and Hibs were not seen as a threat.

'As for Celtic, well, they really were never in our thoughts as serious challengers. We seemed to be able to beat them every time we played and in 1963-64 we had played them five times and won all five.

'Symon wasn't a man to go in for speeches, so you had to guess what he was thinking. I can't recall him saying anything more than a few words at the Cup banquet, but I'm pretty sure he was thinking the same as I was, that the team was good for a good few more years of winning trophies in Scotland and maybe even doing something big in Europe. Symon had never really been fully accepted by those Rangers supporters who had grown up and lived through the Struth years, and I think that hurt him a bit, though he never spoke about it. That just was not his way at all.

'But I do know there were some of those older fans who had started coming round to Symon when we won the Double in 1962-63, and more became convinced when we won the Treble. The football we played couldn't have done anything else but convince them. Baxter was a genius, while Millar and Brand were devastating together, and there was plenty of excitement on both wings with wee Willie and Wilson.

'Those older supporters who liked power were happy at John Greig's emergence. He had the sort of strength and ruggedness they had loved watching when Struth was around. So what was there for us to worry about?'

Certainly, everything Shearer told me when we spoke a quarter of a century later, conformed to what I thought when, as a teenager, I returned from the excitement of watching two late goals win an epic Scottish Cup final. It was the third successive year I had been to Hampden to watch Rangers lift the Scottish Cup. And the only thing that had changed in the two years since the start of that three-in-a-row run – a 2-0 win over St Mirren – was that Rangers had become better.

For the generation who had grown up supporting Symon's Rangers there was, in April 1964, no reason to suppose the club would not go on and continue to eclipse all others as regularly as Struth's teams had done for thirty-four years. After all, Symon was about to celebrate only his fifty-third birthday three weeks after watching his team climb Scottish football's summit. And when a matter of six months later, with season 1964-65 only eight weeks old, Symon was back at Hampden watching his Rangers beat Celtic 2-1 in the Scottish League Cup final, all of that confidence seemed entirely justified.

Symon had been forced into changes, with Henderson out with bunion trouble, meaning the break up of the Millar and Brand partnership, with Brand moving to the right wing and

Millar dropping deeper and Jim Forrest in at centre-forward. Baxter donned the number ten shirt, but it made no difference. He supplied two trademark passes to put Forrest in for the two goals.

The 2-1 scoreline actually does not paint a true picture of a game. Those of us who were at it remember it as being a fairly comfortable triumph for Rangers. There had been a surprising 3-1 loss to Celtic at Parkhead in September and many Ibrox supporters feared that injuries would take their toll at Hampden. But, with Baxter at his best, normal service was resumed. The season 1964-65 League Cup victory followed the 1963-64 Treble, which in turn had followed the 1962-63 Double into the Ibrox trophy room, meaning six successive trophies had been won by Rangers. It seemed, taking into account the way they had coped with injuries, that there was not a cloud on the Rangers' horizon. But if Symon felt any complacency, or even satisfaction, his and Rangers' world was soon to start crumbling.

It took just three weeks from the Scottish League Cup final win over Celtic for the first storm cloud to burst over Symon in faraway Vienna, when Baxter suffered a broken leg. And it wasn't long before the first real threat to a Baxterless Symon's reign as Scottish football's manager supreme emerged, with the return to Celtic as manager of their former captain and reserve team coach, Jock Stein.

2

SYMON AND THE DEEDLE

THERE was probably nobody else in football who was as close to Scot Symon as Willie Waddell, which is why, way back when I first had the germ of the idea to write this book, I took the chance to get Deedle, as he was known throughout the game, to talk about a man who was his team-mate, his manager, and then, when he became the chief football writer on the *Scottish Daily Express*, one his best contacts.

Waddell had the reputation of being a spikey character who was awkward and who could be brusque to the point of rudeness. When we met in the hospitality suite at Ibrox named after him, he was none of those things. The purpose of my interview was to provide a piece for the Rangers match-day magazine in which Waddell recalled his playing career with Rangers. This was during the time when Graeme Souness was transforming the club in a way that met with Waddell's approval. However, Waddell's association with Rangers also, of course, encompassed his time as manager, general manager and managing director. He had given up his job at the *Express* when Rangers needed him. Two years after Symon was sacked, and when it became clear his youthful successor, Davie White, could not compete with Jock Stein, Waddell answered the SOS. At that point I broached the subject of Symon, and to start with, Waddell was clearly lost in misty memories of some great games in which the two of them – colleagues under Bill Struth for nine years – had played at a time when Rangers rolled over everyone on their way to silverware.

Waddell, recalling the Scot Symon he got to know when they shared a dressing room, observed, 'People always said that he was aloof and reserved as a manager, but the truth is he was just a quiet man who was shy. He didn't make friends easily and didn't talk unless he had something to say. I liked him from the start. In fact, we were probably drawn to each other because we were the new boys in the team. The dressing room was full of legends who had been around forever. There was Jerry Dawson, Dougie Gray, Jimmy Simpson, Alec Venters and Bob McPhail. Willie Thornton was the other new boy and he and I struck up a friendship which lasted way after the football ended.

'We both got on well and were pals, but Scot was never like that. You could not get close to him. But he could play all right. He was just the sort of player old Struth loved. He had real Rangers style. Scot played with his head up and was an old fashioned left-half. His job was to tackle, win the ball and then pass it. In those days Rangers liked to play at a high tempo and Symon was perfectly suited to that.

'Of course the way players tackled in the Thirties was a lot harder than you would get away with in the modern game, but even by the standards of the day, Symon's tackling was fierce. When he hit an opponent that opponent stayed hit. And then he would pass it. Long low passes of sixty yards or more up the inside-left channel to McPhail, down the left wing or diagonally to me on the right.

'When Scot got the ball I knew it was time to get ready to move and I got on the end of many of those passes and crossed for Thornton to get a headed goal. Waddell and Thornton was the double act the press and the fans went on about. But it was really a trio, with Symon the third man.'

But what about how Symon thought about the game? Did Waddell, who proved to be a shrewd and astute student of football, ever see any signs in Symon which hinted that one day he would return to Ibrox as manager?

Waddell said that there were so many players who Struth regarded as what were known back then as his 'gaffers' on the park, that Symon was well down the list of names. Waddell went on, 'We all thought the old man would go on forever and when Scot left in 1947 nobody in the dressing room saw the need to start thinking about a new manager even though Struth was seventy-one years old. Remember that a couple of years later Rangers won the first-ever Treble, or the Triple Crown as it was called then.'

Waddell's recollections some forty years after the events were accurate, but things changed a couple of years later as time started to catch up with Struth. The dressing room was ageing and the manager no longer had the same influence, with season 1953-54 showing that Struth's time as manager, stretching back to 1920, was coming to an end.

The previous season had seen a typical Rangers roar of defiance. After having been the 1950 champions, they finished a distant second to the Hibernian side of the Famous Five forward line in 1951 and 1952. Somehow, even with Struth ailing, the Rangers dressing room, overloaded with veterans which contained Waddell, Willie Woodburn, George Young and Thornton, managed to hold off Hibs a year later to win the Scottish Championship by the old-style goal average.

In truth, it was a last parting shot from the era of the Ibrox Iron Curtain and fitting, perhaps, that while Hibernian's Famous Five scored more goals, Rangers' resolute defence conceded fewer and took the title. Struth soldiered on, unable to give up his grip on the most important thing in his life, Rangers.

Waddell recalled, 'Old Struth was really just that by then. The Old Man had serious health problems and had not the vigour to replace Thornton, who was at the end, and Tiger Shaw, who had gone. The difference that season to 1951 and 1952 was we were second to Hibs, but in 1954 it was Celtic who were champions and that was a shock to everyone at Ibrox. You had to go way back to 1938 to find the last time that had happened.

'It was really only then that the talk really started about who was going to be the new Rangers manager. I know it's hard to understand, but back then a lot of players were only part-time. I had trained as a journalist on the Glasgow *Evening Citizen* and worked on the sports desk. The funny thing was that I learned more from colleagues there and journalists on other newspapers about what was going on with Rangers than I did from inside Ibrox.

'There were a number of names being quoted, all of them former Rangers players. At the time it was unthinkable that anyone who hadn't played for Rangers could possibly become manager. Even though Struth had never played football, he had been the Rangers trainer before becoming manager and one school of thought was that Jimmy Smith, who had been a legend when he played for Rangers and who was the Old Man's trainer, would follow in the same footsteps.

'But the favourite was Davie Meiklejohn. Even today there are old-timers who believe Meek was the best player Rangers have had and the greatest captain. He had been doing well enough as Partick Thistle manager and his name figured in a number of newspapers. The trouble was Meiklejohn was fond of a drink and the fact was well known. Struth had known about it for years and it was something that stood against Meiklejohn ever succeeding the Old Man.

'But he did still have a close relationship with Struth. The two talked in a way the old man never spoke to any of his former players. And it was when I was speaking to Meiklejohn that I first heard Symon's name. Meiklejohn told me that Struth had spoken to Symon when he retired as a player and went to take over as manager of East Fife, who were in the Second Division, in the summer of 1947. Struth had told Symon to keep in touch and promised he would keep a special eye on how his career as a manager was going.

'Those of us who had been around Ibrox for long enough knew that it was Struth's dearest wish to do one last thing for Rangers and appoint the man he believed could best succeed him.'

According to Willie Waddell, when I spoke to him in 1987, from the moment Davie Meiklejohn revealed that story to him in the spring of 1954, he knew Scot Symon would be the new manager of Rangers.

3

IN THE BEGINNING

THE James Scotland Symon story began at eleven-thirty on the evening of 9 May 1911 in a house called Viewbank in the Perthshire village of Errol, not far from Perth. His dad was also James Scotland Symon and his mother was Isabella, neé Bruce. Scot Symon's background was modest. His dad, like his father before him, was a roads contractor, and his mum had been a domestic servant.

The world Symon was born into over a century ago was a hard one for many in the second decade of the twenty-first century to understand. George V had ascended to the throne as King–Emperor the previous year and His Majesty's government presided over a British Empire which encompassed a quarter of the world's land mass.

At Ibrox, Rangers, under manager William Wilton, had won the Scottish Championship in the spring of 1911, four points clear of Aberdeen. Falkirk were third, Partick Thistle fourth and Celtic a distant fifth, eleven points behind Rangers. Wilton was the supreme ruler of all he surveyed, and when the Symon family of Errol celebrated baby Scot's first birthday a year later, Wilton's Rangers were crowned champions again. Bill Struth had not long become the trainer at Clyde and it was not until after Symon's third birthday that the man who was to have such an impact and influence on his career and life arrived at Ibrox. Struth became manager in 1920 after the tragic drowning of Wilton.

James Scotland Symon's parents had married in the Established Church of Scotland in Inver, Little Dunkeld, on 29 December 1899 when Queen Victoria was still on the throne. James Scotland Symon senior's father was Peter Symon and his grandmother on his father's side was Margaret. His maternal grandfather, Isabella's father, was John Bruce, who worked as a labourer.

With two James Scotland Symons in the one house, it was not long before his mum started calling the younger by an abbreviation of his middle name and old family name on his father's side, Scotland. From that day until now, James Scotland Symon was styled Scot Symon – with one 't'.

Symon's early years were spent at the local primary school where he showed enough intelligence and aptitude in the classroom to start on the path, as so many from humble backgrounds had done thanks to Scotland's then much-envied education system, as a typical lad o' pairts, by winning a place at the highly-regarded Perth Academy. Life in the early 1920s must have been tough for the teenage Symon, travelling back and forth from Errol to Perth, studying and showing his teachers he had an aptitude for sport. Academically, Symon was above average, without ever giving any indication that he would go on to university. Technical subjects appeared to be his strength, with veteran sports journalist, Rodger Baillie, who knew Symon, believing a career as an architect would have followed for the Perthshire lad if football had not beckoned.

Perth Academy was not the place for Symon's football skills to be nurtured, as its preferred winter game was one which uses the oval ball. There is no record of Symon ever showing any interest in rugby, though the school's summer game, cricket, was one he took to and he developed a love affair with the sport, becoming an international class bowler capped by Scotland.

But the football field was where the teenage Scot Symon really stood out and where even the then quiet young man could really express himself. His first club was Perth West End, a juvenile side, and although one of the youngest players in the team, he was soon spotted by one of the east coast's Junior giants, Dundee Violet. He was still just nineteen when he made the step up to senior when Dundee made him a full-time professional footballer, and he enjoyed five seasons at Dens Park, maturing into an outstanding left-half.

It was during this period in the first half of the 1930s that Symon was first brought to the attention of Bill Struth. Struth liked what he saw. In fact, Symon was everything Struth looked for in a Ranger. He was tough, he was competitive, he never squealed, he could tackle and he could pass with pace and accuracy. And off the field he was a quiet, dignified type, of the sort Struth believed should represent Rangers. But he did not move to sign Symon, simply because there was no vacancy in the team for him. George Brown was the Rangers left-half and was the best in that position in Scotland, if not in all of Britain. Ahead of Brown, at inside-left, there was another of the true greats from the Ibrox Hall of Fame, Bob McPhail.

So when Symon made the step up, it was not to Rangers. Instead, the twenty-four-year-old, and as yet unmarried, Scot Symon left Dundee and headed for the south coast of England to sign for Portsmouth. Fate can be a strange thing. For it was in Portsmouth that Symon met and married Doreen, the wife who was to become the bedrock of his life and who he returned home to in bad times to take refuge from the slings and arrows which came his way. Family life, as we will discover, was what Symon lived for when he was not attending to the needs of

Rangers. It sustained him to attend to those needs so success-fully after he became manager. So, perhaps if Struth had decided to sign Symon in 1935, even though he didn't need him, his life would have been very different. As well as not meeting and marrying Doreen, he may not have been given the chance at Ibrox to become the much-admired player he did become, or to work so closely for so long with Struth, giving the Old Man time to watch and assess Symon, eventually leading to him being the chosen one when it came time to find someone to be named by Struth as his successor.

Struth's side, which had reigned from the mid-1920s, was begin-ning to grow old. Captain Davie Meiklejohn had gone, centre-half Jimmy Simpson was showing signs of wear and tear, Bob McPhail was nearing the end, as was the elegant George Brown. It was time to rebuild. Struth had not forgotten Scot Symon, and the player needed no persuading to join the team which, even as a youngster, had always meant something special to him, even though there is no record of him visiting Ibrox to watch them. In those days such a journey was beyond a young man from a modest background and, anyway, Symon was too busy playing.

He did, though, have to convince Doreen to leave her home, but when she saw how much the move meant to her husband, it is unlikely Mrs Symon put up too much resistance. Symon signed for Rangers and made his debut in a 3-3 draw away to Arbroath on 24 September 1938.

The first Rangers team Scot Symon was ever associated with was: Dawson; Gray and Shaw; Symon, Simpson and Brown; Main, Smith, Thornton, McPhail and Kinnear. The new guard was forming, with Jock Shaw at left-back and Willie Thornton at centre-forward, while Symon would soon switch to left-half and Willie Waddell burst on the scene as an awesome outside-right.

Symon and Waddell formed a lifelong friendship, the two new Rangers men sharing a flat near Ibrox until Symon could arrange for more suitable accommodation for his wife and family and bring them up from England. It was therefore fitting that in the last weeks of Symon's life, his old Ibrox friend Waddell was able to broker what was at least a partial reconciliation between Symon, who had served Rangers so well, and the club which had treated him so shabbily in the autumn of 1967.

A number of those who played with Symon, as the 1930s gave way to the war years and Bill Struth's Rangers marched on at the very top, unchallenged in Scottish football, will testify to Symon's outstanding playing ability. But it is interesting to take note of the view of one great Ranger who was departing as the guard changed, but whose career at Ibrox overlapped with Symon's by one season. All too often in these days of mangled and cheapened language, the word 'legend' is bandied about carelessly. But it was never better used than when it was the title of Bob McPhail's memoirs, *Legend: Sixty Years at Ibrox*. McPhail remembered, 'Scot was already an experienced player when he signed for Rangers in September 1938 and he played behind me for my last season. He was a hard player and a great passer of the ball. He drove the ball hard to your feet. He always seemed to deliver the ball on the ground, making it easy for you to take quick control of it and do what you had to do with it.'

Symon won his only cap for Scotland in a 1-1 draw with Austria in Vienna and helped to make it a fitting farewell season for McPhail, as Rangers won the championship in season 1938-39, the last before the world was engulfed by war as Britain fought for survival and for the freedom of the world. Football was restructured on a regional basis, with a league continuing and the Scottish Cup replaced by the Southern League Cup. In the first season after war broke out, Rangers competed in the

Scottish Regional League, which they won. The next six seasons it was the Southern League Championship and it was won every year. Three Southern League Cups were also hoisted, plus, as Britain celebrated winning the war, the Victory Cup in 1946.

By the time football was back to normal, Symon was thirty-five years old and was beginning to feel the pace. It was very much business as usual for Rangers, as they won the first peace-time title, but once again Struth was changing the guard, with Bobby Brown replacing Jerry Dawson in goal, Willie Woodburn secure at centre-half and Ian McColl starting to make an impact after his move from Queen's Park. Sadly for Symon, the ten league games he played did not qualify him for a medal when Rangers were duly crowned kings of Scotland.

Symon's last appearance was on the final day of the season, 12 April 1947, a 4-0 win over Hamilton Accies at Ibrox. He hung up his boots and left Ibrox to become the manager of East Fife. Scot Symon may have thought that was him finished with Rangers, but the grand Old Man of Ibrox, Bill Struth, had other ideas.

4

FIRST STEPS AS A BOSS

SCOT SYMON'S managerial journey began in the summer of 1947 in the humble surroundings of Methil, with East Fife of the Second Division. Bayview must have been a bleak place then and in direct contrast to what Symon had known at Ibrox. I visited the old ground a couple of times in the mid-1990s and spent some time in the almost claustrophobic cupboard which passed as the manager's office at the time when Steve Archibald was in charge.

It was a somewhat strange feeling to be sitting in that wee dookit with a man who had once played for Barcelona, knowing that it was here that one of the greatest managers in Scottish football history, Scot Symon, started to cut his teeth as a boss. The old Bayview was a rundown and dingy enough old ground by the 1990s, so it is only fair to imagine what it was like in those austere immediate post-war years when everything in Britain which had not been connected with the war effort was run down and dirty after a six-year struggle for the freedom of the world.

But Symon set about bringing some light, some colour and some drama into the lives of the Fifers who followed East Fife, as the club enjoyed its greatest-ever period. That spell began in Symon's first season in charge when he immediately showed his skill in blending a team and sending it out to cope with the demands of the environment in which it had to compete. Symon liked skilful players, but the old second tier of Scottish football in the 1940s demanded strength. It was a rough and tumble place to play.

Symon's success at coping with this was there for all to see when, at the end of the campaign, played in outposts where hot water was seen as unnecessary luxury during a bitter, biting winter and on bare and bumpy pitches, Symon's side gained promotion to the top flight. But that was only the half of it. For Symon planned and plotted a glory run in the League Cup which saw East Fife, while still in the Second Division, reach the Hampden final of the Scottish League Cup, where they faced Falkirk. The game ended goalless, but in the replay East Fife were unstoppable, winning 4-1 to hoist the silverware. Though goodness knows where they kept the trophy secure at the old Bayview.

It was a remarkable achievement and one which the grand Old Man of Ibrox, Bill Struth, duly noted. He was to continue noting his protégé's success over the next six years. Just a couple of years later and season 1949-50 saw Symon and East Fife back at Hampden to win another League Cup, beating Dunfermline 3-0 in the final. And this time in getting there, Symon, the pupil, actually got one over on Struth, the old master. In the semi-final at Hampden before 74,000 people on 8 October 1949, East Fife defeated Rangers 2-1. One can only imagine the scenes at the old ground after the game, with Struth suffering at the defeat of his beloved Rangers, while at the same time feeling a glow of pride in his protégé's achievement, offering his hand in congratulations. Symon, who revered and respected Struth, must also have felt mixed emotions.

The Rangers team beaten by Symon's side was strong, with a defence so impassable it was known as the Iron Curtain. Also on parade were Willie Waddell, Billy Williamson and Eddie Rutherford up front. But the team Symon had moulded was pretty formidable, with the wonderfully gifted Jimmy Bonthrone pulling the strings; Andy Matthew, later to join Symon at Ibrox, on the left wing; plus Bobby Black and the rock of a centre-half, Willie Finlay. It was Finlay who recalled, 'Symon put the team together and let us play our own game and that was much the style of managers when I played. We all liked him and respected what he knew about football and we knew the team he put together was a good one. In fact, it lasted even after he left the club as we won the League Cup again in season 1953-54 when we beat Partick Thistle in the final.'

Struth did have the final word when it came to duels with the man who was to succeed him. But once again, by taking such a small club as East Fife to the Scottish Cup final in April 1950, Symon showed his increasingly impressive managerial credentials, although this time he finished a loser, with Rangers winning 3-0.

Finlay said, 'We all knew that Symon would not stay for too long at East Fife and there had been talk among the players that he would go to Rangers. Some of us even joked that we hoped if he went there he would take us with him to Ibrox.' However, in the summer of 1953, with Struth ailing and Rangers clearly in need of rejuvenation, a strange thing happened. Symon left East Fife, not to return to Ibrox, but to move to England and become manager of Preston North End. It is reasonable to believe Symon wanted to become manager of Rangers, but after six years of success at East Fife, with no offer from Ibrox, he believed the chance to take over a then top English club was too good to miss.

Circumstances beyond his control, and also beyond the control of the grand Old Man of Ibrox, combined to prevent what would become inevitable, happening twelve months before it actually did. At the time, Struth's health was failing and he had been in and out of hospital, following having had his lower leg amputated, and it is extremely likely that it was during a period of Struth's hospitalisation that Symon was spirited away to England and to Preston North End.

Among the top stars who made Preston an attractive and formidable team in the early 1950s were Scotland wing-half Tommy Docherty and the legendary England forward Tom – later Sir Tom – Finney, the Preston plumber. Many good judges rated him above even Sir Stanley Mathews, as Finney, essentially a right-winger, could also play with great effect on the other wing, plus at inside-forward and at centre-forward. Craig Brown, who was a youngster under Scot Symon at Ibrox before being sold to Dundee, remembers having conversations with Finney about Symon and recalled that the great man had nothing but praise for him. Brown said, 'Sir Tom and Symon no doubt got on very well, for they were both gentlemen, and when you see the sort of players Symon favoured throughout his career as a manager there can be no doubt he enjoyed having a player of such skill as Finney in his team. Sir Tom always spoke very highly of Scot Symon.'

Docherty, too, had praise for Symon, saying, 'He did not go in for shouting at players. He liked to look at what players could play with others in a certain way and put his team together that way. He tended not to interfere too much as far as tactics were concerned. Symon believed that if he had the right players, put together in the right blend, the team would be able to sort things out on the park. Getting the blend was one important lesson I learned from playing under Symon.'

Symon spent just one season in England as Preston North End manager and came within a whisker of adding another trophy to his increasingly impressive managerial CV. Symon steered Proud Preston to the 1954 FA Cup final at Wembley. It is a match which I often heard talked about by West Brom veterans when I worked in the Midlands, and it is a game that, according to the lore in the English Midlands, was one of the most exciting finals of the period, though it is always overshadowed by what had happened the previous season when Blackpool came from behind in the closing minutes to beat Bolton in the mystical Matthews final. But there can be no doubt Preston North End and West Bromwich Albion produced a footballing feast of a final before Symon's team was edged out 3-2.

Symon, though, did not have long on which to dwell on his disappointment. Struth, irritated at missing out the previous summer – and by now far too ill to continue at the Ibrox helm – initiated contact with his former player and James Scotland Symon was soon on the train north to Glasgow, where in June 1954 he became only the third Rangers manager in the club's eighty-two-year-old history.

5

TAKING OVER FROM STRUTH

LOOKING back to the era that came to an end when Bill Struth left after thirty-four years in the manager's chair gives a clue as to why Scot Symon has failed to find such an honoured place in the pantheon of Rangers greats. Especially when so many others who are spoken of with such admiration did not contribute nearly as much to Rangers as did Symon in his thirteen years as manager. For a start, those who had grown up, and even grown old, knowing no other manager than Struth found it hard to accept a successor to the man Rangers players only ever addressed as Mr Struth. It was a point made to me by Willie Waddell when he said, 'There was never any question of us calling him "gaffer" or "boss", and when you were one of the younger players you actually called him "sir", like the headmaster of some exclusive school. In private, he was "Old Struth" or "the Old Man" when we were talking among ourselves and I know that's the way the supporters spoke of him in the last ten years.

'Scot was never going to have that sort of respect. When he arrived there were players who had played with him. Willie Woodburn, George Young and I could hardly go from calling him "Scot", to "Mr Symon". We settled on "boss" and that set the tone for everyone else, so right away there was a different feel to the place.'

It was a point well made by Waddell, but there was something else about the aura of Struth which prevented that generation of Rangers supporters from ever embracing Symon with the same affection and, indeed, adoration. Too much of what he did was compared to how it had been in Struth's day, and supporters of my generation grew up hearing their elders and betters compare Symon's efforts to what Struth had achieved. It was seldom a favourable comparison.

My granddad had started as a regular at Ibrox on returning from fighting in Russia with the Highland Light Infantry, and him becoming a regular coincided with Struth taking over in 1920 and building Rangers into such a formidable force. From season 1920-21 until the end of 1934-35 – a total of fifteen campaigns – Struth's Rangers amassed an amazing twelve Scottish championships. Then, from season 1935-36, when my dad started going to watch Rangers regularly, there were thirteen more years – including wartime – when Rangers won the title in the nineteen years from the start of that period until the Old Man retired. No wonder people of their generation would not hear a word against Bill Struth, and certainly the facts and statistics show just how much he deserved such a favoured place in the affections of so many generations of supporters. However, it was only when I grew to manhood's estate and started looking closely at the concluding years of Struth's reign and at what frankly was the mess Symon inherited with an ageing team and how circumstances, especially the life ban to Willie Woodburn during the new manager's first season, affected things, that I came to realise the truth of the matter.

The press, too, had an inglorious part to play. In today's world, newspapers would soon have pointed out just how bad things had become at Ibrox and the magnitude of the task Symon faced, and, therefore, the level of what he achieved would have become obvious. But he was unlucky in that many supporters from the generations to which my granddad and dad belonged were still regulars at Ibrox long after Symon had gone, and those fans rarely mentioned him. Slowly but surely enough, his contribution to the Rangers story was lost and it was the new generation, attracted by the glamour of the big names from England, signed when Graeme Souness sparked the Rangers revolution, which finally buried Symon's name.

That Souness era was gathering pace at the time I interviewed Waddell, and when I asked him if he thought not enough had been made of the mess Rangers were in at the time Symon took over, he admitted it hadn't been something he had considered before. But there was then, had been before, and certainly is not now, anyone better placed to consider that proposition. As a big-name player, Waddell had enjoyed some of Struth's great managerial years and was still around as the Old Man started to ail and lose his grip. He also worked as a journalist, moved on to manage Kilmarnock to the 1965 Scottish title, became the chief football writer on the then biggest-selling daily newspaper in the country, the *Scottish Daily Express*, before going back to become the Rangers manager who steered the club to its 1972 triumph in the European Cup Winners' Cup and then took a role in the boardroom. So, as well as seeing football from every perspective from the inside, he was also as media savvy as any of the game's modern managers. Waddell said, 'Of course Struth had been ill for some time and could not have the same influence as before, and, equally, the team Symon took over was not as strong as it had been four years before. However, the newspapers didn't make a big thing of it and Scot was not the type of person who would try to make friends with journalists and give them stories in return for favourable write-ups.

'As well as changes in football, there were changes in newspapers too, and a lot of the younger guys who had been overseas fighting during the war had taken over some of the top jobs. They were less respectful and wanted help . . . Scot just would not play the game with them.

'Let me tell you, there's no way I would have kept quiet. I would have been on to a few of the top reporters and let them know quietly that there were plenty of problems left behind. But that was not Scot's way. To be fair, the papers did not give Scot a hard time at the start. However, they never got it across that he had been left with not a lot to work with.

'From the war years, Rangers had been winning, based on counter-attacks. When Churchill made his Iron Curtain speech the newspapers soon started calling the Rangers defence the Ibrox Iron Curtain.' Which means that Walter Smith's crafty tactic of parking the bus, which brought the club so much success in Europe in the first decade of this twenty-first century, was nothing new. Smith had merely adapted Struth's Iron Curtain, the one he no doubt grew up hearing about from his granddad.

The names which rolled off the tongue were: Bobby Brown, George Young, Jock Shaw, Ian McColl, Willie Woodburn and Sammy Cox. It was so good there was even a campaign to play it for Scotland behind an attack of the Hibernian forward line of Gordon Smith, Bobby Johnstone, Lawrie Reilly, Eddie Turnbull and Willie Ormond, known, of course, as the Famous Five. The selectors who picked the Scotland teams in those days never took that piece of advice from the press. Perhaps they should have. In the year Rangers and Hibs tied at the top on forty-three points from thirty games – two points for a win back then – Hibernian's Famous Five bagged an astonishing ninety-three goals, while the Ibrox Iron Curtain conceded only thirty-nine – and that was the formidable defence beginning to wane. When the championship had been won in 1950, with the Iron Curtain at its peak, just twenty-six goals were lost in thirty matches.

But by the time Scot Symon arrived, Brown had been replaced in goal by the much smaller George Niven, Jock Shaw had retired, Sammy Cox was thirty and becoming increasingly prone to injury, while the pivot who held everything together – centre-half Woodburn – was thirty-five and starting to creak. Struth's slipping grip had failed to replace those who had left with players of a similar standard. This re-appraisal of Struth's final years is not meant to be critical of this Grand Old Man of Ibrox, or to take anything away from his many remarkable achievements over such a long period – eighteen Scottish championships from the twenty-eight available, plus all six wartime titles speak for themselves – but as the 1940s moved into the '50s, illness took a grip of Struth. However, his was a generation known for its fortitude and he fought on, refusing to loosen his grip on Rangers. History and the dip in the club's fortunes as far as trophies won during those final years can deliver their own verdict.

But there is one story from that period, told to me by that great Northern Ireland centre-forward who bridged the Struth and Symon years, Billy Simpson, until recently a regular at Ibrox and a man I last spoke to at a supporters' dinner in the summer of 2010. Simpson, recalling the circumstances of his signing for Rangers in 1950, said, 'I came across from Northern Ireland on the old ferry which sailed right into the middle of Glasgow at the Broomielaw and then I got a subway to Ibrox. Struth wasn't there, so I was taken to his flat, which was about five hundred yards away, up a close in Copland Road. He had been very ill and was just out of hospital after having had a leg amputated.'

Simpson's simple story gives a startling insight into just how ill the ageing manager who ran Rangers for the next four years was and explains why Symon inherited a difficult situation. And one which was made even harder when Woodburn, the man who Symon hoped would soldier on and buy him time to rebuild the team, was suspended *sine die*, a ban without limit.

6

THE WOODBURN BLOW

WILLIE WOODBURN never forgave himself for the flare-up which saw him suspended *sine die* and wrecked his friend Scot Symon's plans to build a new Rangers around the presence of this formidable centre-half. Even more than thirty years after that swingeing Scottish Football Association life ban on him, Woodburn was still bitter and also angry with himself. I had gone through to Edinburgh to interview him and, as we sat in the sunshine of a pub garden in the west of the capital, Woodburn, then seventy, still looked lean and craggy, clearly the same man who had dominated the Ibrox Iron Curtain for more than a decade. In fact, big Woodie looked as though he was fit enough to pull the boots back on. So goodness knows how long he could have continued, rock-like at the heart of the Rangers defence, had it not been for the SFA. For he was the man Symon was relying on to shore up the team and allow him time to slowly find and introduce new players. And when the players reported for pre-season training, that is exactly what Symon told his former team-mate.

Woodburn told me, 'When we played together, I liked Scot. He was a good colleague. I know I had the reputation of being a hard man, but there was nobody to match Scot. His tackling was fierce. But he was also a gentleman and that was something he retained when he moved into management. When he arrived back at Ibrox, Scot did not make a big thing about it with the players. There were still plenty in the dressing room with whom he had played, including me, and it could have been awkward. However, those of us who knew him also liked him and we were all keen to help him in his first years.

'I was thirty-five years old and knew I was coming to the end and was exploring the possibility of moving into sports journalism. But when Scot arrived he took me aside for a quiet talk and asked me to give him two years. The thing about Scot was that, although he was quiet to the point of shyness, he could be persuasive when he spoke to you privately in his soft voice. He told me he knew I had always been naturally fit and that I had no weight problems.

'He also explained what he wanted to do and that his plans involved keeping the defence intact for as long as he could. George Young was highly experienced at right-back and Eric Caldow was gaining experience at left-back and had speed. Scot knew that Sammy Cox had injury problems so he wanted me to stay and buy him time.

'He said he did not want to rush into getting a new centre-half and had it in mind to ease Duncan Stanners in from the reserves for a few matches to see if he could be my eventual replacement. There was no way I could turn down Scot so I said I would work even harder at keeping myself fit and if I felt I was still doing myself justice I would play on for another couple of seasons.'

Symon must have been heartened by his old friend's reaction. What history has told us is that the new Rangers manager was no reckless gambler. He was a careful man who moved slowly and in his first season in charge he did not make any major signings. However, the best-laid schemes, etc . . . Symon's carefully laid plans lasted fewer than four matches and were blown apart even before the League season kicked off.

Symon's first match as Rangers manager was a Scottish League Cup sectional tie against Stirling Albion at Annfield on 14 August 1954 and Rangers won 5-0 with goals from Billy Simpson (3) and John Prentice (2). The first Rangers team picked by Scot Symon was (in the old 2-3-5 formation): George Niven; George Young and Johnny Little; Ian McColl, Willie Woodburn and Willie Rae; Willie Waddell, Derek Grierson, Billy Simpson, John Prentice and Billy Liddell. So far, so good. And the League season was not due to start until 11 September, with Rangers scheduled to meet Hibernian and the Famous Five at Ibrox. The easy sweeping aside of Stirling Albion was followed by a 1-1 draw with Partick Thistle at Ibrox, then a 3-1 away loss to Clyde. By that time Symon could see for himself the problems he was facing. He had little notion of just how they would escalate when Stirling Albion visited Ibrox on 28 August. Rangers won 2-0, with Johnny Hubbard (pen) and John Prentice scoring.

But the story of the day was the sending-off of Woodburn. As we sat in that sunny garden in Edinburgh, Woodburn relived that black day for me and said, 'The truth is, I should never really have been playing in the first place, as I had a knee problem and had to have it strapped up. Maybe that is why I lost my temper, because the knee was sore. But I had a short temper and never held back. Whatever, there was no excuse for what I did, especially as the game was won with only a couple of minutes to go.

'Stirling Albion had a player called Alec Paterson, and I think he was maybe trying to make a name for himself. We had been tussling all of the game and the truth is, I was getting a bit fed up with it. Eventually I tackled him, took the ball cleanly, but he locked both his legs around my strapped knee. He knew all about my problems because there had been plenty of stories in the papers about it. At that point, and with the way I was feeling, there was no doubt in my mind that Paterson was deliberately trying to do me damage and I lost my temper and head-butted him. Of course, it was wrong, and, of course, I had to go.'

It was what happened next which incensed Woodburn and shattered Symon's plans for the season. Woodburn had previously been sent off three times in his career, and by today's standards would have got a two, three, or at the most four-game suspension. But when he appeared before the SFA Disciplinary Committee on 14 September, the verdict was *sine die*. Woodburn was never to be allowed to play again. Woodburn said, 'I felt as though I had let down Scot, for I knew how much he was depending on me. The truth is, I have regretted it every day of my life since. I was never able to look Scot in the eye again, although being the gentleman he was, he never had a bad word to say to me about it.'

It is was one of the rare occasions which produced an on-the-record quote from Symon, who had seen Woodburn as the castle he would build around. Symon said, 'I was not allowed to go into the committee room with him, but when the door opened and I saw Willie's face, that one look was enough to tell me the verdict. My own feelings were immediate. I knew what the loss of Woodburn meant and it felt as though the old Castle which sat on the top of the main stand at Ibrox had come tumbling to the ground around my ears.' He may not have said much in public, but that quote proves he could have lived with the best of the modern managerial masters of our soundbite media culture. The new Rangers manager had to re-think and, at first, he tried Woodburn's deputy, Duncan Stanners, who played in the second League game of the season, a 2-0 loss away to champions Celtic.

It wasn't long before Stanners dropped out, with Geordie Young switching from right-back to lend his height and power to the heart of the defence. But the rearguard was seldom settled, with Johnny Little or Eric Caldow in Young's old position, while Sammy Cox stepped back to left-back on the few occasions he was fit, leaving Willie Rae and John Prentice – both of whom were not really up to it – trying to take over from Cox at left-half.

And all the while the spectre of Celtic loomed large, hovering over Symon's shoulder in a way they had not been able to trouble Struth, until his last season. Celtic had not won back-to-back titles throughout Struth's reign and when the second of the two Old Firm matches which were played in those days took place at Ibrox on New Year's Day 1955, a hat-trick from Johnny Hubbard and another goal from Billy Simpson damaged the hopes of Celtic retaining their crown.

But it was not Rangers they were locked in a fight with at the top. It was Aberdeen, who proved too strong and who took the title with forty-nine points from thirty games under the old two-points-for-a-win system, with Celtic runners-up on forty-six points and Rangers in third place with forty-one points.

It is interesting to wonder what would have happened to Symon had Celtic won the New Year game and gathered momentum to take the crown, or had Aberdeen buckled to give Celtic a second successive title. For there had been no consolation for Rangers in either of the Cup competitions. They went out of the League Cup to Motherwell at the quarter-final stage and lost a third-round Scottish Cup tie to Aberdeen.

Symon had not made one signing during his first season as manager, an astonishing contrast to nowadays when a manager arrives and promptly signs at least half a dozen new players. But he had not been inactive. Which was just as well as, with

Woodburn already gone, Waddell, who had managed just thirteen league games, many when only half-fit as he struggled with hamstring problems, and Cox both retired.

Fortunately there was a young right-winger who had just stepped up from junior club Camelon Thistle by the name of Alex Scott. He had made his debut as an eighteen-year-old against Falkirk at Ibrox on 9 March 1955 and immediately lit up the ground with a hat-trick in a 4-1 win. Scott was to be the man looked to do just that – light up Ibrox. For the next few years the manager went around the country using his eye for a player, his nose for a bargain and his shrewd football mind to see how they could all be blended to form a new Rangers.

7

ALEX SCOTT AND
KITCHENBRAND ARRIVE

WHEN I first started being taken to Ibrox by my dad and granddad in the late 1950s, our favourite place – providing one or the other of the two had had a good week with overtime – was the wee enclosure just a few yards or so outside the eighteen-yard line at the Copland Road end. And there was no better vantage point than that to view what, from 1955, had become one of the most exciting sights in Scottish football – Alex Scott dashing down the right wing in a blue blur of speed. 'The Flying Scott' he was known as, with a nod in the direction of the most famous steam locomotive in the world, the *Flying Scotsman*. And I swear that, just like that majestic old engine which snorted steam and bellowed smoke, when Scott took off down the right wing he came as near as is possible for a man to resemble that great old loco of my childhood. In some ways, Alex Scott was the man who did more to establish Scot Symon as the new Rangers manager, as he picked up at the start of Symon's second season, 1955-56, where he had left off when he first burst on the scene as an eighteen-year-old at the tail end of the previous campaign.

Rangers supporters had loved Waddell's dash and power on the right and they had been sad to see their hero's injury-ravaged decline and final demise. But Scott soon took over as the player supporters looked to to get down the touchline and swing the ball across, or cut inside and let loose with a shot. Symon knew when he was on to a good thing and gave the teenage Scott his head. Scott played in all thirty-four league matches, bagging the creditable total for a winger of nine goals, plus he had a hand in so many of the goals bagged by those who thrived on his variety of crosses, such as Billy Simpson, Max Murray and Don Kitchenbrand.

Ah, yes . . . Kitchenbrand. Big Kitchensink. The Rhino. Symon signed the burly, big, wholehearted South African from Delfos in September 1955 and the powerful centre-forward who simply refused to accept there was such a thing as a lost cause quickly split the support right down the middle. I have no recollection of ever having seen this colourful character play, but my granddad would simply laugh whenever the name was mentioned and call him a big haddie. My dad was more generous and just as expressive with the sort of colourful Scots tongue you seldom hear in these more coarse days. To my dad, Kitchenbrand was no more than a breenger, or, in English, someone who just barged into things. Kitchenbrand missed as many as he scored, but Symon once remarked, 'He is always in the right position to miss the chance. I will start worrying when he is no longer in the right position.'

Symon was the first man to use what has become a hoary old pundit's cliché in recent years. But for all that Kitchenbrand's misses were often spectacular, his scoring rate was even more so. Kitchenbrand played in twenty-five of that season's league matches and netted an astonishing twenty-four goals. Those strikes were vital and made a telling contribution to the eighty-five notched by an all-out attacking Rangers team, which amassed fifty-two points to take the title, six points clear of Aberdeen, with Hearts a further point adrift, edging Hibs into fourth spot on goal average and Celtic – a sign of things to come – an irrelevance back in fifth spot, trailing champions Rangers by a massive eleven points. Two points for a win, remember.

Alex Scott recalled that season and said, 'I don't care what anyone said about big Don, I loved him. I was just a laddie and it was all fun for me. Ian McColl was behind me at right-half and he could tackle, use the ball and give it to me at my feet.

'The crowd were very kind to me and when McColl slipped a pass to me I could hear them getting excited and that made me get my head down and push the ball beyond the left-back. I had speed and more often than not could get clear and get the cross over, and big Don terrorised centre-halves and scored a barrowload, and the fans loved it. Even the ones who often laughed at the big man got excited when he hurled himself in, even if my cross had been badly placed. Billy Simpson was another who could turn a not-so-clever cross into a good one.'

When he looked back, Scott realised just how important that second season was to Symon after Rangers had followed an unsuccessful final campaign under Struth, with another under the new manager. You had to go back to the height of the First World War to find the last time Rangers had gone three successive seasons without the title. Scott recalled, 'I was too young to feel pressure from history and I think that was true of some of the other new players – big Don, Max Murray, Sammy Baird and Bobby Shearer – but later on I knew how the old-timers, George Young and McColl, must have felt.' Young, now safely slotted in at centre-half, was the anchor, the link with the past, with tradition and the captain, while there was a variety up front, in the shape of Kitchenbrand and Simpson, who often operated as a modern-style twin striker despite wearing the number eight, which back then was the inside-right, a sort of playmaker and forward all rolled into one.

Max Murray added another – and once again unorthodox – dimension, after being signed from Queen's Park. Murray had a kind of whirlwind style and often seemed to have a problem with his balance. According to my granddad, he scored more goals from a sitting position than he did when standing. The language, while sort of industrial, was tough, a bit more graphic. Murray played golf off scratch and in later life became secretary at Falkirk Golf Club and, again, according to my granddad, for a gowfer he wisnae a bad fitba' player. Or was it the other way around?

But what started to become clear that season was that Symon had a happy knack of signing players who could give his team a short-term boost, while promoting youngsters such as Scott, to give Rangers dash and exuberance and also, planning more long term, with the signing Bobby Shearer for £5,000 from Hamilton which, even in those days was a steal. Shearer gave the team a brilliant boost when, in January he went in at right-back, allowing Eric Caldow to switch to his more favoured position at left-back. Once again Symon showed he knew how to balance the team and keep the books balanced, too. The immediate impact Shearer had trailblazed an Ibrox career which saw him play 407 times, win five championships, three Scottish Cups and three League Cups and go on not only to skipper Rangers, but with his no-nonsense, take-no-prisoners style, win himself that most wonderful of nicknames, 'Captain Cutlass'.

Shearer admitted, 'Of all the things I won with Rangers, that title was the most important, for it was my first honour and also because I knew what it meant to the boss. By the time I made my debut in January 1956, the team was on a great unbeaten run and that day we beat Airdrie 4-0 at Broomfield. As a Hamilton boy, I lapped that up and can remember big Sammy Baird getting a hat-trick and Johnny Hubbard the other. And it wasn't a penalty.'

The unbeaten run Shearer recalled started with a 2-1 win over Falkirk at Brockville on 5 November and did not end until a 2-1 defeat away to East Fife on 9 April. The run encompassed twenty-three matches, with twenty won and three drawn. It launched Rangers right to the brink of glory.

Aberdeen, the champions the previous season, did their best to stay in the Rangers slipstream, but when they visited Ibrox on 18 April they knew their crown had gone. Alex Scott, fittingly, scored the only goal of the game to clinch the championship with three games to spare. With the club's twenty-ninth title secured, Rangers lost two and drew the other of those matches, leaving a slightly distorted picture as far as statistics are concerned. But the season was still pretty impressive. Just four defeats, two after the title was secured, with a goals-against column that the Iron Curtain itself would have been proud of – just twenty-seven – while Hibernian's Famous Five would have been happy to boast of the eighty-five scored.

The Cups had not brought a similar reward, with a narrow 2-1 semi defeat to Aberdeen in the League Cup and a bad day at Tynecastle seeing Hearts win 4-0 in the Scottish Cup quarter-final. The League championship, however, was the prize everyone at Ibrox craved and the prize Symon, in his second season as manager, knew he had to deliver if he was to be given the time to build the Rangers team he dreamed of. It was to be a few years before Scot Symon managed that and there would be times when it must have seemed he would never be widely accepted as a worthy successor to Struth. But, at least in the summer of 1956, with Rangers champions again, Symon could take some time off to watch his beloved cricket.

8

SYMON GAINS POWER AS BOSS

THE importance of that first title to Scot Symon cannot be over-emphasised, which is not to say that had Rangers not won the championship in 1955-56 he would have been sacked. For that period over half a century ago was a more tolerant time in football as far as managers were concerned. Walter Smith once said that Rangers were only ever three defeats away from full-blown crisis and, as ever, Smith was correct. No, had Rangers not taken the title in his second season, Symon would not have been fired, but he would have been in the position of just soldiering on.

No, by winning it, and winning it so well and with so much dash and excitement, Symon started establishing his power as manager. Of course, that power never reached the level Bill Struth enjoyed. Indeed, even when he was at the top of his game, Symon still had to submit the team he had chosen for Saturday's match to the Ibrox board, which met on Thursday night. Unfortunately, Symon never spoke about what happened at those meetings and whether the board ever attempted to get him to change his selection. What is more likely is that the directors were merely attempting to ensure Symon never became as all powerful as Struth had been, and while I am sure suggestions were made to him, Symon's selections were never changed.

But it must have been an ordeal for Symon, particularly in his first two seasons in charge when Struth, by then still a director, was present at the board meetings. For Symon, the ill and ailing Old Man remained a father figure. Events have a way of sorting themselves out, however, and Symon's first title in the spring of 1956 and his growing confidence to change things all coincided with a steep decline in Struth's health, and the grand Old Man of Ibrox died in September 1956, aged eighty-one. One thing Symon must have felt was a sense of a duty being fulfilled to his mentor, as he had given Struth the pleasure of seeing the man he had chosen to succeed him put Rangers back on top.

For all of the fact Symon had to attend a board meeting and present his team selection to the directors, he was in the mid-Fifties a manager ahead of his time. It may be hard to take that concept on board as Symon, in his latter years in charge, was seen as a man out of his time. Someone belonging to a passing era and who had been overtaken by the methods of the modern managers who donned a tracksuit and went out onto the training field with the players. The comparisons, notably with Jock Stein at Celtic, were not favourable to Symon. But in the mid-Fifties it was actually Symon who was the modern manager, the professional football man who made the football decisions. Indeed, any comparison with the way Celtic were run placed Rangers and Symon firmly in the up-to-the-minute mode.

For instance, at Parkhead the Celtic manager was the club's legendary centre-forward Jimmy McGrory. But McGrory, the professional football man, was not allowed to manage. Amazingly, McGrory, who had become Celtic manager in 1945, had to defer to chairman Bob Kelly in football matters. Kelly picked the team, handed the written selection to McGrory and told him to get on with it. This system hampered Celtic greatly and perhaps the greatest example of how boardroom meddling at Celtic ensured Symon was always in control occurred in the 1963 Scottish Cup final replay when, after a teenage Jimmy Johnstone had played so well in the drawn first game, Kelly dropped the winger, re-shuffled the team and handed the mess to McGrory. Symon, on the other hand, made one change, the veteran Ian McMillan in for the injured George McLean. Rangers simply toyed with Celtic that night and won 3-0.

But the fact that Symon was more or less allowed to manage went beyond the boundaries of team selection and signing players. It also extended to the manager choosing his own back-room staff, such as it was in those days, and a decision Symon made after winning the title in 1956 provides a clear indication of both his growing confidence in his own authority and his clear-sighted vision for the future and mark him, for his era, the very essence of a modern manager.

There was no such thing as assistant manager in the fifties. Nor was there a platoon of coaches. Coaching was nonexistent and training was left to a trainer, often a club worthy or former player who put the players through their laps of the track and sprints. On match day the trainer, with no formal qualifications, would run on, carrying a bucket of water and a sponge to attend to anyone who was injured. Symon saw this was not good enough.

The trainer Symon inherited was Jimmy Smith, an Ibrox legend who had starred as a full-blooded forward from 1927 until 1946 before Struth made him trainer. It was the position Struth himself had stepped up from to become manager in 1920, and there were many who thought it was in Struth's mind that Smith could follow the same path. But by 1956 Smith's methods were out of date and Symon wanted his own man, someone he knew and someone who was a qualified physiotherapist. He turned to former Rangers left-winger, Davie Kinnear, someone he had played alongside. However, Symon, always the gentleman, didn't just dispense with Smith's services. There was no brutality about Symon the manager. Smith had been a particular favourite of my granddad's, who had often spoken about him and always with a smile of affection and I therefore felt the tug of sentimentality when I interviewed the then seventy-six-year-old Smith in 1987. Smith said, 'I knew the way the wind was blowing and, although I had played with Scot, I was aware he wanted to change things. When he told me, it was a blow, but I could understand his thinking. Scot knew that Rangers had been my life so I was grateful to him when he told me I still had a part to play in the new Rangers and that he wanted me to join the scouting staff. I appreciated that.'

The fact is that, despite moving with the times in some ways, in many others Symon was rooted in the methods which had been so successful for so long for Struth. That meant he was seldom seen out of his office during the day when, in those days before the club acquired the Albion, the players trained at Ibrox, lapping the running track which went around the park, or having a kickabout on the big grassy areas behind each goal. Tuesdays and Thursdays were the days when he would take a seat in the stand and observe proceedings. He kept that routine when training moved across the road to what was then the old Albion dog track and is now a car park. Symon, wearing suit, overcoat and trademark soft hat, crossed Copland Road to the Albion and watched the players being put through their paces by the trainer.

And from 1956 that trainer was his own choice, Davie Kinnear. There were many significant signings made by Symon and there can be no debate his best was Jim Baxter and perhaps his shrewdest was Ian McMillan. But the importance of how he went about replacing Jimmy Smith with his own man, Kinnear, has always been overlooked. It was, in a typically modest Symon manner, his own understated way of showing just who was now running the Rangers show.

9

STAMPING HIS MARK ON RANGERS

THE period just after Rangers won their first championship under his guidance was the time in which Scot Symon started to grow into the responsibility of his job and, if you like, at the age of forty-five – younger than Alistair McCoist when he took over – Symon came of age as Rangers manager.

The arrival of Davie Kinnear as his righthand man, the person who was as close to a confidant as the deeply private Symon ever had, was one example of this increasing self-confidence. But there are many others. Symon was acutely aware that, despite that Rangers were champions, much of what he had done to the team was make-do-and-mend. With the exception of the arrival of Bobby Shearer, there was no clear long-term plan. No blueprint. That was something Kinnear talked about when I interviewed him at the end of the 1980s. Even at such a distance, and also allowing for the fact Symon had died four years earlier, Kinnear was still guarded and circumspect about the things Symon discussed with him. It is a recurring theme when talking to those Symon trusted. The loyalty he engendered in them speaks volumes for what sort of man he was. It also gives us a fair idea of what a sound judge of character Symon was. Judgement is an important thing for a manager to have and that judgement must extend beyond having an eye for a player.

Symon knew a player when he saw one. He also recognised other qualities.

Now, if Kinnear's words and memories are examined with care, they show how Symon was thinking as he moved on from Rangers' 1956 title triumph, planning for the next. And then the next again. Kinnear recalled, 'Scot wanted power and pace in the team and knew he needed younger players, so that period was a busy time. Jimmy Millar had been bought from Dunfermline halfway through the previous season, but that summer Sammy Baird arrived from Preston, where he had played for Scot, who had originally signed him for Clyde, and Davie Wilson stepped up from the juniors, where he had been with Ballieston.'

Kinnear, a quiet, modest man, had to be pressed to talk about his involvement in the arrival of another signing. A man who was almost the identikit of what so many believe a Rangers player should be. He was tall and genuinely tough, fearless and determined, and with a set of personal standards which brought him into conflict with the cavalier Jim Baxter many years down the line. Harold Davis was a genuine hero who had been badly wounded while fighting in the ranks of the Black Watch in a gallant action during the Korean War. Some of the shrapnel was still in his chest as Davis, with the help of his physio, fought the good fight back to fitness and resumed his football career as a determined right-half with East Fife. That physio was Kinnear before his return to Ibrox.

The way Davis went about his fight for fitness impressed Kinnear and he kept a close eye on things when his patient started playing again. Kinnear said, 'Harold impressed me as a man and a few football people told me he was a fair player, too. When Scot asked me to join him at Ibrox, Harold was one of the first names I mentioned. Nothing happened for a wee while, but that was the way Scot worked. Eventually, a couple of months into the season, he signed Harold.'

At the time it was clear the career of Geordie Young could not last much longer. In fact, season 1956-57 was to prove to be this giant's last. One aspect of Symon's management was his belief he could move a player from the position he had played in when he signed for Rangers and mould him into another. It was a flaw in his managerial make-up and the only hint of any vanity in Symon I have been able to uncover in all my research into the man and the manager. Perhaps he saw Davis as the man to replace Young at centre-half and that was certainly where he began his career as a Ranger. He switched between the pivot's position and left-half in that first season, but failed to spark any belief that he could rise to meet the demanding standards required by Symon and Rangers supporters.

It wasn't long though before Symon realised just what a golden nugget of twenty-four carats he had in Harold Davis. Davis was subsequently moved to right-half and soon found a place in the affections of Rangers supporters who, with a nod towards the shrapnel from his war wound that he carried in his chest throughout his career, plus his uncompromising tackling, promptly christened Harold Davis 'The Iron Man'. In fact, after Symon realised Davis was not the answer to his problems at centre-half, he spent most of the following couple of campaigns at left-half. Perhaps Symon saw something of himself in Davis and wanted to see him in his old shirt.

The truth is that Davis, for all that he could tackle like Symon, could not pass the ball nearly as well. He also lacked pace. But, just as Bobby Moore was for England years later, he made up for that with an acute sense of position. He was often there to snuff out trouble before it began. Now, I saw plenty of Davis, and of Moore, too, and not for a moment am I suggesting the

Rangers man was in the same elevated class as Moore. But Harold
Davis was a much better player than some gave him credit.
Indeed, when Symon finally switched him to right-half in 1959,
Harold Davis provided a major initial plank in the framework
of the team Symon built to become the dominant, exciting and
fine footballing outfit of the first half of the 1960s.

Those historic days were still a few years off and Symon took
a team, which was a mixture of ageing Struth survivors and the
men he believed could forge more glory for the club, into season
1956-57 attempting to retain the Scottish championship, a feat
Rangers had not managed since 1950 and which would see a
new challenge to Ibrox from the east.

The Hibernian team of the Famous Five was on the wane,
while Aberdeen's great title-winning side of two seasons earlier
was no longer as powerful. However at Tynecastle, Hearts
manager Tommy Walker had fashioned a side of which many
had to be fearful. Rangers and Hearts, two fine, old traditional
clubs, and Symon and Walker, two fine Scottish gentleman
managers of the old school, were to be locked in the first of
many fascinating and fine battles for honours which excited
Scottish football for the next six seasons. That Symon emerged
from this period as having had the better of it says much for his
wiles. That he should have achieved that while dealing with the
fresh challenge of the previously unchartered waters of Europe
and going so close to success there, while all the time piecing
together such a fine side as the one of the early '60s, is a measure
of just what a remarkable manager James Scotland Symon was.

10

EUROPE – THE EARLY YEARS

EUROPE! The very word conjures what must have been bitter-sweet memories for Scot Symon. He went close. Oh, so close. Not once, but twice. And he trailblazed there more than any other Scottish manager. Nowadays everyone is as familiar – or maybe even more familiar – with the stars from Paris to Prague and from Milan to Moscow as they are with who plays for Dundee United or Dunfermline, because of television. But in 1956 when Symon took Rangers into the European Cup for the first time, things were very different indeed. The 'continentals', as all teams in Europe were called, were an exotic blend of the dangerous, the devious and the unknown. They employed the sort of under-hand tactics that were not quite cricket. Not British! That much was apparent when one of the stars of the first Rangers European adventure, Max Murray, recalled those days with a memory that was vivid and gives an insight into attitudes within Scotland towards those continentals in those far-off pioneering days more than half a century ago.

Murray was one of the many players signed by Symon who split the opinions of supporters. At times awkward, often infu-riating, but even more frequently a top-flight finisher. Despite his goals ratio of 121 in 154 games for Rangers being mightily impressive, there were often cries from the Ibrox terraces of 'Taxi for Maxie', after a Murray miscontrol or stumble. The fact is that in season 1956-57, with Don Kitchenbrand suffering injuries, Murray stepped in to more than fill the breech, missing just two matches and scoring an astonishing twenty-nine goals in a league campaign which saw Rangers retain their crown. Murray also holds the unique distinction of scoring the first goal recorded by Rangers in European football.

The Rangers team which Symon sent out at Ibrox to face French champions Nice in front of a 65,000 crowd on 24 October 1956 to make history by being the first Scottish title winners to compete in Europe's blue riband tournament was: Niven, Shearer and Caldow, McColl, Young and Logie, Scott, Simpson, Murray, Baird and Hubbard. This is not a statistical chronicle of the facts and figures of Rangers when Scot Symon was the manager; there are plenty of other books around which do that. But the occasional historic occasion demands some of that detail. It is Murray's memories which matter more and he looked back to the culture shock of going up against the best in Europe, until then unknown men of mystery. Murray said, 'The continentals were up to all sorts of underhand tricks. They did things we didn't do in Scotland. Things like tugging you back by the jersey when you got past them. But the worst of them all was spitting. That was just so foreign to us. Nobody in Scottish football ever did that sort of thing.

'I remember we struggled to cope with all of this and they scored first. But we then got into our stride and I equalised with a header before Billy Simpson scored another to give us a 2-1 win. However, things got out of hand and we reacted to being spat on and some of the boys waded in with good old-fashioned Scottish shoulder charges, which the French didn't fancy at all. In fact, the famous English referee Arthur Ellis actually stopped the game and called all the players into the centre circle for a lecture.' That is another example of just how different European football was back then, with an Englishman taking charge of a tie involving a Scottish team.

Murray was then involved in a controversial incident when the two teams met in Nice for the second leg. He was fouled for a penalty which Johnny Hubbard tucked away and then he looked to have stretched that lead when he scrambled the ball over the line Murray-style, only for the referee to blow for half time at the precise second Murray's effort crossed the line. Even at what was then a distance of over thirty years, when I spoke to Murray he still could not understand that, saying, 'He had awarded us a corner and when the ball came over he did not blow and when Nice failed to clear he still didn't blow. But just as my shot went in he blew.'

Rangers lost their concentration and Nice scored two second-half goals, the one which levelled the aggregate coming just a couple of minutes before the end. In those days there was no away goals rule or penalty shoot-out, and the tie went to a play-off. Rangers lost the toss and the third game was played in Paris. Murray said, 'That was the only time I ever saw a player being sent off for being punched on the jaw and flattened. Our left-half Willie Logie was hooked, but the referee sent him off and we lost 3-1.'

But if there was to be no initial glory for Rangers in Europe, on the home front they reigned supreme, beating Celtic home and away, but more importantly seeing off Hearts twice too. The Edinburgh side back then always provided the real challenge to the champions. It was far from plain sailing, though, and Symon had to show that his Rangers had the same sort of courage and resilience Struth's sides had so often displayed. They did that in one match against Murray's old club, Queen's Park, then still in the top flight. Queen's had held Rangers to a 3-3 draw at

Ibrox in February, but worse looked to be on the cards when, with the title tussle red hot, Rangers went to Hampden in April.

Despite missing a fourth-minute penalty, Queen's were 4-1 up after thirty-nine minutes, but Rangers held their nerve and launched a comeback to win 6-4. Murray got two that day and recalled, 'Scot never went in for shouting and bawling, but even by his standards he was quiet that day. He just looked at us in a way that made me feel I had betrayed him. George Young was in his last season and I think he sensed all we needed was a gee-up. He just kept telling everyone we could still win, that there was nothing to worry about.' But there had been plenty for Rangers supporters to worry about when, on 12 January, the champions lost 1-0 to Ayr and fell nine points behind leaders Hearts. Rangers had three games in hand, but it was the era of two points for a win.

Symon, though, kept his head, Rangers went on another remarkable run, this time a sixteen-game unbeaten spurt, with fourteen wins and two draws, which took them to the end of the season and clinched the Scottish championship with fifty-five points to Hearts' fifty-three. And the main man had been Max Murray with that astonishing twenty-nine-goal haul. Murray got another four in the League Cup, where Rangers went out at the section stage, plus two in the Scottish Cup before the Ibrox club exited and there was also his historic first-ever Rangers goal in the European Cup for a total tally of thirty-six. Not bad for someone who so often inspired the cry of 'Taxi for Maxie'. He said, 'Whatever anyone said about me, I scored a lot of goals for Rangers and that season I beat Willie Thornton's post-war record for a season and that held until Jim Forrest came along.'

It was as well for Symon that Murray had made such a massive contribution to entrench him in the manager's position, thanks to back-to-back titles, for season 1957-58 was to start just about as badly as possible for Rangers, testing Symon's mettle almost to breaking point. However, it was from the very lowest point that Symon made the signing which bought him the time needed for him to begin the climb that took him to his managerial peak.

11

THE WEE PRIME MINISTER

AFTER the second successive title in 1957, Scot Symon saw no need to be rushed into making summer signings, and when his team kicked off the League Cup campaign the team was, broadly speaking, the same. That all was far from right was soon obvious after League Cup section defeats by Raith Rovers and Hearts, plus a draw against Third Lanark saw Rangers fail to reach the competition's knockout stages. This was followed by a terrible start in the league. A draw at home to Third Lanark was followed by another, this time away to Celtic, with a defeat away to Airdrie by the preposterous 5-4 scoreline followed by a 2-1 loss to Dundee at Ibrox.

Something had to be done before the campaign ran away from Rangers and Hearts were handed a cakewalk to the title. Alex Scott, who felt he was not getting the right service, was the man to whom Symon once again turned to provide the spark on the park. So he went out and bought the best scheming inside-forward in Scotland at the time, Airdrie's Ian McMillan. The dapper McMillan belonged to a breed long since extinct. A skinny, hunched, slightly delicate-looking chap, with his shirt cuffs pulled down over his hands, spindly legs sticking out below shorts that were too long and a big backside. Athletic-looking he was not. Indeed, McMillan worked as a quantity surveyor, trained just two nights a week, had a certain studious demeanour and was both shy and modest. In those last two, he mirrored his new manager.

Symon paid Airdrie the then formidable sum of £10,000 for the inside-right who made his debut in a 4-4 draw with Raith Rovers at Ibrox on 18 October 1958. McMillan scored, as did Scott, along with Sammy Baird and Johnny Hubbard. But it was the supply of passes released by McMillan to the wing which once again unleashed the still young Scott as Symon's most potent weapon. The manager had found what he thought was the perfect partnership. However, he was to better it just four years later when a young Willie Henderson took Scott's place, with a style even more suited to gaining maximum advantage from McMillan's passing wiles.

Scott said, 'As a winger, I relied on a wing-half or inside-forward feeding passes to me and at that time I just was not getting enough of the ball. But when McMillan arrived he spoon-fed me and I was able to be more active and make a bigger contribution. McMillan was very good for me.'

It was not long before Rangers supporters came up with their own special way of making sure everyone knew just how he ran things. Harold Macmillan was the man in 10 Downing Street and soon Ian McMillan became the Wee Prime Minister.

There were other changes to the team, with Symon deciding McMillan needed protection. Harry Davis settled in behind him at right-half, while the captaincy, with McColl left out, went to Bobby Shearer and a tall straight-backed left-half by the name of Billy Stevenson forced Symon to find a place in the team for his strong running. At inside-left, Ralph Brand was Symon's choice in front of his own signing, Sammy Baird. A typical team picked by Symon, after the season settled down, was: Niven, Shearer, Caldow, Davis, Telfer, Stevenson, Scott, McMillan, Murray, Brand and Wilson. There were changes, with Hubbard on the left and Billy Simpson at centre-forward. But Symon's team was taking shape, and I got my first chance to see it when my mum decided I was old enough for my dad to take me to Ibrox for the first time.

The momentous day on which my love affair started was 15 November 1958 and the opponents were Falkirk. I was seven years old. There are bits and pieces of the day that I remember. Rangers wore red shirts with collars. I was shocked. My dad had to explain that in those days, if there was a clash of colours, the home side changed, so Rangers had to switch to red as Falkirk wore blue. Red jerseys or not, I recall Rangers won 3-0 that day. We sat in the main stand, my dad having to fork out after Mum insisted I was still too wee to be in a crowd. I also recall Billy Simpson scored two, but I had to resort to Robert McElroy's magnificent book, *Rangers: The Complete Record*, to find that the other scorer was Scott. Strange that, for in those early years, Scott became a particular favourite of mine.

After that first visit, I can't recall being back at Ibrox again until the last game of the season, but there were to be plenty of twists and turns to the season before then and more than a fair few on that last day, too. In fact, compared to what happened that day, the original 2003 Helicopter Sunday, and the 2005 version, were tame affairs. Before the grandstand finale could be set up, Rangers needed to start winning and that's what they mostly managed to do, the only defeat being 2-0 to Partick Thistle at Firhill in January before they went to Tynecastle on 11 April, at the top of the table, four points clear of Hearts. The Edinburgh side won 2-0 to cut that gap to just two points going into the last day.

And what a last day the fixture list produced, with Hearts going to Parkhead to face a Celtic team only just in the top half of the table. While Rangers were at Ibrox where Aberdeen were the visitors. Yes, that's right, Rangers and Celtic were both at home, and both matches kicked off at three o'clock on the Saturday afternoon. The past is, indeed, a foreign country. To add spice, Aberdeen were fighting to avoid relegation and knew that to keep their fate in their own hands they had to beat a Rangers team which knew it had to win to be sure of holding off Hearts and being crowned champions. That was the first I can remember of the many happy Saturday afternoons I would spend in the wee enclosure with my dad and granddad. And it started well when Scott flew clear again and teed up Davis for a shot, which was blocked but fell to Ralph Brand, who turned it into the net.

Now, back in those faraway days, there were no goal flashes on big screens and no mobile phones, none of the modern marvels of technology to feed information in the blink of an eye. It was even before the Swinging Sixties when transistor radios, pressed to ears, became a common sight. So, when Rangers suddenly lost their nerve and fell behind to two Norrie Davidson goals, my dad, granddad and I, along with more than 41,000 others, had nothing to shout about. The game finished 2-1 to Aberdeen, and I have a dim and distant memory of boos and of leaving a sad and sullen Ibrox.

Alex Scott's memories were more vivid. He told me, 'We were all convinced we had blown it. Hearts were a very good side and Celtic were no great shakes. We knew how good Hearts were as they had beaten us the previous week. There was no sign of Symon in the dressing room afterwards, but that wasn't unusual. I remember somebody coming in and saying they heard Celtic had won, but nobody believed him. Then the results were read out on the radio and Celtic had won 2-1.'

Celtic supporters had many years and reasons to curse their team's victory that day, for it not only handed the title to Rangers but ensured Symon was under no pressure, either that summer or early the next season, and that he remained around to build the Sixties side which so very often heaped humiliation on the Parkhead club. What would have happened to Symon had Celtic, as they were expected, lost that day and Hearts won the title? For at that time, Symon's long-term future as manager, despite those back-to-back titles, had still to be secured. He was still living in Bill Struth's shadow. In many ways, his position was similar to that of Alex McLeish's almost half a century later. Despite having won the two Cups in his first six months as manager and the League Cup at the start of his first full season in charge, had McLeish's team not held off Celtic's late challenge and gone on to take the 2003 title, he would surely have been sacked.

Nobody knows for sure just how close Symon came to being handed a P45 in the twenty minutes between the final whistle, signalling a 2-1 defeat by Aberdeen, and the news of Hearts losing to Celtic at Parkhead becoming official. According to Alex Scott, the players did not see him. There is no record of Symon's reaction to the winning of his third championship in his fifth year as Rangers manager, but what the Rangers chairman Bailie John F. Wilson said may give us a clue as to what he was thinking and how close Symon may have been to losing his job. The Ibrox chairman said, 'We did not play well and will now have to review our entire resources.'

As for me, I was heading along the Paisley Road towards Kinning Park subway station with my granddad and dad. A sullen wee eight-year-old whose scone had been well and truly stolen, when a few supporters ahead of us spotted a busload of Celtic fans heading west. They called for their team's result and, on hearing that Celtic won, started a cheer, which soon spread along the thronged pavements as disbelief was replaced by joy. My scone was not only returned, but was spread with treacle on one side and jam on the other. So, too, I suspect, was James Scotland Symon's.

12

THE FIRST EURO GLORY RUN

WHATEVER it was that chairman Bailie John F. Wilson meant when he spoke about having to 'review resources', Scot Symon obviously did not agree for he did not make a single significant signing in the summer of 1959. And the resources he had available proved to be enough to ignite Rangers' first major glory run in Europe. A thrilling seat-of-the-pants rollercoaster adventure which took the Ibrox side on a nine-game run that carried them to the semi-final of the European Cup. But in the end what happened was that Symon's lack of tactical acumen was exposed, something which prevented Rangers from making that final leap forward and winning a European trophy.

Scot Symon's managerial strengths and style were much the same as those of Bill Struth. He had an eye for a player and also knew just what sort of character would fit the demands placed upon a Rangers signing. He also knew about balance and could piece together the jigsaw of a team with great insight. For instance, on the right, he had the tackling of Bobby Shearer and Harold Davis to provide a barrier behind the physically weak Ian McMillan and the attacking dash of Alex Scott. However, at a time when continental coaches, inspired by the Hungarian side which demolished England twice, were working on evolving ever more sophisticated tactics, Symon stuck, in the main, to the old Struth methods of picking his team and then letting them get on with it, leaving any changes needed after the action started to his captain and other senior players.

The formula remained a success in Scotland until Jock Stein arrived at Celtic, Symon's methods were good enough. Europe, though, was a different matter. Ian McMillan, recalling what happened at half timewhen Rangers played the first leg of their European Cup semi-final against Eintracht Frankfurt, made the point well. He said, 'Eric Caldow equalised with a penalty after Eintracht had taken the lead and even missed a spot-kick. We were lucky to escape being out of the Cup before half-time. Eintracht had watched us before we faced them and knew how to exploit weaknesses. But at the interval there was no guidance from Scot. He did nothing to try and make us more defensive so that we could keep the score down and give ourselves a chance in the second leg at Ibrox. Sitting in that dressing room in Frankfurt, I had a wee sense of what was coming, and I was right, for Eintracht took us apart in the second leg and won 6-1.'

McMillan was right when he made that assessment. The fact is that back then Rangers did not need a range of tactics when playing in Scotland. It was unthinkable for there not to be two wing-halves, one defensive and one more creative; two inside-forwards, one creative and the other a goalscorer; plus two wingers who rarely dropped deeper than the halfway line; plus a centre-forward.

Season 1959-60 was when Jimmy Millar came into his own and became a key man in that European adventure, after being switched into the centre-forward position when Rangers were short after an injury to Max Murray when on pre-season tour in Copenhagen. Legends and myths often grow up over events in football and then become entrenched in people's memory banks as facts. That is what happened when Scot Symon switched Millar into the centre-forward role, which was to be his stepping-stone to greatness as a Ranger. Millar, however, is able to tell the truth about how it all came about. Millar told me, 'The fact is that playing at centre-forward was nothing new to me. When I was at Dunfermline, the manager was Bobby Ancell and he tried me in a number of positions before he put me in the number nine shirt. I enjoyed the position and that is where I was playing when Rangers bought me. But for the first few years at Ibrox I was not used there. Scot, though, knew I had played there and must have remembered.'

Millar's career, which until then had been on the south side of solid, then took off and became spectacular. But there was more to his slow start than the position he played in. There was National Service. Until the start of the 1960s, all young men under the age of twenty-one had to spend eighteen months to two years doing National Service in one branch of the Armed Forces. This disrupted the careers of many players signed by Scot Symon, including Davie Wilson and Millar. Millar's memories make for strange reading for those who were not around back then. He said, 'I signed for Rangers for £5,000 in 1955 and played just two games before being called up. Actually I wore the number nine shirt in one of them against Aberdeen. After that, I not only didn't play for Rangers for two years, I didn't kick a ball at all for all of my time in the army.

'I was unlucky and think I was the only professional footballer who did not get a posting to somewhere where he could play football. I was in Suez when we invaded in 1956 and also in Malaya for the emergency there. I had signed for Rangers for £16 per week, which was about twice what a tradesman got, but I had to get used to army pay which was fifteen shillings per week.' In those pre-decimal currency days that was the same as seventy-five pence.

Millar remembered, 'By the time I was back at Ibrox in 1958, Max Murray was scoring a lot of goals so there was no chance for me at centre-forward until that night in Copenhagen.' The move paid off for Symon, for Millar soon captured the love of the Rangers crowd. He had a strange style and looked flat-footed, giving him a running style which many thought was a waddle. He could leap and win headers despite his small, chunky frame and soon fans began calling him 'The Penguin'. But as seasons rolled along and Millar's bravery and brilliance never wavered, the nickname changed to the one which endures to this day, with Millar part of the team of legends who are match-day hosts at Ibrox. Jimmy Millar will always be 'The Old Warhorse'. He missed just two matches in that European adventure which ended when Eintracht won the semi-final second leg at Ibrox 6-3. The Germans were to go on to take part in that never-to-be-forgotten Hampden European Cup final in 1960 when they lost 7-3 to the fabled men of Real Madrid.

Rangers had beaten Anderlecht, Red Star Bratislava and Sparta Rotterdam, after a play-off at Highbury to get to the semis, proving that, even if he had no great tactical awareness, Scot Symon's team-building skills and eye for a player were pretty good. In the league, though, Rangers were dogged by inconsistency. This was the season when I became a regular at Ibrox and saw my first Old Firm game. Rangers were magnificent on that September day in 1959 and I can still remember my eight-year-old joy as they gave Celtic a 3-1 beating, which could have been more.

Years later, when working for the *Sunday Mail*, a crowd of us, which included Billy McNeill, were enjoying a convivial afternoon in the Montrose Bar, just off the Broomielaw, and I recalled the match. I told Big Billy I knew he hadn't played, as I had vivid recall of Millar putting the ball through the legs of the Celtic centre-half that day, Scotland captain Bobby Evans. My memory also recalled that two of the Rangers goals were scored by Scott and Millar, but couldn't conjure up the name of the third marksman. It was Wilson. At which point, one of the company asked me who scored for Celtic. I admitted I hadn't a clue. 'It was me, and it was my first Old Firm goal,' said the questioner, McNeill's best pal and a first-class gent Mike Jackson. I would have loved to have rushed home to tell my granddad and dad the story, but sadly they were long gone by then.

That victory over Celtic was probably the high point of a league campaign which saw Rangers finish third on a mere forty-two points, twelve behind champions Hearts and eight adrift of runners-up Kilmarnock. It was that fine Kilmarnock side, managed by Willie Waddell, which lay in wait at Hampden for a Scottish Cup final which was the last chance for Symon to take silverware and which was played just three days after Rangers' 6-3 Ibrox mauling at the hands of Eintracht. It was also the first Scottish Cup final I attended. Jimmy Millar was to be the hero whose two goals ensured Rangers lifted the oldest-surviving trophy in the world. But the star of the show was a blast from the past after Symon reached back through the years to the last survivor of Bill Struth's Iron Curtain and coaxed one last stirring performance from Ian McColl.

Harold Davis, so important to Symon's team, had been badly injured against Eintracht and even the Iron Man could not fully recover. There was no obvious replacement for such an important match against such formidable opposition. Symon and McColl had been team-mates as far back as 1946, McColl's first season as a Ranger and Symon's last as a player. There was, therefore, a sort of poignancy about the whole thing, which I admit did not impinge on my nine-year-old consciousness at the time. But, looking back, I can see Symon and McColl, the Struth old boys, coming together to serve the cause so dear to the old man one last time and while recognising what was happening, showing no signs of the emotions they must have been feeling. That was their way.

Symon's strategy paid off. McColl was magnificent, Wilson tormented Killie out on the left, Sammy Baird gave his last outstanding big-game performance before making way for Ralph Brand, while McMillan gave Scott the service he thrived on, in order that he could deliver the crosses Millar fed on. Millar said, 'Killie had a bit of bad luck early in the game when their centre-half Willie Toner took a knock and with no substitutes he had to carry on and that made it a bit easier for us. Jimmy Brown was the Kilmarnock keeper and he was a character who wore a scarlet jersey at a time when other keepers wore yellow, and again unlike the others who wore old-fashioned cloth caps – bunnets – Jimmy wore a matching scarlet-coloured baseball-type hat. He had been the Hearts keeper at the time I was growing up as a Hearts fan and was a great favourite of mine. I managed to outjump him twice and headed the two goals.'

The Scottish Cup triumph was all the sweeter for Symon in that it was his first and broke a bad run in both Cups for him since he had taken over. It was also the first time Rangers had lifted the trophy since 1953 and put an end to any talk of a hoodoo, similar to the twenty-five years which Rangers went without the trophy before 1928, starting to build up.

Symon was aware, though, that despite the end-of-the-season cheer engendered by lifting the Scottish Cup, he had to win the league again and to do that the team needed to be more consistent and tighter at the back. He attempted to address those problems with two summer signings.

13

BAXTER

WHEN Raith Rovers had beaten Rangers 3-2 at Ibrox in November 1959, the man who did the damage was a slim, wraith-like figure, operating on what we would now call the left side of midfield. His name was Jim Baxter, who had not long turned twenty. Scot Symon was impressed and kept tabs on him for the remainder of the season. The trouble was that Baxter's best position was left-half and Rangers already had an outstanding player in that role. Billy Stevenson was so good, skilful and powerful that there were some who compared him to the Manchester United and England legend Duncan Edwards, so tragically killed in the Munich air disaster. But Symon felt he must have Baxter and in the summer of 1960 he was both preparing the Scottish record bid to get him and concocting a plan to fit both Baxter and Stevenson into his team.

One of the many traits Symon had learned from Struth was that, as well as ability, a player's character mattered if he was to play for Rangers. Certain standards applied. Therefore, before Symon signed any player, background checks were made into how the player conducted himself as a man. All of which made the fact that Symon was willing to move heaven and earth to sign Baxter surprising, for Jim Baxter was almost exactly the opposite to Symon in every way. Where Symon was quiet, Baxter was loud. While Symon was genteel, Baxter was coarse. Where Symon valued tradition, Baxter rebelled against authority and, as a player, where Symon tackled like a demon, Baxter couldn't tackle a fish supper. But, where Symon was an outstanding passer of the ball, Baxter was even better.

Who knows? Maybe deep inside the buttoned-up Scot Symon was a subdued rebel who had given up the fight to get out. Perhaps Baxter was the man Symon wished he could have been. What we do know is that Symon once said, 'I heard all the stories about Baxter and what he was supposed to have got up to. But I chose not to take any notice because the truth was that as a player he never let me down and I always felt I had his loyalty. It was also a time when things were changing in the world and Baxter belonged to a generation people from my time could not understand.'

As for Baxter, despite his taste for wine, women and song and his total disregard for tradition and authority, Symon, who exemplified tradition and authority, was someone who he admired. Years later Baxter told me, 'Symon was good to me. Okay, I know I was good for him, but I always felt I owed him and I tried my best for him in big games. That was really true when it came to beating Celtic. The truth is I had more pals in the Celtic dressing room than I did at Ibrox. Pat Crerand, Billy McNeill, Mike Jackson and John Colrain were all close friends. But I knew how much old Scot loved to beat Celtic, how much it meant to him, so I tried to give him that bit extra when we played them. It was my way of paying him back and thanking him for turning a blind eye to some of my wilder moments. I'm sure he knew about my escapades.'

The fact is that Jim Baxter became the best Rangers player I or anyone else from my generation ever saw. If I live to be a hundred it is doubtful I will ever see a better performer. I hope

I do, though. Playing for Rangers and better than Baxter! Wow! That would be some player. If that ever happened, something my granddad taught me would allow me to admit it and recognise another Rangers player's ability as being superior to the sublime skills of Slim Jim Baxter. George Brown, a silky and gentlemanly left-half from the Rangers sides of the 1930s, had been a particular favourite of my granddad's, but such was the impact Baxter made on all the generations of Rangers fans who saw him, that my granddad, by then a man in his sixties set in his ways and opinions, was willing to concede Jim Baxter was better.

The remaining great years of Symon's reign were linked to Baxter. But all that lay ahead when Baxter climbed the marble stairs at Ibrox for the first time and on 20 June 1960 became a Ranger for the Scottish record transfer fee of £17,500. That very same day another major signing was made by Symon.

Symon had continued his search for a centre-half after signing Willie Telfer in the autumn of 1957 as a stop-gap and thought the answer lay in Bill Paterson, signed in 1958 from Newcastle. At the time there was an actor called Hugh O'Brien who played the title role in a television western series called *The Life and Times of Wyatt Earp*. Paterson was a dead-ringer for the actor and soon everyone was calling him Wyatt Earp. When I laid eyes on him for the first time in a quarter of a century, at a gathering of a great many of the players who had performed for Rangers, to which I had been invited by the man who organised it, Alex Willoughby, I immediately greeted the former centre-half by exclaiming, 'Wyatt Earp!' The mild-mannered Paterson, who was at that time running a guest house in Inverness, smiled and told me I was the first person to call him that in over twenty years.

Paterson, however, failed to fulfil his potential and Symon's search for a centre-half took him to Airdrie where, on 20 June

1960, the same day Jim Baxter signed, he handed over a cheque for £17,000 for Doug Baillie, a twenty-three-year-old man-mountain of a defender – six-foot-two and almost as broad as he was tall – who had been a regular in the Airdrie side since his seventeenth birthday.

Symon placed a great deal of faith in Baillie's ability to dominate in the air and use his strength on the ground to be impassable. Symon's plan also involved trying to fit Baxter in slightly further forward than he was used to playing. He wanted to try this out early in a season that would see Rangers take part in the first-ever European Cup Winners' Cup and which opened with them in the same League Cup section as Celtic, along with Partick Thistle and Third Lanark. Things backfired, though, and after they beat Thistle in the first League Cup match, Rangers lost to Thirds at Cathkin ahead of the visit to Ibrox of Celtic for the first big test to be faced by the two new big-money signings, Baxter and Baillie. They both failed, with Baillie being given a particularly torrid time by the young Celtic centre-forward that day, John Hughes. Celtic won 3-2 and Baillie's career never really recovered, although he remained at Ibrox for another four years. The Celtic curse, which had done for John Valentine in the same competition, had struck again.

Symon recalled Paterson to the heart of the defence, allowed Baxter to roam at will from left-half and Rangers started to settle as they exacted fierce revenge on Celtic, with two wins in seven days, scuppering any hopes there may have been at Parkhead that Rangers were there for the taking. On 3 September Rangers went to the east end of Glasgow for the return League Cup clash and won 2-1 with goals from Harry Davis and Ralph Brand, while in the league, on 10 September at Ibrox, Baxter gave a taste of how he was to continue to put Celtic to the sword for the next five years. He was in his element teasing and tormenting with the passes which helped Alex Scott, Jimmy Millar, Ralph Brand, Davie Wilson and Harold Davis get the goals in a 5-1 win.

The League Cup campaign went all the way to the Hampden final where the opponents were once again Willie Waddell's Kilmarnock. Baxter just loved the big occasion and he revelled in the 2-0 win, with Scott and Brand scoring. Rangers lifted the League Cup for the first time under Symon and set sail for a new and even greater European adventure, plus an assault on the Scottish championship. Scot Symon's truly magnificent team was now recognisable and only a couple of pieces short of the one which so many recall with so much fondness.

14

BAXTER AND SYMON:
CHALK AND CHEESE

IN a perverse sort of a way, the signing of Jim Baxter and the changes in the way Scot Symon was forced to manage for the rest of his time at Ibrox actually became a prelude to Symon's eventual demise. In Winston Churchill's famous phrase, it was the end of the beginning for Symon. It is extremely important to examine the changes which occurred after Baxter and his lavish lifestyle, disregard for authority and, frankly, loud mouth arrived, along with his equally lavish skill, to invade a Rangers dressing room which was a bastion of tradition, conservatism and respect for authority.

If Baxter united all Rangers supporters who grew up watching him, that was certainly not the case inside the Ibrox dressing room, where Baxter upset the old hands and actually usurped Symon's authority. Until then, Symon had managed Rangers in much the same way as Struth had, and not just in a football sense, either. He continued to enforce the old man's iron code of discipline on players and the way a Ranger was expected to behave, not just at Ibrox and in training, but in every aspect of their life. It was a code the old hands, such as Harold Davis, Eric Caldow and Ralph Brand were happy to conform to and comfortable with. They did not take to Baxter's waywardness and felt a sense of bewilderment at how Symon let this young Fifer get away with so much.

Brand explained, in a way which perhaps lends weight to my theory that Symon secretly wished he could have been more like Baxter, 'Symon had a soft spot for Jim and I don't think he did him any favours by letting him off with so much. Symon's normal thinking seemed to be clouded over when it came to Jim. The rest of us could see what was happening and morale in the dressing room was affected. There were bust-ups in the dressing room and, if Jim was involved, Symon would invariably take his side.' The fact that such an assessment and insight comes from Brand adds weight to it being the authentic voice of reflection of how Scot Symon was bent to Baxter's will, instead of it being the other way around, because Brand had a genuine affection for Baxter and the two became close and life-long friends. Indeed, at Baxter's funeral in Glasgow Cathedral in 2001, Brand delivered a eulogy of sincere eloquence and was visibly moved.

Baxter was known to supporters as 'Slim Jim' and he referred to his own magical left foot as 'The Glove', such was the control that left foot exerted on a football. But it was Brand who gave him the name all his friends in football called him for the rest of his life, 'Stanley', after the famous Scottish comedian Stanley Baxter.

One player in that early Sixties dressing room was Iron Man Harold Davis. The former soldier, who knew what it was like to be in battle and who had suffered such horrific wounds, knew how important discipline was and valued it. Something which brought him into open conflict with Baxter and which diminished Scot Symon in his eyes. Davis said, 'Nowadays you hear a lot of talk about how this or that manager has lost the dressing room. We didn't use the phrase back then, but I know exactly what it means, for when Symon started to pander to Baxter that is what happened. Symon lost the dressing room. You could smell the drink on Baxter most mornings when he turned up for training. And even on match days there was a smell of booze on Baxter. We didn't like it and there would be the odd flare-up, but the truth is we were all waiting for Symon to sort him out. But he never did.

'It wasn't as though Symon was not a strong man. He was and showed that when he took over as manager. Bill Struth had been ill for some time and the captain, George Young, had virtu-ally taken over and was running things, but when Symon arrived and, despite the fact that Young was the Rangers and Scotland captain and a strong personality, Symon put him in his place and made sure everyone knew he was in charge.

'He did not do that with Baxter, so discipline suffered and Symon lost face. He made a rod for his own back and by allowing Baxter too much leeway at the start, he was never in a strong enough position to rein him in. By the time he had been there a few months there was nothing Symon could do. If he had told Baxter to toe the line or else, Baxter would only have asked, "Or else what?" Then Symon would have been forced to back away from a confrontation.'

It would be easy to dismiss the Davis view of how Symon behaved and attribute it to that of an old pro who may secretly believe Baxter shortened his own time with Rangers. Certainly by 1962, Davis, never the quickest, was finding the extra work-load by Baxter's refusal to cover and run hard to handle, and he found himself replaced by the younger and more energetic John Greig. The truth is that Greig was not only younger, but also a better player. And Symon was right to make the change as it improved the team. However, there is another voice which adds even more weight to the argument that Baxter's arrival at the club and Symon's unwillingness to impose the same stan-dards of discipline on him as he applied on everyone else led to the players losing respect for their manager.

Eric Caldow had been signed by and played for Struth and idolised the Old Man, so much so that he became bitter about how Symon became guilty of double standards where Baxter was involved. There is also a hint in the former Rangers and Scotland captain's verdict that he believes Symon actually started to fritter away the Struth legacy. Caldow said, 'It annoyed the rest of us that Symon let Baxter get away with so much instead of stamping down on his bad behaviour right at the start. By the time Jim settled and started to play so well and to have such a tremendous influence on what we did on the field, he was allowed to do more or less what he liked off the park. Symon was never a tactician and the only instruction he gave us at that time was to give the ball to Jim, and that showed just how important Baxter became to that team.'

There is a case to be made for Symon, despite the criticism of how he handled the Baxter situation, even when made by such experienced and revered old Rangers men as Brand, Davis and Caldow, who, incidentally remains the best left-back Rangers have had in the more than the half a century which has passed since I first saw them play. It is that Scot Symon's dream was to change the image of the Rangers team while attempting to keep as many of the club's traditions alive. But if he had to bend and sacrifice any of those Rangers traditions to get near to his footballing dream for the team, he was enough of a pragmatist to do so.

During Symon's career as a Rangers player, the team was known for its adherence to safety first and the Iron Curtain defence. The Rangers method was swift counter-attacks, many of them launched by Symon's own passes, as the main weapon, with dashes on the right by Willie Waddell, followed by crosses to Willie Thornton, who was deadly in the air. Symon as manager wanted more. He wanted a range of passing from a variety of areas. Ian McMillan gave him just that on the right side of the park, while the arrival of Baxter provided the extra final dimension to the shape Symon wanted. With Brand and Millar linking for a twin-pronged strike partnership and Davie Wilson always a threat out on and coming in from the left, while Alex Scott did the same on the other side of the pitch, Symon had the team he wanted, playing the skilful, silky, subtle soccer he believed would win Rangers not only trophies, but credit as exciting entertainers. But, however important Scott, McMillan, Millar, Brand and Wilson were, none of what Rangers achieved from August 1960 until the end of 1964 would have been possible if it had not been for Baxter. Scot Symon knew that and it is a measure of the man that he was willing to sacrifice his reputation inside the Ibrox dressing room, even among men he respected, in pursuit of his personal dream and his commitment to what he believed was best for Rangers.

15

BEATING CELTIC

IF Jim Baxter was right and Scot Symon allowed him to get away with so much, all because he loved beating Celtic, then the uniquely gifted left-half certainly delivered for his manager. From the time he signed for Rangers in the summer of 1960, until he broke a leg in Vienna in the autumn of 1964, Baxter lined up against Celtic seventeen times. Rangers won twelve of those Old Firm encounters, drawing three and losing only twice. It is an extraordinary record and at no time in the history of Old Firm matches has one side so dominated the other for such a lengthy period. It is also worthy noting that one of those two defeats came in August 1960 in Baxter's first match against Celtic for Rangers, making what followed all the more remarkable.

At that time television had started showing old movies that my parents recalled seeing in their courting days, leading to my mum often exclaiming, 'We've seen that film before, Andy', which also then led to my dad remarking, as he and I left Ibrox with my granddad after watching Baxter waltz Rangers to another win over Celtic, 'We've seen that movie before, David.' Heading to Ibrox on the subway from Kelvinbridge in those days, the talk I listened to was not so much about whether or not Rangers would win the Old Firm game, but by how many goals they would win it by. If Symon was extra-pleased with these triumphs, as Baxter believed, he never gave any sign of his pleasure in public. There were no jigs of joy on the touchline and no frantic shouts from the dugout. Symon, as was common with the managers of that era, was nowhere near the pitch.

Symon was soberly dressed on match days and he watched the action sitting, showing no emotion, in the directors' box. But, despite any outward sign of emotion from the Rangers manager, Alex Scott, who had fond memories of Baxter's first season, the 1960-61 campaign, recalled that he believes it was the only period when he thought Symon looked relaxed. Scott said, 'Whatever some of the others thought about the way Baxter lived his life, in that first season he had not yet really started to go off the rails and we all enjoyed what he gave the team.

'Baxter was a master and Ian McMillan was a pure footballer whom I enjoyed performing alongside. His passing set me up so often and Baxter's ability to sweep the ball from the left and his inch-perfect diagonal passes gave me more freedom than ever before. I had been a regular for five years by the start of that season, but the next two years saw the best Rangers team I ever played in.

'I know people rhyme off the Greig, McKinnon and Baxter side which came along a couple of years later, but, from 1960 until 1962, Rangers were better. That was because McMillan was still at his peak. By the time the team Rangers fans remember came along, Ian was not the same player. He was near the end.'

Of course, Scott's views were no doubt coloured by the fact that by the time the fabled team emerged, his own star had waned and Scot Symon had found a new favourite to play at outside-right, wee Willie Henderson. However, to back Scott's claim, Rangers had the club's best run in Europe, something which was not to be equalled until 1967. Rangers entered the new European Cup Winners' Cup and their adventure took them all the way to the final. So, despite the romantic view supporters who remember the era attach to the side which evolved over the next few seasons, Scott's view is backed by sound and solid evidence, plus my own memories of a Rangers side carefully constructed by Scot Symon, which played not only winning football but exciting and skilful stuff, good enough to give the continentals a run for their money.

Rangers played fifty-eight games in the season which saw the club reach its first European final, ten short of the number notched up in 2008 when the club reached its fourth. But, unlike now, there was no squad system in those days, just a first eleven and a few experienced reserves, plus a handful of youngsters. In fact, as history shows, despite his outward aura of conservatism, Symon believed in blooding young players, as he had shown in 1955 when an eighteen-year-old Alex Scott became a regular. For the most part, the Rangers team in season 1960-61 read: Ritchie or Niven, Shearer, Caldow, Davis, Paterson, Baxter, Scott, McMillan, Millar, Brand and Wilson. But, the future was signalled on 11 March 1961, when Willie Henderson, then still just seventeen, made his debut in a 2-1 win over Clyde at Ibrox. I was at that game and can recall the buzz of excitement every time Henderson, so different in style from Scott, got the ball. My dad, like Henderson, a Lanarkshire man, worked as a fitter engineer on the steam locos in Coatbridge and had heard Henderson's name mentioned with favour by some of his workmates who had seen the winger in action for Airdrie schools. Symon was well aware that he had unearthed dynamite, but knew it had to be handled with care and wee Willie managed just three appearances, all in the league.

Around the same time, just three days earlier in fact, another name which was to become embedded in the memory of Rangers fans made its first appearance on the team sheet, Ronnie

McKinnon. But it was not as a centre-half that McKinnon took his bow, but in the position in which he had been producing impressive performances for the reserves for eighteen months, right-half. My memory may be playing tricks, but I am sure McKinnon's debut was a floodlit game against Hearts at Ibrox. Robert McElroy's *Rangers: The Complete Record* records a 3-1 win. But the vivid recall I have is of just how impressive the then twenty-one-year-old was. McKinnon played just once more that season and it was to take the famous Russian tour, followed by the latest in a long line of centre-half crises, before McKinnon became a regular and finally solved the No. 5 problem that had dogged Symon since the life ban on Willie Woodburn.

The small group of players Symon relied on that season, therefore, had to be fit to cope with the rigours of playing, not just through a Scottish winter, but with an often-soaking heavy ball on mud-patch pitches. They also had to cram into an old-fashioned bus and take to the pre-motorway road system, plus cope with the vagaries of pre-jet plane flights through Europe. And not cosseted on a charter either, but on scheduled flights, which often involved at least one change.

Whatever Harry Davis, Ralph Brand and Eric Caldow may have thought about Baxter's disruptive influence on the dressing room, Symon must have succeeded in seeing they remained enough of a close-knit bunch to cope with horrendous playing conditions, to endure travel hardships, to go on from their early-season capture of the League Cup to retain the title in thrilling last-ditch style and still manage to blaze a trail abroad by becoming the first British team to reach a European final.

Once again, history places Scot Symon in a place of honour.

16

EUROPE AGAIN

WHEN Rangers returned to the European arena in 1960-61, the season after their humiliation at the hands of Eintracht Frankfurt, they were an entirely different team. Not in terms of personnel, where Jim Baxter was the only new face, but in terms of style and class, it soon became obvious that Rangers had improved immeasurably. Scot Symon must, therefore, have been pleased to hear a neutral verdict on his side from Richard Kress, someone who had been part of the Eintracht team that had demolished his side the previous season. Rangers had survived a scare in the first leg of their opening tie against the Hungarians, Ferencváros, a team that included the legendary Flórián Albert. When they took the lead at Ibrox, things looked bleak, but Rangers recovered to win 4-2 and, in the era before away goals counted as double in the event of an aggregate draw, a two-goal cushion looked decent. That confidence evaporated when the Hungarians struck twice to level the tie, before Symon's favourite goal-poacher Davie Wilson cashed in on a moment's hesitation in the Ferencváros defence for the winner.

But it was in the two matches against the German side, Borussia Möenchengladbach, that Symon's team, with Baxter at the centre of every move, Ian McMillan revelling in the extra space found in Europe in those days and Ralph Brand and Jimmy Millar forging their famous M and B double act, that Rangers came of age in Europe. The first leg was switched to Dusseldorf's larger Rheinstadion to accommodate a huge Ibrox support from the British Army of the Rhine, but it was a visit from old foes Eintracht to watch the team they had humbled a few months earlier which must have made Symon smile quietly to himself.

After watching Rangers demolish his fellow countrymen 3-0, one of those Eintracht stars, Richard Kress said, 'I cannot believe the change there has been in Rangers since we played them. I am amazed in the improvement in the quality of their football in such a short time.' There is no record of Kress providing an opinion as to why that should be the case, but one of the scorers that night, Ian McMillan – Alex Scott and Millar got the others – had his own view. He said, 'The team had taken shape and I found it enjoyable to play with so many good players around me. Jim Baxter had arrived and he was a marvellously talented player. Jim and I were in the middle of the park with Harry Davis behind us and he won the ball and just slipped it forward to one of us.'

McMillan had been critical of Scot Symon's failure to make any tactical switch in the previous season's European Cup semifinal in Eintracht, with the half-time score still 1-1, but his analysis of the way Symon had altered the shape for the next season and added Baxter's brilliance, is another indication of the manager's ability to find the right blend.

It is also interesting to note that when he spoke about Baxter there was none of the rancour some others from that era displayed towards the Fifer's wayward lifestyle and disregard for traditions. That, for me, is significant, for McMillan is a modest man and the sort of person one would expect to be particularly unsettled if someone arrived to upset his habits and quiet way of going about things. There was also a mutual admiration society between the two supremely talented ball-playing midfield men who were the architects of so much of the thoughtful football Rangers played during Symon's best and most successful years as manager. For Baxter, commenting on the Wee Prime Minister, said, 'Ian was terrific and so quiet you sometimes forgot he was there. But you never forgot about him when he started playing. We were chalk and cheese. He spoke quietly and I can't ever recall him swearing. Not even using the mildest word. But on the park we knew each other and were great together. Of all the players I performed alongside at Rangers, McMillan was my favourite.'

McMillan and Baxter certainly worked their magic together when the Germans arrived in Glasgow for the second leg and in the worst downpour seen for years and on a mud heap of a pitch, Rangers hit top gear, living up to the praise of old foe Kress with a thumping 8-0 triumph. Ralph Brand, with a hat-trick, Millar, with two, along with Baxter, Scott and Davis were the scorers. Rangers looked unstoppable and the countdown began as soon as they were drawn to meet Wolves in the semi-final. Baxter recalled, 'They called it the Battle of Britain. I know there have been a few since then, but this was the first and we so much wanted to beat the English team. Wolves were a big deal then.'

Baxter was right. In the Fifties Wolves pioneered European football before the European Cup even started and their win over the magical Magyars of Honved was the stuff of legends. They had been English champions in 1958 and '59 and won the English FA Cup in 1960. They were very much a side still at the top, even after Billy Wright had retired, as others such as Eddie Clamp and Ron Flowers were formidable players.

I was one wee boy who could hardly wait and I pestered my dad and granddad so much that they gave in and took me. Ibrox has never seen a night like that one on 29 March 1960. There were 80,000 packed into the old ground, thundering songs down from the steep terraces, egged on by the Rangers Accordian Band which marched around the track pumping out the club anthems. But, despite the anticipation and the fervour, there was a real worry about whether Rangers would be up to this extremely difficult and dangerous task. That stemmed from the absence at centre-forward of Jimmy Millar, who had been out since mid-January, suffering from a back injury. Symon brought in Max Murray for a spell, but he failed to recapture his old goal touch. A young inside-forward called George McLean – not to be confused with the player of the same name signed at a later date – also wore the number nine jersey. But it looked as though Murray was going to be the man to lead the line against Wolves when he scored in a 2-2 draw with Motherwell at Ibrox four days before the big night.

Then disaster struck. Murray was injured and out. So, too, was McMillan. Symon's solution to that was to change the whole pattern of his side, for there was nobody who could take over McMillan's role as playmaker. Davie Wilson wore the number eight jersey, with youngster Bobby Hume on the left wing. But there was no obvious solution as to who was to play at centre-forward. This was when Symon gambled. For such a serious, studious man welded to tradition, Symon often surprised with his ability to throw the dice. He was to do it again in the 1967 Cup Winners' Cup final and his reputation never recovered when the gamble backfired. But the first time Symon pitched a centre-half in at centre-forward, it worked a treat.

Doug Baillie had played in just three league matches since his Old Firm debut debacle and had not appeared in Europe. But Symon turned to the big, no-holds-barred centre-half and asked him to become a big rummle-'em-up centre-forward for the night.

Things looked bleak and seemed about to go from bad to worse after a mere nine minutes when Davis suffered a leg injury and, in those pre-substitute days, had to limp on. Others may have limped off, but the Iron Man was made of sterner stuff. The trouble for Rangers was that Wolves took control, hitting the crossbar and having efforts cleared off the line by Bobby Shearer and Eric Caldow. Then with thirty-three minutes gone, Alex Scott took off on a flying run, which left Flowers struggling, and shot beyond Wolves' Scottish keeper Malcolm Finlayson.

The goal changed nothing about the way the game was played, with Rangers defending desperately. But with just seven minutes, Wolves made the fatal mistake of thinking Rangers were there for the taking. Clamp played a sloppy pass across his own area and Brand pounced to give Rangers a 2-0 lead to take to the English Midlands. 'When Rangers went to Wolverhampton Town' remains a song played on the tannoy and sung by supporters to this day. The second leg was the stuff of legend and the 10,000 who follow-followed to Wolverhampton was the biggest travelling support by far seen in Europe at the time.

Four days earlier, England had crushed Scotland 9-3 at Wembley. Shearer and Caldow were in that side though not, remarkably, the best player in Scotland, Baxter. So, as well as the glory of Rangers, the honour of Scotland was at stake. And once again Scot Symon showed he knew a thing or two about team selection. This time, having seen the damage Scott's speed could do, he switched his flying winger to centre-forward, Wilson to the right, partnered by the fit-again McMillan. Symon's stroke worked again when Brand slipped a pass to create an opening for Scott to score and when Wolves tried to hit back with a pile-driver, Billy Ritchie leapt, arched backwards and produced a save still talked about by the legions who took over Molineux that night. Another Wolves great, Peter Broadbent, got the equaliser with just over twenty minutes left, but Rangers held steady and Scot Symon became the first manager to lead a British side into a European final.

Jimmy Millar recalled, 'I was the one who was sent out to wave to the fans from the balcony of the team hotel and, to be honest, I felt a bit of a fraud, but I became even more determined to be fit for the final.' Unfortunately, Millar was not ready for the final – then played over two legs – when Fiorentina visited Ibrox. Symon tried his Scott-at-centre-forward trick again, but this time it didn't work. The Italians took the lead when Davis left a passback short and Luigi Milan scored. Davis said, 'I know I got the blame, but Ritchie was responsible, too. He was an outstanding keeper when it came to shot-stopping, but wasn't too keen on leaving his line.'

Rangers had the chance to equalise with a penalty, but Italian keeper Enrico Albertosi's goal line prancing – then illegal – put Eric Caldow off and no retake was given when he blazed wide. Milan got a second and Rangers went to Florence for the match on 27 May with faint hope. That hope was lifted with the news that Millar was back, though he later admitted he was not fit, as he had not played for four months. The great 1958 World Cup final winger from Sweden, Kurt Hamrin, produced a cross for Milan to score again and by the time Scott scored on the hour mark the final was lost. But Scot Symon's patient team building had ensured Rangers became the first Scottish team to reach a final and leave their mark on Europe, and he did it by adding the style of continental class to Scottish power. Those who saw how his Rangers team played in Europe that season cannot help but assess the manager as being up-to-date in many ways as the Sixties got underway. Rangers, under Scot Symon, were swinging.

17

THE PRIVATE SYMON

FEW outsiders ever got beyond the barrier Scot Symon erected between himself and the rest of the world. It is, therefore, surprising that the one person who did and who was given privileged access to the Rangers manager as a man, was a journalist. And a very young one at that. Rodger Baillie went on to become the chief football writer for the *Sunday Mirror*, *Daily Record* and *The Sun*, but during the spell between the late 1950s and the early 1960s he was a very junior sportswriter on the *Record*. What made him unique, though, is that he was stepping out with Symon's only daughter, Carolyn. Courting or, if you like, the old Glasgow word, winching.

Rodger, now in his seventies, is still an active journalist, whose vast experience, superior range of contacts and treasure trove of memories are often still called upon by *The Sun*. Those memories include often visiting Scot Symon's house in Dalkeith Avenue in Dumbreck, and he recalls the house was an imposing Victorian villa and says his visits gave him the opportunity of seeing a side to Symon which was unknown outside of his family and an extremely small circle of friends.

Baillie said, 'He was much more relaxed when he was at home. I was having this teenage romance with Carolyn and it must have been a curious position for him because I was nineteen and I had only gone on to the *Daily Record* sports staff in August of 1959 and started going out with Carolyn in that autumn. He must have thought that I was a young thruster trying to make my name by getting on the inside of stories that he would give me.

'It wasn't like that, but, looking back, I could understand if he felt that way. However, he never showed me anything but courtesy, even if he was a bit wary at the start. I suppose most fathers are wary whether you are the Rangers manager or otherwise.'

One thing which has always intrigued me is what Symon sounded like. Nowadays, managers of even the most lowly clubs are on the airwaves almost every day. But I cannot recall ever hearing Symon being interviewed on radio or television. Baillie was able to fill in that blank, revealing, 'He had a Scottish accent, but not West of Scotland, maybe more a very slight Perthshire accent. The whole picture I got of him at home with his wife, Doreen, who was English, and they had met when he played for Portsmouth and was a charming woman, Carolyn and his son Kenneth, was of a perfectly normal family.

'In fact, interestingly enough, something which you could never have now, or have had for many years, is that his phone number was in the telephone directory, JS Symon, 6 Dalkeith Avenue. If you looked from the outside and forgot he was manager of Rangers, he lived like millions of others. There was nothing out of the ordinary about him.

'I don't know how much his salary was, but he drove a Rover and then an Austin Cambridge, which were the sort of cars middle management, bank managers or headmasters had in those days and he took his holidays in Arran for years before venturing to Majorca when that became a popular destination.

'Socially there were the sort of parties where a few neighbours were invited for drinks, but he and Doreen seldom went out for a meal. Back then, there was only one good hotel in Glasgow, The Central, and hardly any restaurants. My feeling was that he took his strength and his solace from his family and when he got home he closed the door behind him and just tried to shut out the world.

'When I visited and we spoke it was really just chit-chat, although we did sometimes talk about football, about players mostly. He did talk to me about the team sometimes and told me one day that Rangers had a lad who had suddenly shot up six inches. He said they had all been calling him wee John Greig, but that they were going to have to find something else to describe him and that was the first time I heard Greig's name.

'Apart from that, I could not tell you if he had any other interests, whether he played golf or bowls, went to the theatre or what kind of music he liked listening to. As for friends from outside football, the only one I ever knew of was an imposing figure from Bermuda called Alma Hunt. Whatever his antecedents were, they qualified him to play cricket for Scotland and he and Symon played an international together against Australia in 1938 and formed a lifelong friendship.'

The picture of the Symon that Rodger Baillie knew emerges as the painting of a generous-spirited man. As Baillie said, 'He was good at introducing me to people and the man I remember most was Stan Cullis, who was the manager of that great Wolves team. But even after I was no longer going out with Carolyn and going to his house, he always treated me with courtesy. I was sent to do a story on seeing off Rangers when they travelled to London for the European Cup Winners' Cup match with Tottenham Hotspur. I was not going to be covering the game and tickets were like gold dust, but Symon gave me three tickets, which made me very popular with two pals.

'To be honest, I was very much a junior reporter at the *Record* and had very little to do with covering Rangers and didn't get involved with him professionally on a regular basis until I moved to the *Sunday Mirror* in 1963. The relationship between the manager of Rangers and the press and media access was like a parallel universe compared to today. Symon did accept phone calls from journalists at Ibrox and at home, but after a game there were no interviews with the manager. Reporters stood outside the front door and tried to get players to stop and talk.'

Something else which has changed, too, is the way managers and media mingle these days when abroad. A recent example is the press pack joining in with Scotland manager Craig Levein for a five-a-side match. Symon, apart from once, kept himself to himself during Rangers' European adventures, even though the press and the club often shared the same hotel. Baillie's memory bank, though, can recall the one exception to Symon's rule and its humorous postscript. He said, 'The one episode which was different was when Jim Baxter broke a leg in Vienna. It had been an afternoon game and the tradition in Europe was to attend an aftermatch banquet. Symon was affected by Baxter's injury and when the press went into the bar he joined us and entered into the chit-chat quite freely. He drank Dubonnet and soda.

'In those days, most newspapers had either a Rangers player as a columnist or had someone on the payroll to supply them with gossip. The talk got onto this and Alec Young, from the *Daily Mail*, claimed his newspaper did not indulge in that, but Symon told him he knew he went up Jimmy Millar's backstairs to his house. So, he was certainly, in his own quiet way, well aware of what everyone was getting up to. In the morning Gair Henderson, of the *Evening Times*, who had not been at the previous night's session, remarked to Symon that he was sorry he had missed a great night. Symon, though, was back in character and told him the zip was up again, making a motion to his mouth.

'He didn't like the press, but he was not as unco-operative as his image, and he wasn't immune to using the black arts of leaks and spin himself when he felt it could help him. The reporter he used for this was Robert Russell, who was the number two on the *Scottish Daily Express*, then the biggest-selling newspaper in Scotland. If Rangers had a bad result, Robert was summoned to Ibrox and Scot poured out his heart to him. The best example of that was the week after the 7-1 League Cup final defeat against Celtic in 1957. Russell had exclusive stuff from Symon.'

Later, when he was courting Carolyn, the bold Rodger was to benefit from this, just two days after Eintracht Frankfurt had thumped Rangers 6-3 at Ibrox in the European Cup semi-final and the day before the Scottish Cup final against Kilmarnock in the spring of 1960.

Baillie said, 'I met Carolyn and she said her dad had told her to tell me Rangers were going to sign Jim Baxter. I rushed into my office and told my sports editor, but he was far from convinced and made me telephone Symon and ask him if this was true. When I did, he just growled that he had told Carolyn to tell me that and slammed the phone down.' Rangers were far from favourites to beat that fine Killie team and it seemed Symon reasoned the best time to get in his retaliation for any defeat was before it happened and chose his daughter's boyfriend to be the messenger. As it was, Rangers won the Scottish Cup.

Baillie went on, 'Clearly, though, he was left behind in these black arts when Jock Stein arrived. Just like Sir Alex Ferguson went to Manchester United and said he wanted to knock Liverpool off their perch, Stein's idea was to knock Rangers off the back page.'

However, one thing Baillie refuses to go along with is the idea which grew up towards the end of Scot Symon's time at Ibrox, that he was tactically naïve. The veteran reporter, who had some privileged access to Symon, insisted, 'No, I don't think that view of him is right. But, whether by accident or design, and I believe it was more by design than anything else, he built a Rangers team which, for two or three years, could match any of the teams which followed and probably anything that went before. So, he could not have been as naïve as he is sometimes portrayed.'

So what about those criticisms of the way Symon handled Jim Baxter and the belief of many older players that Symon started to lose his authority because of it? Once again, Baillie is the man to turn to for answers. For as well as having had the opportunity to study Symon in his own lair, he became close to Baxter when he ghost wrote the player's *Sunday Mirror* column, to such an extent that when Baxter married, Baillie was his best man. Baillie said, 'Jim certainly gave Symon respect, but it was an era when players were almost becoming pop idols and Matt Busby had very much the same problem with George Best. I always felt that to some degree some of the older guys didn't like all the publicity, which was not about Rangers, but about Jim.'

As Baxter's career really took off and his demand for more money saw the player Symon so loved and depended on and Rangers deadlocked to such an extent it seemed as though Symon was going to lose his prized asset, Baillie played a major role in keeping the best player in the land a player at Ibrox. For the moment, though, it is enough to take on board the insight into Symon the man, the husband and father, provided by one of the finest and most respected football reporters to operate in Scotland for the last half-century. Rodger Baillie was someone who got closer to him than anyone outside his immediate family, at a time when Scot Symon was ensuring Rangers were the best team in Scotland and establishing their status and reputation as a force in Europe.

18

THE PAST IS A FOREIGN COUNTRY

JUST to prove that however much has changed in football since Scot Symon was in his managerial heyday, some things remain the same. Rangers found their run to the final of the European Cup Winners' Cup can was a hindrance to the club's priority, which was winning back the title Hearts had taken the previous season. Just as the rigours of reaching the UEFA Cup final in Manchester in 2008 and the SPL's disgraceful bowing to Celtic chief executive Peter Lawwell's ungracious demands that nothing be done to level the playing field, so Symon's team had to cope with whatever the fixture list threw at them. In the opening weeks of the season that meant coping with the ten games needed between 13 August and 23 October to go all the way to Hampden and win the League Cup. These matches were on top of the eight games in the championship over the same period, plus the first two European matches. That is a total of twenty games, many, such as three Old Firm fixtures, of high intensity, all before the clocks went back.

By the time Rangers brought down the curtain on season 1960–61, Symon's team had played fifty-three matches and travelled the length and breadth of Europe, including the then hazardous and uncomfortable trip behind the real Iron Curtain to the Soviet satellite of Hungary at the height of the Cold War.

It was also the season in which Hearts were overtaken by Kilmarnock as the main threat to Ibrox ambition. Despite having beaten Kilmarnock in the League Cup final, Rangers could not get to grips with them in the league and the Ayrshire side left Ibrox with a 3-2 victory in November. Titles, though, are neither won nor lost in November.

That defeat to Killie was the second Rangers had suffered, the first being when Dundee won 1-0, again at Ibrox, in October. Then came a result which had everybody talking and saying Rangers were not as good as they thought they were, which must have annoyed Symon for he was not given to making boastful claims either in public or in private. What must have rankled with him even more was the display from his team when it went down 1-0 to lowly Ayr United on Christmas Eve. The only consolation was that this time the Rangers loss had not been at Ibrox.

Three defeats before the turn of the year was hardly the stuff of champions, though, especially as Kilmarnock were in such fine form and the next three games Symon faced were against the outstanding Motherwell team of that era at Fir Park, Partick Thistle, managed by his old team-mate Willie Thornton at Ibrox and then at home to Celtic on 2 January. The Old Firm match was, by tradition, played on New Year's Day, but in 1961 that was a Sunday, so in that more religiously-respectful era for the sabbath, it was moved. Baxter had played in those defeats to Dundee, Kilmarnock and Ayr United, giving credence to what Harold Davis said about him and the problems Davis thought he caused. Davis said, 'The only thing Scot ever told us about how to play was just give the ball to Jim. Which was fine if he was playing well. The problems arose when he was having a bad day, and there were a lot more of them than people who lived through that time are willing to admit.'

Certainly, my memory of Baxter's performance in that game against Celtic adds weight to what Davis insists is a memory of Baxter distorted by the years. Rangers had recovered from the shock to their system in Ayr and beaten Motherwell 2-1, with goals from Ian McMillan and Ralph Brand, while Brand, along with Jimmy Millar and Davie Wilson, accounted for the Jags 3-0. They went into the New Year Old Firm game swaggering with confidence. Or, at least, that's what it looked like as far as Baxter was concerned. Maybe he thought it was going to be all too easy and, in fairness to him, that is what it became in later years. But at that time he had yet to impose his superiority on the minds of Celtic's players and when he tried to be too clever, too casual and, frankly, too disrespectful inside his own penalty area, he was robbed of possession by Johnny Divers, who put Celtic into the lead.

George Niven was the goalkeeper that day, although his reign as top choice was coming to an end, and he only played because Billy Ritchie was injured. He recalled, 'Jim was just too cocky and I hated to see anyone trying to footer about in my penalty area.' Niven was a modest man, but despite his small stature, a first-class keeper whose career was extended beyond Rangers by five years when he moved to Partick Thistle. When I interviewed him, he lived quietly in the Highlands, working for British Rail in Dulnain Bridge, just thirty miles outside Inverness. His memory of that game, clearer than the recall of a nine-year-old me, was, 'It was Harold Davis who turned that game for us. He tackled and covered and made sure Celtic never got the chance to settle on their lead. I think Baxter was maybe knocked out of his stride after his mistake. But Harold was never beaten and we came back. I remember we equalised with a goal from Ralphie and wee Davie Wilson got the winner.'

The record books show Niven was correct. However, they do not tell the story of the match and of how Davis rose to the occasion after Baxter's blunder. Davis has always insisted that his criticism of Baxter and the way Scot Symon let him get away with things he would never had allowed others to do, is based on how much he damaged the camaraderie of the dressing room. There are other theories. I have already noted that, as Davis grew older and was less able to cover ground and plug gaps, Baxter was still reluctant to tackle back. Another reason could well have been that until Baxter's arrival at Ibrox, Davis had been very much a favoured player by Symon, who had first come into contact with him when he was manager of East Fife and then taken him to Rangers. However, he was replaced in Symon's special affections by Baxter. Human nature is what it is and Davis, Iron Man though he was and remains, would not have been human had he not felt some resentment.

Whatever the dynamics of the dressing room, Symon could not seem to coax a real run from his team, even after those three big wins. Five days after they beat Celtic, there was a draw away to Airdrie, another draw away to St Mirren, and that was followed by a 4-2 defeat from Dundee at Dens Park. By then, Jimmy Millar was sidelined with a slipped disc and Max Murray could not form the same sort of partnership with Brand. From seeming to have had a comfortable lead after the wins in late December and against Celtic, Rangers found Kilmarnock breathing down their neck.

That gap was closed further going into the home straight when Rangers travelled to Ayrshire and went down 2-0 to Kilmarnock, the challengers and the team managed by Symon's old Ibrox team-mate and the man who was his closest friend in football, Willie Waddell. Alex Scott, another who, like Davis, had enjoyed favoured status as far as Symon was concerned, recalled the aftermath of that defeat to Killie, with a mere three games remaining and the diversion of a European final intruding. Worse was to follow, for the next week Rangers hit rock bottom and crashed to a 6-1 defeat to Aberdeen at Pittodrie, which must have been another of the bad games Baxter had and which Davis rightly insists have been airbrushed from history. It looked as though the unthinkable was about to happen and that Rangers were about to stumble on the finishing line and be overtaken by Kilmarnock.

Scott said, 'Symon did not talk to us at any length very often. His team talks actually became simpler as the years went by. Instead of ordering others to try and get the ball out to me on the right, his instructions had become, "Just work hard, win the tackles and look up and find Jim." But two days after that horrendous defeat at Aberdeen, he must have sensed the title could be lost.

'We did not usually see him at the Albion training ground the day before a game, but he appeared before we were due to meet Hibs at Ibrox. Also, unusually for him, he gathered the players around him and told us we were the best team in Scotland, the best Rangers team he had managed and that he had every confidence that we would win our last two matches and become champions. I remember a few of us who had been around for a while looking at each other and thinking that if Symon said that then he must believe it and it must be true.' Those few words from this man of few words certainly worked their magic. There were no fireworks against Hibs, but sleeves were rolled up and there was a gritty old-fashioned determination to regain pride and to repay Symon for the faith he told the players he had in them.

It was far from plain sailing as Rangers went in without long-term injury victim Millar and Eric Caldow also sidelined. Symon also felt forced to risk Ian McMillan, even though the schemer was not 100 per cent, switching Scott to centre-forward and putting the teenage Willie Henderson in at outside-right. It took just half an hour for all of Symon's plans to go up in smoke. Football is a bit like war, in that whatever plans you make they can mean nothing when the action starts. Henderson was carried off with ligament damage. He remembered, 'I was in tears with the pain and tried to hobble back on, but there was no way I could continue and then I was in tears again, for I had left the team with just ten men. Remember, there were no substitutes in those days.' Henderson need not have worried, for a McMillan goal was all that was needed to send Rangers into the last game of the season, a single point clear of Kilmarnock, needing a win to be certain of the championship. The opponents were the honest men of Ayr United who had inflicted such a sore wound on the Rangers pride earlier in the season.

I was among the 45,000 at Ibrox that afternoon and what a day it was for the fabulous football Symon wanted to see from Rangers. There was no tannoy music to pump up the atmosphere before kick-off, no songs of triumph, apart from the 'Follow Follow' chorus which rolled down from the terraces, and no lap of honour from the players. There was no appearance in front of the crowd from Symon either, though the players deserved to take a bow, as did Symon, for he had galvanised them from that 6-1 defeat at Aberdeen into a fighting ten-man win over Hibs which came straight from the history book of Rangers tradition and onto an outstanding title-clinching 7-3 win triumph over Ayr. Scott, in at centre-forward again, claimed a hat-trick, with Wilson and Brand netting a brace apiece.

Rangers added the title to the League Cup they had already won, ahead of going to be the first British team to play in a European final. Symon's achievements in 1960-61 were considerable, but could not extend to the Scottish Cup.

Which takes us back to Baxter. He had been superb in the second-round tie at Fir Park and Rangers, thanks to two goals from Murray, were cruising. Then Baxter was injured and had to play out the game as a limping passenger on the left wing, allowing Motherwell to come back and force a replay. Baxter was missing when Motherwell visited Ibrox and Rangers were comprehensively beaten 5-2, with the Ibrox gates being closed after 82,000 had paid their cash at the turnstiles.

19

FIRMLY ENTRENCHED

BY the summer of 1961, with Rangers champions again, Scot Symon was firmly established as the manager. If there had been a moment two years earlier when his job had been in danger, then it had long gone. This was an era when, unlike today, clubs did not chop and change managers at the drop of a hat. That was particularly true as far as the Old Firm were concerned. Across the city, Celtic were managed by their former centre-forward, Jimmy McGrory, who had taken over in 1945. He won his one and only title in 1954, along with the Scottish Cup. Then came the 1957 League Cup. But those were his only honours, yet he survived until 1965.

Symon, therefore, by the summer of 1961, was firmly entrenched. The 1960-61 championship had been his fourth in the seven seasons since he took over from Bill Struth, and there had been a Scottish Cup and a League Cup won, too, on top of Rangers becoming the first British team to reach a European final just a year after the run to the semi-final of the European Cup. But what must also have given Symon deep and private satisfaction was the acknowledgement that Rangers had evolved under his guidance and grown into a team where the accent was on skill. He may even have entertained the thought that summer, while on his annual family holiday in Arran, that he had escaped from Struth's shadow.

In one rare interview given by Symon after he left Rangers, he admitted that he found his early years a sore trial, made more difficult by the presence of Struth around the club. It was a similar situation to that Bob Paisley endured after taking over from Bill Shankly as Liverpool manager. Shanks continued to turn up at the training ground and take part in five-a-sides and the players continued with their ingrained habit of calling him 'boss'. In the end, in order that Paisley had authority, the Liverpool board had to tell Shankly to stay away. This was not an option open to Symon, even though he must have felt it awkward that Struth continued to spend some of each day at Ibrox, where Symon now sat in the office the Old Man had directed and dictated from for thirty-four years. Symon spoke only briefly about that period when he was interviewed by Ian Peebles for the book which celebrated Rangers' centenary, *Growing with Glory*, published in 1973.

There is a chapter in the book devoted to Symon, but a combination of his refusal to give much co-operation, plus the fact that at that time it was just six years on from his sacking, meant wounds were still sore. Not just on his side either, for Rangers realised the damage chairman John Lawrence had inflicted on the club's image by the way he so brutally sacked Symon. However, his brief comment on how he felt about taking over from Struth, and the Old Man's continued presence, gives us some sort of grasp of how difficult his task was between 1954 when he arrived and Struth's death two years later. Symon said, 'Although Bill retired, he never left Ibrox. There was nowhere else that he could go and nowhere else that he wanted to be. He had spent a lifetime at the ground and enjoyed being there. As a director, he was entitled to be there and there were many mornings when he got to Ibrox before I did. I had to be constantly on my guard not to do anything which would offend or hurt him because I had too much respect for him.'

It says much for Symon's sensitivity and loyalty to the Old Man that he treated Struth so well and with such consideration during a period when he was having to pick up the pieces Struth had left behind. A lesser man may have not been so considerate. Symon, though, as so many stories about him reveal, if only with a glimpse, was a generous-spirited person.

For all of that, there is no overlooking Symon's determination to do the job his own way and be his own man. He was not merely a clone of Struth. That is an easy mistake to make when looking back over more than half a century and seeing what appears to be obvious similarities between the man who made Rangers great, Bill Struth, and the man he chose to carry on the club's greatness, Scot Symon. Both were dapper, tidy and well dressed, though – especially in pictures of him when he was a younger man – Struth was more flamboyant in his dress sense. Both valued tradition and discipline, though both could indulge anyone they deemed to be special. It was Torry Gillick with Struth and, of course, Jim Baxter, as far as Symon was concerned. Both also always managed to look older than their years. In Symon's case, it could be said of him that he was one of those men who appeared to have been born middle-aged.

But probably the biggest difference between them was that Symon was a football man. Struth had been an athlete – a professional sprinter – while his successor had come up through the junior ranks and played for Dundee, Portsmouth and Rangers. Struth had been the Rangers trainer who became manager when Willie Wilton died in a drowning accident in 1920. Symon had learned how to be a manager at East Fife and Preston North End, and the Rangers he took over were a bigger and more important club and Scottish institution than they were in 1920. To underline other differences, it is interesting to get a take on what Struth was like from one of the few players who enjoyed almost equal time playing for both managers, George Niven. The goalkeeper was signed for Rangers by Struth in 1947, made his debut at the end of season 1951-52 and became the regular first choice, replacing Bobby Brown, at the start of the following season. He remained at Ibrox until 1962, eight years into Symon's reign, during which time he had been first choice for most matches.

Niven, recalling Struth, said, 'Old Struth always had a word for you no matter who you were. Right from the youngest laddie in the reserves to the biggest star in the first team, he took an interest. He was a man who really cared about his players and you realised how much he thought of you. But he did have an aura about him and even though he was quite an old man by the time I knew him and walked with a stick after having had his lower leg amputated, everyone knew he was very much the boss.

'However, he never shouted and bawled at players. If you had played badly then he would let things lie for a couple of weeks and then speak to you to try and find out what was wrong. After I had made it into the first team, there was one game when I didn't do too well. I had forgotten it a fortnight later when I was told Struth wanted to see me in his office. I tried to remember what I had done wrong, but when I got there he wanted me to tell him if there was anything bothering me. He said that if I had any problems I should tell him and he would help in any way he could.

'When I told him there was nothing wrong, he said that was all right and that he didn't mind someone having a bad game now and then, just as long as he knew they were giving their very best and trying as hard as they could for the club. Struth really was a wonderful man and he used to make the team wait until just before we left the dressing room before we put on our shorts so that they were crisp and fresh. In the dressing room, though, he would sometimes give Sammy Cox a rap with the walking stick because Sammy would often swear and Struth did not like that.'

The picture painted by Niven of Struth is of a paternal figure, sometimes more concerned with the personal life of a player, and driven to uphold high standards of appearance. Symon, though, was much more of a professional and the idea of him whacking one his top players because of bad language is too ridiculous to contemplate. Baxter would have been black and blue. Though, as the story told by Rodger Baillie about John Greig revealed, there was a paternal aspect to his interest in the younger players on the Rangers books and he certainly never flinched from giving youth its head. He was rewarded for this adventurous streak by the contributions made by such as Alex Scott, Davie Wilson, Willie Henderson and – the by then no longer wee – John Greig. In fact, the season which lay ahead, 1961-62, was to see Symon prefer Henderson to Scott, even though Scott remained Scotland's first choice, once again underlining his modernity.

Unfortunately for Symon and his lasting reputation, although he had escaped the clutches of Struth's shadow inside the dressing room, there were still many fans who turned on every Rangers slip-up, departure from tradition or signing that did not work out by declaring that it would never have happened in Struth's day. It is that attitude which was fed to a new generation of Rangers supporters and which has continued down through the years, diminishing Symon's legacy to the Rangers story and which this biography seeks to put right.

20

SYMON'S SETTLED SIDE

IT is a measure of how happy Scot Symon was with his team and with the younger players who were coming through that the summer of 1961 saw him make just one signing, centre-forward Jim Christie, for £10,000 from Ayr United. Christie had scored a hat-trick against Rangers on the last day of the season. Signing a player who had performed well against his team became a pattern of Symon's time as manager. He knew that the one position where he needed cover was at centre-forward, where there was no suitable replacement should Jimmy Millar have again succumbed to the slipped disc problem which had side-lined him for most of the second half of the previous campaign. Christie was raw and rugged, a Boys' Brigade captain from Maryhill who I often saw wearing his uniform in the area, although I have to admit the Scouts was my choice of youth organisation. At a glance, Christie had the sort of scoring record any centre-forward would be proud of. A goal a game. But that broke down to eight goals in as many matches. He was not a Symon success story.

Basically, Symon's first-choice team had not altered from the one he would have gone for the previous season, given an injury-free dressing room. It read: Ritchie; Shearer and Caldow; Davis, Paterson and Baxter; Scott, McMillan, Millar, Brand and Wilson.

It was the team Symon sent out at Cathkin on 12 August to open the campaign with a 2-0 League Cup win over Third Lanark, earned by two Davie Wilson goals.

It was another Rangers team that played that same day which remains firmly imprinted in my mind, the reserve side which beat Third Lanark's second string 11-0 at Ibrox. I was there with my granddad, whose love of watching the future generation had been passed to me. It came from a time when travel to away matches was either too difficult or too costly, or both. That is why reserve matches in the old days attracted decent crowds. There were around 5,000 at Ibrox that afternoon and the team we watched was: Norrie Martin; Davie Provan and Bobby King; Ronnie McKinnon, Doug Baillie and Billy Stevenson; Willie Henderson, John Greig, Max Murray, Willie Penman and Bobby Hume. By the time the season ended, Baillie had had a long run before McKinnon claimed the centre-half role, Henderson had usurped Scott, and Greig had deputised regularly for McMillan at inside-right. Later, Provan was to become a Rangers and Scotland regular at left-back following Eric Caldow's broken leg.

The strength and growing contribution to Rangers' future made by so many of its players is another testimony to Scot Symon. He was never afraid to spend big money – relative to the times – to get what he believed was the best for Rangers, but he was also shrewd in spotting and developing young talent. Having cracked his League Cup hoodoo a year earlier, Symon plotted a course back to Hampden and a final against Hearts which ended in a 1-1 draw, with Millar scoring. The replay was held over until the week before Christmas and on a foggy midweek night, Millar, Ralph Brand and McMillan scored in a 3-1 win.

The defence of the league title was something Symon soon realised was going to be harder to manage as Dundee took over from Kilmarnock as the team ready to challenge. Once again,

Celtic were an irrelevance. Rangers began their title defence with an eight-game unbeaten run, which included five wins and three draws, before Dundee were due at Ibrox on a mist-shrouded day in November. Many Dundee supporters were turned back by police before they got to Glasgow in the mistaken belief the game was off because of fog. Symon ended the day wishing it had been postponed. Rangers were demolished 5-1. But a story of what happened after the match again serves to illustrate the measure of the man.

Years later, when I was working as a young sportswriter on a group of weekly newspapers in north London, my job was to cover Tottenham Hotspur. Alan Gilzean was still playing for Spurs. When I first approached him for an interview, he insisted we go to the Bell and Hare pub next to White Hart Lane. Gillie gave this young fellow countryman his time and his thoughts, then after buying a second round, asked me what team I supported and smiled when I answered that I was a bluenose. I also told him that I had been at Ibrox when he scored four goals in that 5-1 win and that, despite him turning my team over, I had become a fan. It was the plain and simple truth. Gilzean then told me that when Dundee were leaving Ibrox, Scot Symon was walking Dens boss Bob Shankly – brother of Bill – down the marble stairs when he spotted Gilzean. Gillie said, 'He must have been hurting, but he came across towards me with his hand outstretched and told me that I had done well and that he had no complaints about how his team had played as there wasn't much any of his players could have done to stop me. No opposition manager before or since has ever done that.'

With Alex Hamilton at right-back, Ian Ure at centre-half, Andy Penman in midfield, Gilzean up front and Gordon Smith, adding a last chapter to his glorious career, out on the right wing, Dundee were a fantastic team. The truth is, Rangers were lucky to escape with a 5-1 defeat that afternoon but did well to stay with them right into the home straight and the last day of the season.

After Dundee slipped, Rangers began to look as though they could recover ground, but when their trip to Dens ended in a goalless draw there was a sense of a missed opportunity and Rangers finished their campaign, having run out of steam with three draws, while Dundee clinched the title by beating St Johnstone in Perth on the campaign's closing day. Gilzean scored two of their three goals in a runaway romp.

But, as well as retaining the League Cup, Rangers successfully defended the Scottish Cup and, in doing so, Symon showed that he was very much a manager who valued youth. Willie Henderson celebrated his eighteenth birthday on 24 January 1962 by laying on the goals for Millar and Brand in a 2-1 win over Partick Thistle at Ibrox. He was a growing presence in the team, sometimes when Alex Scott was injured, but on other occasions when Symon showed a preference for the teenager over Scott, who had turned just twenty-five in December 1961 and was at the peak of his prowess.

It looked as though matters had come to a head and had been decided in Scott's favour in February 1962 when Henderson got caught up in a traffic jam on his way to Ibrox for an important European Cup tie against Standard Liege of Belgium. Rangers had lost the first leg 4-1, with Henderson in the side, but it had been an uncharacteristic performance by a side weakened by the absence of Caldow and McMillan, and Symon must have felt that with these key men restored for the second leg there was a chance of pulling off a famous comeback. Certainly that was the feeling among the supporters and, ironically, the near-80,000 who set off for Ibrox actually helped contribute to Rangers' downfall, for they created the snarl-up which brought Glasgow to the standstill and marooned Henderson, forcing Symon to turn to

Scott. In the event, Scott did well while a Caldow penalty and a Brand strike took Rangers to within a goal of a play-off.

Many felt that Henderson would find it hard to gain Symon's forgiveness, though Scott later explained that he was one who wasn't surprised when the manager forgave the teenager before the season was much older. He said, 'Symon loved wee Willie. You could see him give a quiet smile when Willie was laughing and joking with the rest of the team. The wee man was a character and I sensed that my time was running out, for Symon was treating Willie in much the same way as he had me when I first started playing for him when I was the same age as Willie.

'But I knew my time was up when the team was pinned up for the Scottish Cup final and wee Willie was in. I had played for Scotland against England at Hampden the week before and we had won 2-0. It was the first time Scotland had beaten England at Hampden for twenty-five years and I was full of it. I thought that after all I had done for him in his first years as manager, I deserved an explanation from him, but Symon said nothing.' That was often the case, though when put into the context of his other many human qualities, this failure was more likely to be because of Symon's shy nature rather than any hard-heartedness. Scott, understandably, was angry at his treatment and the next season left Rangers for £45,000 and joined Everton where he starred in their great championship-winning sides of the Sixties.

The Scottish Cup, though, was to throw one slice of luck Symon's way. Jim Baxter could not get away from National Service duty to play against Motherwell in the semi-final in the spring of 1962 and Billy Stevenson was also unavailable, leaving Symon with a headache he did not need, especially as Millar was injured. He turned to his reserve side and Ronnie McKinnon, switching him from right-half. Max Murray got two and Wilson the winner in an epic 3-2 triumph, but the man of the match was McKinnon, who had a blinder.

Throughout the season, the hardy perennial problem of a centre-half haunted Symon again. Bill Paterson had started the season but managed to hang on for one match after the loss of five goals to Dundee. Clearly what Symon had said to Gilzean was the truth, but not the whole truth. Doug Baillie returned, but Symon was still searching and there was a see-saw between the two, with Paterson in against Motherwell. Clearly, though, after his performance against Motherwell, a place was going to have to be found for McKinnon. And, just as clearly, that place was not going to be at left-half. Rangers' next game was four days later and resulted in a 4-0 win over St Johnstone in Perth, with goals from Wilson and Brand, plus two from Greig, still seen as McMillan's deputy at inside-right. But the significant thing in the Rangers team that night was that the man wearing the number five shirt was Ronnie McKinnon. He was to remain there for the next decade and the following season was part of that famous half-back line of Greig, McKinnon and Baxter.

Symon often tried to move players around to see how they performed in different positions and sometimes got it wrong. He could coax a decent or even outstanding performance or short run of performances from someone asked to try a strange position. In McKinnon's case, he got it spectacularly right for the next ten years.

With Henderson on the right and McKinnon at centre-half, Rangers beat St Mirren 2-0 in the Scottish Cup final, with goals from Brand and Wilson. But the player who caught Symon's eye that day played for St Mirren. When Symon created a Scottish record transfer fee to sign him, that player became part of the problem that led to Symon's downfall. But the Berwick disaster was more than five years and an unimaginable world away.

21

SERIOUS REPERCUSSIONS

TWO events which occurred in the second half of season 1962-63 were to have serious repercussions for Scot Symon. One was something the manager had no control over, the death of chairman Baillie John F. Wilson, but the other was the signing of George McLean, who in the end had a devastating impact on Symon's control.

It happened in January 1963 when Symon created another new Scottish record transfer fee by signing the St Mirren player who had been the man of the match in the previous season's Scottish Cup final against Symon's team, George McLean. But that afternoon at Hampden McLean had played at left-half. What on earth Symon wanted with a left-half was anybody's guess. Perhaps he feared that he would lose Jim Baxter, who had, even that early, begun to believe Rangers were not paying him what he was worth.

As it was, in unique and strange circumstances, the money was found, from another source, to keep Baxter at Rangers. Symon's part in this scheme will be revealed later by the man at the centre of it, the by then chief football writer on the *Sunday Mirror*, Rodger Baillie. For the moment Symon had to find a place in his team for McLean, a tall, strikingly good-looking guy with a dress sense which went beyond merely stylish and fashionable and earned him the nickname in the newspapers of 'Dandy'. Some supporters who never took to him had another name for him. They called him 'Mince McLean', with more than a nod in the direction of that old Glasgow insult which branded anything not quite up to the mark as 'mince'.

Once again Symon indulged in his habit of finding a position for a player other than the one the new arrival had operated in at his previous club. There was certainly a case to be made for finding a successor to Ian McMillan, who was due to turn thirty-two in March 1963 and who was increasingly prone to injuries. He managed just twelve of the thirty-four league matches played that season. Symon persisted with McLean in that inside-right role, even though it soon became clear that he was not the right sort of player to provide a supply of passes for Willie Henderson to run on to. Actually, the solution to that problem was already available to Symon inside Ibrox in the shape of a beautifully balanced, polished inside-forward from the old tradition, the then still teenage Alex Willoughby. He made his first appearances towards the end of that season and his touch and vision were much appreciated by supporters.

Perhaps I am biased because Willoughby once conducted a session at the coaching class I attended in Dunard Street Primary School no more than a couple of goal-kicks away from Firhill, but I always felt he was the man who should have taken over from McMillan. For whatever reason, Symon never appeared to fully trust Willoughby, something which, as events unfolded during Symon's last full season in charge, put the manager on the back foot.

The other thing that happened was something Symon had no control over. Rangers chairman Baillie John F. Wilson died. Wilson may have harboured dark thoughts about Symon's future in the twenty minutes between Rangers losing to Aberdeen in April

1959 and the fact that Hearts had lost to Celtic being made official, confirming Rangers as champions, but in the main, he was Symon's champion and did not interfere with the manager's running of the team and club on day-to-day matters. His successor, John Lawrence, was a different kettle of fish. He was, according to Rodger Baillie, not quite in touch with reality at times even as far back as 1963 and, again according to Baillie, by the time the crisis of 1967 broke, was, in the veteran reporter's words, 'ga-ga.'

Unfortunately for Scot Symon, the man who assumed greater importance within the Ibrox corridors of power after Wilson's death and Lawrence becoming chairman was someone about whom I have never heard a good word spoken or read a good word written. His name was Willie Allison and he appeared to work chairman Lawrence like a glove puppet. Allison had been the sports editor of the *Sunday Mail* before getting his dream job as the first press officer employed by Rangers. But after Lawrence took over at the head of the boardroom table, Allison's influence extended way beyond his job description. And it was a malignant influence. Rodger Baillie observed, 'Allison was meant to help with press relations, but he was more a hindrance than a help.'

In his excellent autobiography *Managing My Life*, Sir Alex Ferguson is even more scathing and damning about Allison, who was responsible for making life uncomfortable for him at Ibrox after Symon's sacking, and who eventually helped to hurry Fergie through the exit door. Another example of how Allison worked was when, after Baillie John F. Wilson's death, a vacancy on the board was filled by Allison's crony Matt Taylor. Wilson's son, John Wilson, already a director, became vice chairman, but he was soon out-manoeuvred by Allison in order to put his pal Taylor into the vice chairman's seat. Again, according to Baillie,

Taylor was not far behind Lawrence when it came to being an old man with an increasingly slender grip on reality, thus further strengthening Allison's influence, leaving Scot Symon without a power base or an ally to protect him from the enemy within.

In a way, that actually increases Symon's stature from a historical point of view. For far from spending time, thought and effort on any backstage politics, or being motivated by Machiavellian motives, Symon gave all his concentration and every one of his efforts to the Rangers team. Which is why he deserves to be remembered more and to be given a more prominent place in the club's history. For Scot Symon was an honourable man in the best tradition of Rangers.

Unlike the man who conspired against him, Willie Allison, a man whose low place in history is assured thanks to Sir Alex Ferguson's assessment of his character. Or lack of it. For many years what Allison did to Symon, and then to him, coloured Ferguson's view of the club he grew up supporting and then played for, to such an extent that he refused the chance to leave Aberdeen and become Rangers manager in 1983. However, in the last decade Ferguson has, if you like, returned to his roots and is often heard to speak about what a marvellous club Rangers is. As many of those who hear Ferguson's complimentary comments about Rangers are among the biggest movers and shakers in the football world, he has been described to me as the best PR man Rangers could possibly have.

That is something nobody ever claims Willie Allison was.

22

SYMON AND BILL NICHOLSON

THE nearest I ever got to meeting Scot Symon was when, as a youngster, I stood outside the main entrance at Ibrox and approached this austere, middle-aged man, dressed in much the same way as my dad when he went out at the weekend, and asked him politely and tentatively for his autograph. He did not speak one word, but handed me back my still-treasured leather-bound autograph book bearing the legend JS Symon. However, about ten years later I did get to meet and talk with a man hewn from much the same managerial rock as Symon, the great Tottenham Hotspur manager Bill Nicholson. When I was a young sportswriter covering Spurs for the North London Weekly Herald Group, I had privileged access to Billy Nick. Or, as he was to me then and as he remained whenever we met in later life, Mr Nicholson.

There is a parallel there with another of the great stories told about Symon by Rodger Baillie and which has helped to make this more than just a football book, but which has also set Symon the man into context against the background of contemporary events and more. Baillie said, 'I was very young when I first started courting his daughter and called him Mr Symon. Even when I was made chief sportswriter at the *Sunday Mirror*, he was still Mister to me and it was only many years later I felt senior enough to call him Scot.'

Back in my time covering Spurs, Monday afternoon was my time to call in at White Hart Lane. Directly across the High Road Tottenham was my newspaper's offices and the majority of Mondays, Nicholson was there and was willing to throw open his door to this then young reporter. There were times when I was in and out in ten minutes, after having asked him a few questions about the next match, but there were other Monday afternoons when he ordered a pot of tea and we would talk at length. Always about football, but seldom about his current side, which contained such tremendous players as Alan Gilzean, Martin Chivers and Martin Peters – a particular favourite of mine – plus the best goalkeeper I have ever seen, the majestic Pat Jennings.

Nicholson much preferred to hark back to his Double-winning team and the years that followed immediately after 1960-61. He knew I was a Rangers fan and once told me – this would be in the winter of 1972 – why Derek Johnstone was a better centre-forward than centre-half. That's why I never went along with speculation in the press eighteen months or so later linking Spurs with Johnstone as a replacement for the immense Welsh pivot, Mike England.

One afternoon, after the tea had been called for and work taken care of, Nicholson asked me if I remembered the two ties his Double team, by then reinforced by Jimmy Greaves, had played against Rangers. I did, having been confined to listening to the first game on the wireless, but managing to get my dad and granddad to take me to the second leg at Ibrox. He then wanted to know if I had ever met Scot Symon, which I admitted I had not, but told him the story of asking him for and getting his autograph without a word being spoken. Now, Nicholson was a Yorkshireman and a man of his times and upbringing. He was, as I suspect Symon was, a man of few words. But there were times when he was garrulous and when he was, you listened.

Nicholson told me of his memory of those two ties and of the times before the two teams were drawn to play each other in the autumn of 1962, and it soon became clear to me that Symon was a man and a manager much admired by Nicholson. Which was good enough for me because, young though I was and still relatively inexperienced, I knew enough to recognise in Bill Nicholson a special man. A man of honour and a man of substance whose only concession to flair was to imbue the many Tottenham teams he built with style, skill and swagger.

The gist of what he said was that when Symon had been manager at Preston North End he had admired the way they played and knew that it must have been a hard job for a young manager from Scotland to take over an English team that contained the England legend Tom Finney. Not that Nicholson suggested Finney would have been anything other than a gem to inherit for the new manager. Nicholson also said, 'I knew the Rangers teams he had built and knew how good Jim Baxter was, but felt Dave Mackay could be more than a match for him.' If there was one player who could make the often-flinty Billy Nick come over all moist-eyed, it was Mackay.

The Tottenham manager also spoke about how later that season he had contacted Symon to express an interest in buying Alex Scott but was told that he had been promised to Everton, then managed by Harry Catterick, who was a football friend of Symon's. Nicholson said that from what he knew of Symon he realised it would have been a waste of time trying to open a bidding war to beat Everton for the player. Transfers in those days were conducted by manager-to-manager negotiations and, said Nicholson, Symon had given his word to Catterick he would sell Scott to Everton and so, as far as he was concerned, that was that. It was a case of one man, who I knew to be a man of his word, recognising in Symon a kindred spirit.

That season's European campaign was in the Cup Winners' Cup, and I shall never forget the way it opened with a match against the glamorous Spaniards from Seville at Ibrox on 5 September 1962. A couple of nights earlier had been the big parade of trams through the city for the last night of the Glasgow trams. My wee pal Neil McDiarmid and I went into town to see it and had to go to a shop inside the old St Enoch Station to buy a film for his Brownie 127 camera. Then, as now, we were 'haundless' – another quaint old Glasgow term basically meaning useless – and could not put the film in the camera. It was at this point we noticed a group of clearly exotic guys in the station, who stood out in the monochrome Glasgow of the era, and recognised one as Canario, the man who had played outside-right for Real Madrid in their legendary 7-3 European Cup final win over Eintracht Frankfurt at Hampden two years earlier. He had moved to Seville. We approached him and he fitted the film into Neil's camera and then signed autographs for us. It never occurred to Neil or to me to ask him to pose for pictures.

The next time we saw him and his Seville mates they were left dazed by a Rangers performance out of tune with the mono-chrome era as it dazzled with dash and classy colour and is still talked about with a sense of awe by those of us still around from the 80,000 lucky enough to see it. Symon sent out a team which clicked perfectly and slaughtered Seville with a Jimmy Millar hat-trick and one from Ralph Brand. The second leg saw Seville launch a full-blooded assault on Rangers players, to such an extent Willie Henderson had to take to his heels and take refuge behind the rugged Billy Ritchie. Seville won 2-0, but Rangers went through.

If the meeting with Wolves eighteen months earlier had been billed as a Battle of Britain, then when the draw paired Rangers with Spurs, this tie got the full treatment in the press. No wonder, for Rangers and Tottenham Hotspur were by far the best, most skilful footballing teams and star-studded sides in Scotland or England. It was to be a battle royal. Unfortunately for Symon, no matter how good he or the Rangers supporters thought the team was, the Tottenham team, built at enormous expense by Nicholson, was better. At £17,500, Baxter was by far the most expensive Ibrox player. Spurs had Jimmy Greaves, whose £99,000 fee had been pegged there by the shrewd Nicholson in order that Greaves did not have to carry the burden of being the first £100,000 player.

Nothing Scot Symon had, or, given Rangers' resources, may have had at his disposal could have stopped Greaves, Mackay, John White and Danny Blanchflower and Spurs, exploiting a weakness to crossballs which stopped Ritchie ever becoming a world-class keeper, something which the still-inexperienced Ronnie McKinnon had not yet learned to compensate for. Rangers were ripped apart, losing 5-2 in the first leg. The second game saw Tottenham come out on top again, this time 3-2.

All those years afterwards, Nicholson still appreciated the way Scot Symon accepted those two defeats, especially as they were inflicted on a team he had been building with more than just one eye on Europe, only to be handed, through the bad luck of the draw, British opposition more attuned to exploiting the weakness in the Rangers side than continentals were.

Although Nicholson never came out, even in the privacy of his chats with me, and condemned Rangers' treatment of Symon, he did express his sympathy for the fact Symon lost his job. Strangely, just eighteen months or so after that conversation, by which time I had moved to Birmingham, Nicholson was sacked and in just such a high-handed and brutal fashion by Tottenham Hotspur as Symon had been by Rangers. It was just another parallel between two fine men and managers. One who I met and shared many a pot of afternoon tea with and another who I only ever came into contact with when I asked him for his autograph.

23

MYTHS AND LEGENDS

THERE are as many myths in football as there are legends. One is that, when he was Celtic manager, Martin O'Neill's team dominated Scottish football. A quick comparison of the seven trophies Celtic won in O'Neill's five years in charge, compared to the same number won by Rangers during Alex McLeish's four-and-a-half years at Ibrox, shoots that one down. One other that this book has put firmly in its place is the notion that when Rangers went on tour in Denmark in the summer of 1960 and an injury to Max Murray meant there was a vacancy which was filled by Jimmy Millar. The stories go that this was the first time the player had performed in the number nine shirt. Millar was able to give lie to that by revealing that he had been playing at centre-forward for Dunfermline at the very time Scot Symon signed him. But there is another myth that also has to be nailed and it concerns the emergence of John Greig as a regular in the number four shirt, to become the final piece in the most famous half-back line in Rangers' history, the one put in place by Symon, of Greig, McKinnon and Baxter.

The first time I saw Greig play was for the reserves in that 11-0 win over Third Lanark in August 1961, which was just after Symon had told Rodger Baillie of how he was going to have to find a new nickname for 'Wee' John Greig after the Edinburgh youngster had shot up by six inches over the close season. Greig was an inside-right and it was in that position that he made his debut that season, a 4-0 win over Falkirk at Ibrox. On that occasion, he deputised for Ian McMillan and partnered Willie Henderson. Greig played eleven times in that championship-winning team, scoring a highly creditable seven goals. He was marked down by Symon as one for the future.

When Rangers went on their now legendary summer tour of Russia – an adventure which has assumed mythical status – Jim Baxter was unavailable, on Her Majesty's Service with the Black Watch. His understudy, Billy Stevenson, had a family crisis and could not travel either. Symon decided to gamble on the then still only nineteen-year-old Greig at left-half. Greig had a terrific tour as Rangers trailblazed, beating Locomotive Moscow 3-1, Dynamo Tbilisi 1-0 and drawing 1-1 with the champions of all the Soviet Union, Dynamo Kyiv. All the reports that came back rated Greig, at left-half, as the outstanding find of the tour, which is where the myth started.

Ask any Rangers supporter and their immediate recollection will be that when Rangers started season 1962-63, Greig's performances on the Russian tour had established him as a wing-half, not, of course, in Baxter's number six shirt, but at right-half. This myth was debunked by no less a source than the man himself. Greig said, 'I think that Scot Symon had decided that my future lay as a defender rather than a midfield player, but I did not win an automatic choice at right-half at the expense of Harry Davis when the season started, even though Harry was in the latter stages of his career.

'I reverted to inside-right and that is where I was playing when the big freeze closed football down at the start of January 1963. It was when the thaw set in, making training conditions difficult underfoot, that Harry pulled a muscle in a practice game and I was in at right-half the following Saturday against Dunfermline.'

Greig, therefore, had to wait from returning from Russia in June, until Rangers went east again to East End Park on 9 March, to get in at right-half. Symon did not need any more evidence to convince him of Greig's worth in that role, which at the time was to be the more defensive of the wing-halves, covering the areas behind the Baxter brilliance, McMillan's scheming and the linking of the other inside-forward, Ralph Brand, with Millar as a twin strike force. The truth is that when looked at with hindsight, Symon was slow to react to what Greig had shown he could offer and perhaps reluctant to see the end of Davis, a player and a man he admired and respected. Maybe his loyalty to Davis was a mistake, though the only real damage Rangers suffered in the first half of the season was those defeats in Europe inflicted by Tottenham Hotspur and, with the best will in the world, it is difficult to imagine that the change of Greig in place of Davis would have made much of a difference at either White Hart Lane or the second leg at Ibrox.

Davis, though, was not a completely spent force and his tackling was still formidable, even if his ability to cover ground, plugging gaps, was no longer compensated for by his ability to read a game, uncanny though that remained. It is for his physical presence, though, that Harold 'Iron Man' Davis is still so fondly remembered by all who saw them, including me, and was one of the attributes which endeared him to Symon, no mean man in the tackling department in his own playing days.

Nobody got a closer view of the Davis's tackling technique than the man immediately behind him, Bobby 'Captain Cutlass' Shearer, a red-headed right-back who, as his nickname suggests, could tackle like a demon. But, according to Shearer, he was a pussycat compared to Davis. Shearer said, 'I know what people said about me being a hard man, but really, compared to Harold, I was nothing. He was as hard as nails and had a terrific build. He was extremely strong and every pound of muscle went behind every tackle he made. The truth is that when he tackled someone, if that player somehow managed to keep going, then when I moved in there wasn't all that much left of him to tackle.

'When Greig came in he was pretty tough, too, and he was faster and got around more as well. I was lucky that as I started approaching the end of my time at Rangers, that when Harold went he was replaced by Greig. I know Symon had a special place in his affections for Harold and you could understand why. Maybe he was reluctant to see him go, but the fact is he could not ignore Greig and when you look back on what Greig went on to achieve then you realise why Symon knew the youngster's time had come. It wasn't in Symon's make-up to take Harold aside and explain things to him, but the manager would have agonised over his decision and it was the right one.' Davis, however, still had something to give Rangers before his race was run. Though the first of the two Cups won the previous season, the League Cup, was surrendered at the semi-final stage when Rangers went down 3-2 to Kilmarnock, regaining the crown in the championship was the priority for Symon, especially after his European dream was shattered by Tottenham Hotspur.

After opening with four straight wins, champions Dundee visited Ibrox on 29 September with Rangers determined to avenge that 5-1 beating the previous season. But the game ended 1-1, with Millar getting the Rangers goal. But, as the campaign gathered pace, Dundee found what many a side was to discover in the coming years, a European campaign could have repercussions on the home front, and they slipped away. Instead, the challenge came from a surprising direction, Firhill. Partick Thistle had a superb side, including a top-class and experienced goalkeeper, former Ibrox man George Niven. By the time the New Year's holiday fixtures loomed, the countdown started to an unusual title race crunch clash between Rangers and Partick Thistle in Maryhill on 2 January.

Before that, though, Rangers had to take care of Celtic at Ibrox on New Year's Day at Ibrox at the same time as the other Glasgow derby was played at Shawfield, where Thistle met Clyde. That's right, two games scheduled within twenty-four hours. That was back in the days when men were men. Once again, the irrelevance of Celtic was underlined by the fact that I can recall the talk on the subway to Ibrox was about the Thistle game. It was assumed Celtic would be beaten. And it proved to be another of those films we had seen before, as my dad used to say. It also proved to be a swansong for Davis. On a rock-hard pitch and in freezing conditions, with Greig at inside-right in front of him, Davis scored the opening goal. Millar, Greig and Davie Wilson got the others in a 4-0 humiliation of Celtic. Baxter had his best Old Firm game to date. But even better was to come from him later that season and on an even bigger stage, too.

Thistle drew with Clyde and lost Niven with a wrist injury. That's when the winter got worse and Rangers did not kick another ball in anger until they went to Dunfermline and won 2-1 on 9 March. Niven recalled, 'Thistle were playing really well in the first half of that season, even though we had lost 2-1 at Ibrox early in the campaign. We felt that with a full house of the 30,000 you could get into Firhill in those days, we could beat Rangers. What happened was that by the time we were able to play again we had lost our momentum, while Rangers came back looking unstoppable. To be honest, even without the freeze and even if we had beaten them at Firhill, it's unlikely we would have won the title. Symon's team was unstoppable when it was at its best.' And Rangers were certainly at their best when that rearranged game sent them up to Queens Cross on a wet night which in April saw them produce some astonishing stuff on a mudheap, with Wilson having one of those nights, scoring four in a 4-1 win.

Back to myths, and there are many who look back to that season and describe it as the year Partick Thistle finished runners-up to Rangers. Not true. The Jags collapsed after Rangers ran them ragged and finished third. It was left to Kilmarnock to try and challenge for the title. The truth is that it was a pretty feeble challenge. True, Killie beat Rangers 1-0 at Rugby Park on 13 May, the first defeat Symon's team had suffered since going down 1-0 at Tannadice to Dundee United on 10 November. That astonishing eighteen-game unbeaten run contained just three draws and was the charge which ensured that the title was clinched by a comfortable nine points. That meant that from the moment a Millar hat-trick, along with strikes from Brand and George McLean, in a 5-2 semi-final win over Dundee United on 13 April 1963, Symon was able to concentrate his thoughts on Celtic and the first Old Firm Scottish Cup final for thirty-five years.

24

THE OLD FIRM
SCOTTISH CUP FINAL

IT is hard for those who have grown up on a steady diet of Old Firm Scottish Cup finals to get their heads around the fact that when the pair prepared to do battle in the 1963 final, it was the first time they had met at the ultimate stage of the tournament for thirty-five years. To put that into context, in the thirty-five years which followed 1963, Rangers and Celtic met in the Scottish Cup final in seven seasons. But back then, there were supporters who had grown to manhood's estate never having seen the two great rivals go head-to-head with the old trophy at stake. Alex Scott remembered the tingle and excitement surrounding the build-up and he was no longer even a Rangers player, having left to join Everton in the autumn of 1962.

When I interviewed Scott in the early 1980s for a piece for the Everton match-day programme, he recalled, 'The Rangers players were inundated with people begging for tickets and some of my friends in Scotland even got in touch with me to see if I could help. In fact, some of my old team-mates even phoned. It was bedlam.' The Scottish Football Association had taken the then unusual step of making the final all-ticket and what was also unusual that year was the long wait between the semis and the final. Rangers beat Dundee United 5-2 on 13 April and then had to wait until 4 May for the final showdown. The season had been extended into May because of the backlog of games caused by the six weeks when the weather prevented football being played.

At Ibrox, though, the prospect of the Old Firm final had to be set aside in order that the title be clinched and even after that, Jim Baxter recalled, there were no special preparations or extra talk about the match. When he looked back at that period, Baxter said, 'I can't remember anything special except for the demand for tickets. But inside the dressing room we were all used to big games and we were all used to winning them. As for the manager, I can't recall Scot Symon saying anything to us in the week before the final. It was just a normal week for us.'

That sort of build-up was a huge change to the way things are done now, but one factor that remained the same and with which a comparison can be made with what Rangers had to accept in 2008, was the fixtures forced on them in those spring days before Symon's team was due to face Celtic in that final. Rangers were press-ganged into meeting Hearts on 27 April, Motherwell forty-eight hours later and were due to meet Airdrie two days after the Hampden final. It was as well for Symon's hopes of the Double that the championship was wrapped up before he had to turn his attention to the Scottish Cup. Remember, too, that this was the era of a first eleven, well before the days of a first team squad with rotation, and players rested. But the fact that Rangers had built such a comfortable lead over their nearest challengers, Kilmarnock, meant there was little focus on or controversy about the fixtures faced by the club.

All of the attention was focused on this first Old Firm Scottish Cup final since Rangers had beaten Celtic 4-0 in 1928, a win of supreme significance, as it was the first time the Ibrox side had lifted the trophy for twenty-five years, a barren spell known as 'the Hoodoo Years'. Symon's only Cup final meeting with Celtic had been in the League Cup and he had suffered the bitter experience of that 7-1 drubbing. The two teams had met at Hampden in the Scottish Cup semi-final in 1960 and after a 1-1 draw Rangers had triumphed 4-1. During the build-up to the 1963 final, many of the 1928 heroes were wheeled out to recall that victory with the by then Ibrox director Alan Morton prominent, along with Bob McPhail.

However, as is often the case when the hype kicks in, the match itself disappointed – in more ways than one. For a start, my dad could only get two tickets. He had never been to an Old Firm Scottish Cup final and my granddad had been there in 1928. That meant there was one very disappointed twelve-year-old in the family, especially as I felt sure I was going to miss seeing a famous victory. As it was, after Ralph Brand put Rangers in front, Bobby Murdoch equalised and the countdown began for a replay eleven days later.

This time it was back to the normal procedure for the time of pay-at-the-gate and this time I was there with my dad in the north enclosure and this time there was a famous Rangers victory to be witnessed. Before Rangers returned to Hampden, they had to squeeze in three more league games: Airdrie, Third Lanark and Kilmarnock. It was as well the title was wrapped up, for they lost to challengers Kilmarnock on 13 May, a mere forty-eight hours before the Scottish Cup final. But the talk had not been about the ridiculous programme Rangers were pushed into, but about a selection problem to which Scot Symon had to come up with the answer.

George McLean, who had arrived from St Mirren in February and displaced the ageing Ian McMillan, was injured against Celtic. Symon had to decide on an inside-right to partner the potent Willie Henderson. He knew he had to get his best from wee Willie and knew the man who could bring out that best was

Chairman John Lawrence and vice chairman, Matt Taylor, the two men who conspired to sack Scot Symon.

Willie Woodburn, whose *sine die* suspension was a blow to Symon's team-rebuilding plans in his first season in charge.

Scot Symon looking both bewildered and hurt in his back garden on the day he was brutally sacked by Rangers.

Bill Struth on the day he stood down as manager. Left to right: Willie Rae, Willie Cameron (who manned the front door at Ibrox), Jock Shaw, Struth, Sammy Cox, captain George Young, Willie Waddell, Willie Thornton and Johnny Hubbard.

Scot Symon when he took over from Bill Struth as manager of Rangers in the summer of 1954.

Don Kitchenbrand, an early Symon signing, who always had the Rangers fans arguing.

Symon mobbed by fans going into the St Enoch Hotel after Rangers beat Celtic 3-0 in the 1963 Scottish Cup Final replay.

The first title. Scot Symon and the Rangers playing staff pictured with the first Scottish Championship trophy won in season 1955-56.

Celebrating their 2-0 League Cup Final win over Kilmarnock in October 1960 by carrying skipper Eric Caldow shoulder high. Left to right: George Niven, Ian McMillan, Alex Scott, Bill Paterson, Jimmy Millar, Davie Wilson, Caldow (with trophy), Bobby Shearer, Jim Baxter, Ralph Brand and Harold Davis.

... And Wilson. Davie Wilson in full flight. The memorable forward line of the early '60s was Scott, McMillan, Millar, Brand and Wilson.

The Old Warhorse. A typical leap by Jimmy Millar when he was in his prime.

Wee Willie Henderson. He soon became an even bigger favourite than fans' favourite Alex Scott.

Jim Baxter sticks the ball up his jersey to give to veteran Ian McMillan after beating Celtic 3-0 in the 1963 Scottish Cup Final replay triumph.

Davie Meiklejohn. The 1920s and '30s iconic captain was in the frame to replace Bill Struth.

Ralph Brand chucks a bucket of water over his team-mates as they celebrate a 3-1 Treble-winning Scottish Cup Final triumph over Dundee in 1964. Left to right: Brand, Billy Ritchie, Davie Provan, Bobby Shearer (with the Scottish Cup) on Ronnie McKinnon's shoulders, George McLean, Jimmy Millar, John Greig, Jim Baxter and seated: Willie Henderson and Davie Wilson (wearing the bowler hat vice chairman John F. Wilson had promised him if Rangers lifted the Treble).

The Treble campaign had kicked off with a 5-0 League Cup Final cakewalk against Morton. Left to right: Jim Forrest, Ralph Brand, Alex Willoughby, Billy Ritchie, Davie Provan, Bobby Shearer (brandishing the trophy), Craig Watson, Ronnie McKinnon and John Greig. Crouched in front: Willie Henderson and Jim Baxter.

The poise and elegance which Symon spotted in an eighteen-year-old Sandy Jardine.

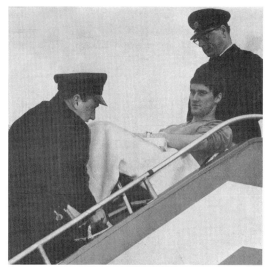

Jim Baxter is carried onto the plane for the flight back to Scotland following his broken leg at the end of a 2-0 win over Rapid Vienna in the European Cup.

Jim Baxter throws the Scottish League Cup high into the air, watched by Wilson Wood and Davie Provan, after beating Celtic 2-1 in 1964.

Scot Symon's last trophy, the 1966 Scottish Cup. Left to right: Davie Wilson, John Greig, George McLean, Kai Johansen, Jimmy Millar, Bobby Watson, Ronnie McKinnon, Willie Johnston, Davie Provan, Billy Ritchie and Willie Henderson.

By this time a pensive Scot Symon must have felt the clock was ticking on his time in the office at the head of the Marble Staircase.

Örjan Persson was one of the signings Symon made in the summer of 1967.

The last time Scot Symon stood with his players for a team picture, August 1967. Left to right: Back row: Symon, Bobby Watson, Davie Provan, Ronnie McKinnon, Erik Sorensen, Norrie Martin, Billy Ritchie, Roger Hynd, Sandy Jardine, Örjan Persson and Bobby Seith (coach). Front row: Davie White (assistant manager), Willie Henderson, Alex Smith, Alex Willoughby, Alex Ferguson, John Greig, Dave Smith, Andy Penman, Kai Johansen, Willie Johnston and Davie Kinnear (trainer).

It was just plain Alex Ferguson back then. And Fergie's style of jutting elbows is captured in a Euro tussle with Leeds United. Leeds keeper Gary Sprake jumps with Ferguson, while Paul Reaney (his back to the camera) and Jack Charlton look on.

Alex Scott, hunched and in full flight. Scott had a curious and highly individual running style and, as he is captured here, was capable of swinging his crosses over while still going at full pelt.

Slim Jim Baxter called his left foot 'The Glove'.

The Partick Thistle team which beat Jock Stein's Celtic 4-1 to win the 1971 Scottish League Cup. Back row: Willie Ross (physio), Hugh Strachan, Ronnie Glavin, Alex Forsyth, Alan Rough, John Hansen, Jackie Campbell, David McParland (manager). Front row: Tommy Rae, Bobby Lawrie, Jimmy Bone, Alex Rae, Frank Coulston, Denis McQuade. Scot Symon was general manager by then, but he gave half of the Cup-winning side their first team debuts.

none other than the Wee Prime Minister. McMillan had been missing from the side since December, so Symon knew he had to give him a run out before the replay and keep his fingers crossed that McMillan came through unscathed during the match against Third Lanark on 11 May. He did, and immediately the old fox of a schemer looked forward to linking with the brash brilliance of Henderson again.

McMillan said, 'The manager told me just to take it easy against Thirds and to feel my way back. I did as I was told and was soon happy to be back playing in a very good side and felt no after-effects from the game. I told Symon I was okay, so he said that was fine. I knew I would play against Celtic. Scot did not have to say any more. I had the pleasure of playing alongside two great Rangers right-wingers, Alex Scott to start with and then wee Willie. They were both completely different in style. Alex liked the ball played into his feet. That suited him because he was strong and could take his man on and get to the deadball line and get his cross in. Henderson had plenty of tricks to beat an opponent, but he preferred to chase the longer pass and use his burst of speed to get clear. That suited me, for I was able to hit the pass inside the full-back and let him run after it and that was my job done.'

McMillan certainly got his job done on that May night against Celtic in the 1963 Scottish Cup final replay. Right from the start he fed passes to Henderson and Celtic closed in to try and stifle space and stop McMillan from creating havoc. All they succeeded in doing was allowing the wily Jimmy Millar to find room for a McMillan-style pass to release Henderson in just six minutes and his cross was met by Brand for a close-range shot, which gave Rangers the lead. From then on, it was a procession as Baxter teased, tormented and toyed with Celtic. Wilson made it two just before half time and Brand added another in the second half. Rangers supporters invented a new chant that night. 'Easy

Easy' echoed from the Ibrox support as Baxter, frankly, took the mickey. The tormenting of Celtic by Rangers supporters must have been music to Symon's ears.

But, as usual, he stayed in the background as the final whistle went and Baxter waltzed away with the ball stuck up his jersey, not for himself, but as a gift for McMillan. That act gave lie to the belief Baxter was not a team player. McMillan recalled, 'Jim knew it was my final fling and it was a magnificent gesture from him. When he signed in 1960 it was clear right from the start that Baxter was a marvellous player. Scot Symon made a tremendous signing.'

Symon's Rangers reigned supreme at the end of season 1962-63 with the Scottish Cup added, in such swaggering style, to a championship which had been won convincingly. Such was the confidence the Rangers manager had in the team he had built that there were no summer signings. Already youngsters such as Alex Willoughby and Jim Forrest were beginning to stake their claim, while Davie Provan had shown he was a more than able deputy for Eric Caldow, who had suffered a badly broken leg while captaining Scotland against England at Wembley. Symon had a supreme and entirely justified confidence that there were even better days ahead, with making a bigger impact on Europe again uppermost in his mind.

In fact, even though that European dream remained elusive, Symon was on the brink of managing Rangers to the club's best season since the 1948-49 heyday of the Iron Curtain side, but doing it with a team a world removed from its predecessors, a side that swept opponents aside with breathtaking brilliance. Symon's team was about to create a legend which lives to this day.

25

HOLDING ON TO BAXTER

BEFORE he could embark on making Rangers even more dominant in Scotland and attempting to make more of an impact in
Europe, Scot Symon had a major problem to solve, one which,
if he could not find a solution to, would see all that he had
worked to build over the previous nine years collapse around
him, turning to ashes his dreams of even bigger and better things
for Rangers. He had to find a way to hold on to Jim Baxter and
keep him happy. How Symon managed to tiptoe his way through
this minefield has remained a secret for half a century and is a
terrific example of just how shrewd he could be. And how much
of a pragmatist he could be in his dealings with newspapers, for
Symon managed to pull off a coup that no football team boss,
no matter how famous for their media manipulation they have
been or are, has managed even to this day.

In the spring of 1963 Baxter's brilliance and his fame were
spreading beyond Scotland's borders. This was the era of the
transfer trade forming the low road to England for Scotland's
biggest stars. Billy Stevenson, pushed out by Baxter's arrival,
had gone to Liverpool, while Alex Scott, having lost his place
to Willie Henderson, moved to Everton. But perhaps a better
example of what was happening and one that was closer to home
as far as Baxter was concerned was Pat Crerand. Pat Crerand

and Baxter were pals who were men about town together in Glasgow. When they faced up to each other at Ibrox on New Year's Day 1963, Crerand was completely overshadowed as Baxter masterminded a 4-0 victory. It was Crerand's last game for Celtic before a £56,000 transfer to Manchester United. With the move to Old Trafford, Crerand's wages immediately shot up to £100 per week.

When I asked Baxter about this and how he felt about it, he explained, 'I was far from happy. Paddy and I were good pals and he was a terrific player. But I was better. And all I was getting at Rangers was £45 a week. It was the same when I was away with Scotland and all I heard was guys playing in England who were on a hundred quid a week and who boasted about it. They were on more than twice as much as I was, but I was more than twice as good as any of them were. It wasn't right, so I asked Symon for a rise.'

At the time, all Rangers first-team players were on the same money, £45 a week, plus bonuses, which were far from lavish, as the then captain Bobby Shearer explained. Shearer said, 'We got a fiver for a win on top and as we won almost every week that meant the weekly pay packet should have had fifty quid in it. But it didn't work that way. What happened was that at Christmas and at the end of the season, you got all the bonus money. There were also extra bonuses if you won a trophy.'

Willie Johnston, then just a teenager, remembers the first time he was called upstairs to get his windfall after being in the team Baxter had captained Rangers to a League Cup final win over Celtic in 1964. Johnston and I were actually sitting in the pub Baxter used to run on Glasgow's Paisley Road when he told me the story on Hogmanay 1981, some time after he had returned for his second spell with Rangers. He said, 'I was waiting at the foot of the marble stairs when Jim came down smiling and fingering a wad which he told me was a couple of hundred quid. I was up those stairs like a shot, but when Symon handed me my money there was only a hundred. I complained, pointing out that Baxter got twice that, but Symon just reminded me I was still just a young player. I accepted it. That's the way it was back then.' And that is the way it was going to stay, for when Baxter tried to use the money Crerand was getting at Manchester United as a bargaining tool, Symon simply stonewalled him and made it clear there was no way the board would break the wage structure for anyone, even him.

Baxter recalled, 'I believe that old Scot wanted to keep me and would have given me a bit more. I wasn't asking the earth and never said I wanted a hundred quid a week. I would have settled for £70, but even that was out of the question as far as Rangers were concerned.'

So the row dragged on during high summer 1963, filling the back pages of the newspapers and making headlines about where Baxter was going, with almost every major club south of the border, including his close buddy's new team, Manchester United. Tottenham Hotspur were also frequently mentioned as Baxter could have taken over from the recently retired Danny Blanchflower. But on one of those winter Monday afternoons ten years later, when I was sitting with Bill Nicholson in his office, he revealed that had always been a non-starter. According to Nicholson, he already had one supremely gifted, hard-drinking Scottish wing-half, Dave Mackay, and did not need another, especially one like Baxter, who, unlike Mackay, a dedicated hard trainer, didn't fancy fitness work.

During the spring of 1963, Baxter's profile in England had risen on the back of a game he played at Wembley. Baxter's performance for Scotland against England in 1967, when the English were World Cup holders, is often cited as the best game he ever played. But those who had seen him at Wembley four years earlier knew better. Scotland had lost Eric Caldow with a badly broken leg just six minutes into the match. But Baxter simply rose to the occasion, took control and scored the two goals in ten-man Scotland's 2-1 win. Clearly, with all of this in mind, Baxter felt he would have the whip hand and that Symon would somehow come up with a scheme to keep Scotland's best player at Ibrox. He did, but not in a way anyone could have predicted and, indeed, in a way that has remained secret until now.

It has to be pointed out that this was long before the time of freedom of contract or long-term deals. The way things worked at Rangers then was that players were offered terms every summer for the coming season. If they did not accept then they could be left sitting in the stand. The club had the legal right to hold the player's registration and the player could not sign for anyone unless the club agreed to release his registration. This was the backdrop to Scot Symon's dilemma in the summer of 1963 as he racked his brains to find a way to see that Baxter was rewarded for his worth to Rangers, but without smashing the strict pay code the club's directors insisted on imposing. At which point reporter Rodger Baillie, by that time no longer going out with Symon's daughter, enters the picture again and it is from his involvement and from what he remembers that we are able to discover just how clever Symon was. At the time, as Baillie has already recalled, many Rangers players picked up a tenner or so extra dough for putting their name to a newspaper column. Over the years, I have been involved in many of these columns, acting as ghost writer for, among others, Andy Gray.

The drill is that the reporter and the player have a brief chat and the journalist then goes and writes the column which appears under the player's name. The player is also expected to keep the reporter fed with bits of information and gossip he picks up in the dressing room. The going rate for a Rangers player working for a Scottish-based paper was around ten quid, well short of what would have satisfied Baxter. Now, we shall never know if Symon's hand was at work, but he knew some of the biggest names in what was then still Fleet Street, where the big money was paid, from his time as Preston North End's manager.

Baillie had by then left the *Daily Record* to become chief Scottish football writer for the Fleet Street-based *Sunday Mirror* and he said, 'Negotiations started for Baxter to become our star columnist and it was agreed that Jim and I should spend a day in London so he could sign the deal. Rangers were back in preseason, so Baxter had to go to Symon and tell him what was happening and ask for permission to take a day off training to go on the trip to London. Not only did Symon agree without hesitation, he told Jim that he had better stay overnight and have the next day off, too.

'It wasn't the sort of thing Symon would usually have done, but he must have known that this was one way in which he may find the solution to the problem of finding a way to keep Baxter happy. We went off to London where the editor and sports editor regally entertained Baxter with an expensive lunch at a top restaurant and then a night out on the town and overnight stay in a swanky West End hotel, all on the *Sunday Mirror*. Baxter was in his element, and I have to admit I enjoyed it all, too.'

And the deal Baxter signed on for with the *Sunday Mirror* was nothing like the tenner his team-mates were getting from Scottish newspapers. It was a whopping £40 a week, just a fiver short of his wages with Rangers. Baxter accepted the £45 a week terms from the club and signed on again. All was well for Symon and his plans to go one better than the Double of the previous season. Baillie said, 'The *Sunday Mirror* provided the solution to Symon's problem. It was a huge sum of money for any London paper to pay for a column from any Scottish player who was playing in Scotland.'

Baillie did not go into detail about how the move from the *Sunday Mirror* to sign Baxter started. But there is one puzzling question which remains after I unearthed this story after it had remained hidden for so many years: Why did Symon so readily agree to giving Baxter a day off and even tell him to take two days to go on the town in London? Did he, for instance, know how much money the newspaper was offering Baxter? If he did, he would have known that such a sideline would subsidise Baxter's Ibrox wage and mean he remained a Rangers player. If that was the case, and if Symon even pulled any strings to get the deal started, it means that Scot Symon was a shrewder manager of men and media manipulator than any who had gone before or who came since, including Jock Stein and right up to that modern marvel, Sir Alex Ferguson.

However it was done, the fact is that Jim Baxter now had a weekly wage packet of £85 quid, of which Rangers were still only paying £45. Baxter was happy. And so, too, was Scot Symon who knew he could now start looking forward to season 1963-64.

26

THE TREBLE

BOBBY SHEARER and Alex Willoughby were at opposite ends of the age spectrum of the players Scot Symon was to call upon for the 1963-64 campaign. Shearer was a gnarled and grizzly old campaigner who tackled like a tiger and wore the love he had for Rangers on his sleeve well ahead of the days when skippers started to wear a captain's armband. Willoughby was the youngster, the slim willowy playmaker of an inside-forward. Possibly he was even more committed to the Rangers cause.

I was fortunate enough to interview Shearer in the late Eighties and then work with him as a double act hosting pre-match dinners for the Ibrox games in Rangers' great 1992-93 Champions League run. I had first encountered Willoughby just about the time he broke into the Rangers side when he was a guest coach at the coaching school I attended in Dunard Street Primary School not far from Firhill. When I interviewed him in the Eighties Willoughby's Rangers connection remained. He ran the Wee Rangers Club and was as committed to the cause then as he had been as a youngster, supporting the team and a young player breaking into the side. We became great pals and his tragically early death robbed Rangers of someone who would be on the club's side through thick and thin. As his years at Ibrox progressed, we will learn of how he believed he should have been given more opportunities. But, when he looked back to the summer of 1963 and the early weeks of what was to become such a momentous season for Rangers, Willoughby was able to recall a feeling of supreme optimism ahead of the campaign. He said, 'I looked around that dressing room and felt that we would be unstoppable. Jim Baxter was at his peak, Jimmy Millar was strong and his partnership with Ralph Brand was a goals machine. Davie Wilson gave the team speed on the left and wee Willie Henderson was a winger I loved playing alongside.

'I knew George McLean would start the season at inside-right. After all, Scot Symon had paid a Scottish record fee for him. But I had been given a few games towards the end of the previous season and believed that if he was injured Symon would give me my chance and that I would take it.

'And when we were drawn to play Real Madrid in the first round of the European Cup there was even more excitement inside the dressing room. I remember Baxter rubbing his hands together in a kind of "Bring them on" gesture. Baxter was frightened of nobody when it came to putting his ability up against theirs.'

Symon, as was his way, said nothing, though Shearer recalled his thoughts when he learned he was to face the fastest winger there had ever been, Real Madrid legend, Gento. His thinking was somewhat different from Willoughby's youthful enthusiasm and Baxter's brash, arrogant confidence. Shearer said, 'Gento was so fast it was frightening, and he was still at his best. Ferenc Puskás and Alfredo di Stéfano were still around, too, and even if they were getting just past their best, that best had been a lot better than anything we had ever faced before. I knew we were good, but wasn't sure if we were ready for them.'

Just over three years earlier, Real Madrid had mesmerised Glasgow when they hammered Eintracht Frankfurt – the 12-4 semi-final conquerors of Rangers – 7-3 in the Hampden European Cup final that Sir Alex Ferguson still talks about with awe to this day. Now Real were coming back to Glasgow, this time to Ibrox to face Rangers in the first leg. And, despite the recent memory of just how good Real Madrid had been at Hampden, there was plenty of confidence among Rangers supporters that their team could tame the old masters. Real, the view was often heard at the tine, were past it, while Rangers had a team in its prime. If Rangers could get a decent lead at Ibrox, so people said, they could go through.

As it was, it was old head Shearer who was proved right and young Willoughby wrong, on a night when Ibrox rocked and rolled as 80,000 roared Rangers on. Willoughby didn't play, but Shearer was in his usual right-back role and in the end his fear of the flying Gento was proved to be justified. But Rangers made a fight of it. The club had controversially increased the price of the cheapest ticket to ten bob, that's fifty pence, and too much for my dad and granddad to be able to stretch for a brief for me. However, also unusual for the era, such was the interest in the game that it was shown live on television.

I was glued to the wee black-and-white screen as Rangers dominated, attacking from both wings as Baxter strolled and posed, revelling in being up against such a side. Brand went close early in the game and then hit the post in the second half. Willoughby remembered, 'The excitement was intense and by the time the game was into its last ten minutes nobody was thinking about building a lead for the second leg. We were all just caught up in the game from minute to minute. There were five or six minutes left when Real showed just what they had up their sleeve. Di Stéfano had hardly had a kick, but he found space just inside his own half and played a pass left to Gento. It was the first time Gento had been given the chance to have a run at wee Bobby, and our defender didn't have a chance. Gento bent a cross around the defence and Puskás hit the ball with his left foot for a shot which Billy Ritchie had no chance of saving. It was so brilliant I nearly applauded.'

Shearer's memory, from the thick of the action, was similar and he told me, 'I tried to get into the best position to cut Gento off when I saw the way Di Stéfano was shaping for I knew he was going to pass it to the left wing. I was prepared to foul Gento to stop him, but Di Stéfano's pass and Gento's speed meant I could get nowhere near him. Even then, he still had to make the pass and after he made it Puskás still had to get off the ground to meet it with a volley.'

Willoughby's cousin, Jim Forrest, was in that night at Ibrox, as Millar was injured, and when Rangers went to the Bernabeau for the return, Willoughby too played, in place of McLean, who moved to replace the injured Brand at inside-left. With reserve left-winger Craig Watson deputising for broken leg victim Davie Wilson, it meant there was not a player in the Rangers forward line older than twenty.

Symon must have feared for his young players, but there was nothing he could do. Millar, Brand and Wilson were missing all at the same time and that time was when Symon had to take Rangers into the most intimidating stadium in Europe back in the early Sixties, the Bernabeau. Symon must also have winced as Real mocked any Rangers' hopes of escaping with their dignity intact, never mind making a game of it. Real Madrid 6, Rangers 0 was the scoreline. Scot Symon's hopes of season 1963-64 becoming the one which would see Rangers make a determined assault on the European Cup were over, shattered by a combination of injuries to key players but, in truth, more by the gap which was still a gulf between the Scottish champions and the then five-time winners of the European Cup. If there is an argument for saying Symon's Rangers team of 1963-64, at its strongest, was one of the best Rangers have ever fielded, there is an even stronger argument for claiming that Real Madrid were the best club side ever seen. And Rangers were not even at their strongest when they faced them.

27

MORE YOUNG PLAYERS

JIM BAXTER remembered the way Scot Symon reacted to the way Rangers were simply taken apart by Real Madrid in the European Cup and how the manager's shrewdness set the tone for everything that followed.

Baxter said, 'Old Scot knew fine well that Real Madrid were a lot better than any of the teams we were up against in Scotland, so he just said nothing. When we got back to Glasgow it was as if nothing had happened as far as Symon was concerned. And that was probably the wisest thing to do. That was clever. Sometimes it's best to do nothing at all.

'The newspapers were all full of how we had been put in our place by Real Madrid and how Rangers weren't as good as we thought, but the truth was they were an exceptional side. However, as far as Scottish football was concerned, old Scot knew he had built an excellent side, so he just let us get on with it. And, in the end, we won the Treble, so he was right. At that time Symon was right a lot more often than he was wrong.'

The Baxter reaction to what had happened when Rangers were taken apart 6-0 in Madrid was equally typical. If Symon adopted the low-key, then Baxter decided just to ignore it and step back into Scottish football with his gallus approach unruffled. Symon had been the Rangers manager for nine years by the time season 1963-64 started and a new generation of Rangers supporters had grown up and were growing up under his era. It meant there were fewer comparisons made with Struth. That was especially the case in Europe, for, although Symon's hopes there had been shattered again, there was no comparison for older supporters to draw as Struth's reign ended before the European era arrived.

If there were going to be comparisons made between Struth's sides and the team Symon unleashed on the new season in August 1963, after having won the Double in the previous campaign, then even Symon's fiercest critic had to admit they must be favourable. If losing seven goals while failing to score one over a hundred and eighty minutes can ever be described as a blip, then that is what those two lessons from the Real Madrid masters were. A blip, forgotten amidst the euphoria which followed. The truth is that in the opening three weeks of the season, in the League Cup and the Championship, Rangers were rampant and saw off Celtic three times in that short spell. There were to be two more Old Firm matches during that 1963-64 season. Of the five encounters Rangers were triumphant in every one. That in itself was a remarkable feat, even taking into account the relative merits of the two teams.

Throughout the Old Firm rivalry, no matter how far one side may trail the other at any point, the underdog almost always manages to lift themselves to stop being completely dominated. Scot Symon's Treble team of 1963-64 ensured that Celtic did not manage even a whiff of a draw in any of the matches against Rangers. As Baxter said, 'We were a lot better than Celtic and I was always determined that we showed just how much better, so I had some of my best games for Rangers against them. The fact that they were always played before 70,000 or 80,000 suited me, too.'

That was how the campaign started, with a full house at Parkhead, as Rangers, who had been drawn in the same section of the League Cup, looked a class apart, winning 3-0. There was no Jimmy Millar at centre-forward to joust with Billy McNeill, who was instead faced with a new and even bigger handful, Jim Forrest. Millar was starting to show the signs of battle scars from his campaigns as the Old Warhorse, and Forrest was clearly the man Symon saw as the future. However, Millar, dogged, determined and much more skilful than he has ever been given credit for, was also able to add craft to the team at inside-right when needed – not that Millar was content to give up the number nine shirt – and by the time the season reached its thrilling climax, the Old Warhorse was back.

But there were few Rangers fans who made the trip to the east end of Glasgow on 10 August 1963 who gave much thought to the missing Millar. Forrest, short, chunky, fast and deadly, simply terrorised McNeill who, by the end of the afternoon, looked bewildered every time Rangers fed the ball to their new pin-up centre-forward. Forrest got two and George McLean the other in that 3-0 win.

If Celtic thought the coming campaign was going to present them with the chance to avenge the 3-0 Scottish Cup final humiliation, they were soon firmly put in their place. There might have been no Millar and no Ian McMillan, but Baxter was still there and that quite simply meant it was the same old story. Or that film we've seen before, as my dad always said, a huge grin on his face.

The League Cup campaign which that win kicked off was followed by routine 5-2 and 4-1 wins over Queen of the South and Kilmarnock before Celtic visited Ibrox. That followed the routine, too, as old campaigners Davie Wilson and Ralph Brand joined new hero Forrest on the scoresheet in another comfortable 3-0 Rangers win. East Fife were beaten 2-0 in the second leg of the quarter-final after a 1-1 draw at Bayview before a final place being clinched with a 3-1 win over Berwick Rangers was marred when Davie Wilson broke a leg. Wilson did not return again until February.

It was during this period that Symon once again showed his willingness to give young players their head, notably at inside-right where he was happy to replace the injured McLean with the then teenage Alex Willoughby. It says something of how Symon's nerve must have been affected by the spring of 1967 when he made the mysterious decision to overlook Willoughby, a decision which Willoughby went to his grave without ever having Symon explain it to him. That lay a long way in the future and when he looked back to the autumn of 1963, Willoughby had nothing but happy memories, especially the Scottish League Cup final at Hampden when the first leg of the clean sweep was carried off. Willoughby's memories of what happened after the 6-0 loss to Real Madrid matched Baxter's recall. Willoughby said, 'Symon said nothing and we just got on with things and our first game back showed we were not fazed for we beat St Mirren 3-0 and I played and scored. The newspapers were saying nice things about me and I was enjoying being in the team with my cousin Jim Forrest, and I hardly dared hope that we would both be in for a Cup final at Hampden.'

But in they were, as Symon decided to give youth its head against Morton, who even though they were in the old Second Division, they were flying, playing some terrific stuff and had the most talked-about scoring machine in Scotland outside of Ibrox, Allan McGraw. Captain Cutlass, Bobby Shearer, remembered the occasion as one of the few times that Scot Symon had any instructions for the team other than simply to work hard and give the ball to Baxter. Shearer recalled, 'Maybe it was because

Morton were a team we were not used to playing against and maybe Symon even worried a wee bit that we would take them too lightly. Actually, there was never any chance of us doing that, not after what had happened to us in Madrid. We were more determined than ever to show what we could do.

'Symon read the way things would go perfectly. He told us we would have to be quick and alert at the start as he expected Morton to fly at us, and that was exactly what happened. But we were ready for them. The manager also said that as long as we concentrated we would not give Morton any chances and that the longer the game went on the more our class would tell.'

Symon got it spot on, though even he may not have realised just how long it would take for his team to blunt the Morton threat and assert their greater class, skill, speed and finishing. For the first half ended goalless as Rangers dug in and made sure they did not give Morton a sniff of a chance to get into a giant-killing position. Then, after the interval, Rangers opened out with Baxter strolling, Henderson scampering, Willoughby scheming and Forrest scoring. The cousins were unstoppable, with Forrest netting four and Willoughby getting the other in a 5-0 win.

Willoughby said, 'I really thought Jim and I had arrived and the newspapers were full of the new young Rangers and of how Symon had built a team which could make it a clean sweep of all three trophies and go on to dominate Scottish football for the rest of the Sixties.' Those scribes were only half right. As for Willoughby's hopes that he had arrived? He played only six times in the championship that season, scoring three times, and did not make a solitary appearance in Rangers' successful Scottish Cup campaign. Symon returned to his Scottish record signing, George McLean, a decision which, had the Rangers manager only known where it would lead, may well have been one he regretted making.

Even as far back as that season, there were many, myself included – and I felt my view was vindicated when I heard my dad and granddad express it too – who considered that the more thoughtful, skilful team player Willoughby was a more worthy successor to Wee Prime Minister Ian McMillan than the mercurial and often selfish McLean. But Berwick and Nuremberg were a long way away as Scot Symon's Rangers moved on from their Scottish League Cup triumph to sweep all opposition aside in an all-conquering campaign.

28

GREIG, McKINNON AND BAXTER

BOBBY SHEARER had fond memories of season 1963-64, which even being left in the wake of Real Madrid's legendary flying machine, Gento, could not diminish. For it was the campaign in which he followed in the footsteps of another legendary full-back who held a special place in the affections of Rangers supporters, Jock Tiger Shaw, to become the second captain to lead Rangers to the Treble, for no other club had managed the clean sweep of Scotland's honours since that Bill Struth-managed trailblazing team of 1949.

Now Scot Symon and Shearer went on the Treble trail during a campaign when the team the manager had so painstakingly put together began to run out of superlatives to do its brilliance justice. Shearer recalled, 'Scot hardly had to tell the team anything. Most of us had played together for a number of years and the youngsters who Symon brought in at times were schooled in his way of playing football. I thought Alex Willoughby was a wonderful player who showed great promise, and although Jim Forrest was an entirely different style of centre-forward to Jimmy Millar, he gave the team a goal threat and maybe even a faster one. Not that you could write off Jimmy, who was always around to push for his place back when he was fit and eventually actually force Symon to prefer him towards the end of the season.'

The early weeks and months of the season saw that demolition at the hands of that magical Madrid side, but then the League Cup was paraded around Hampden after Rangers saw off Morton 5-0. But against that backdrop, Shearer recalled that the team knew it had to build a momentum in the bid to retain the championship, and that is just what Rangers managed to achieve after an opening day 1-1 draw against Dundee at Dens Park. Celtic visited Ibrox and were beaten 2-1 and there followed triumphs over Partick Thistle, Hibs, Third Lanark, Falkirk, St Mirren, East Stirling, Queen of the South and Airdrie before Aberdeen held Rangers to a goalless draw at Ibrox on 9 November.

The following week Rangers went to the Rugby Park home of Willie Waddell's outstanding Kilmarnock side, which was once again providing the only real threat to the dominance of Symon's team. I recall travelling to the game with my dad and that it was a raw, wet day, with the pitch a mud-heap. After a home draw against Aberdeen, Rangers knew they could not afford to go down in Ayrshire. And Shearer recalled just what an important afternoon it was for the rest of the season for Rangers. He said, 'Killie played really well in that game. Our keeper Billy Ritchie took a bang on the head and was as white as a sheet during the second half. There was no substitute goalkeeper and I was worried that I might have had to take over from him in goal. I had done that once against Hearts at Tynecastle. But Billy managed to get through the match. The mud was up to our ankles, but it didn't bother Jim Baxter, and it was no worry to Jimmy Millar. He was at inside-right that day and the truth was that Jimmy could play just about anywhere.'

Ralph Brand scored with a penalty for a 1-1 draw, which was followed by another away day, this time to Fife, where Rangers beat Dunfermline 4-1. The following week Hearts visited Ibrox and shockwaves shuddered through Scottish football. Rangers were beaten. But not just beaten, they were outplayed, outsmarted and outclassed by Hearts. The scoreline was 3-0 for the Edinburgh club. Shearer admitted, 'We got the runaround and had just one of those days even the best teams can have. The manager was forced to make changes because of injuries, including to Symon's key player, and Baxter did not play.'

It was an object lesson in just how important Baxter was to Rangers and puts into context just how wide of the mark those players who criticised Scot Symon for indulging him were. To be fair, though, Baxter was not the only missing link. For, instead of drafting in a replacement for his main man, Symon chose to switch Ronnie McKinnon to left-half and recall Doug Baillie to play as the pivot. Ian McMillan made one of only four league appearances. With Baxter still out going into December, Symon restored McKinnon to the heart of his defence and called up Wilson Wood from the reserves to wear the number six shirt, and Rangers beat Dundee United 3-2 at Tannadice before drawing 3-3 at Motherwell and then losing 3-2 to St Johnstone in front of a disbelieving Ibrox crowd. All of which meant that Symon had to ensure he got team selections spot on as Rangers went into a three-games-in-five-days hectic schedule. And for the first, on 28 December, the visit of Dundee to Ibrox, there was still no Baxter.

Shearer knew what was happening and also how long Symon must have thought about his selection. He said, 'Of course, Jim was a huge miss and it didn't help the manager that I was injured, too. Davie Wilson was still recovering from a broken leg and Ralph Brand was another on the injured list. Jimmy Millar was there, though, and I think Scot placed a lot of faith in him.

'I knew that Baxter was nearly ready and could probably have played, but we were due to go to Parkhead on New Year's Day and Jim just terrified Celtic at the time, and I am sure the manager chose to keep him for that. I remember it was one of the few times I heard him say much before a match. Although I was not playing, I was in the dressing room and he laid it on the line that the team had to find extra fight and not allow Dundee to get into their stride. He was preaching the right sermon to the right men.' Shearer put that beautifully, for Symon moved John Greig back to his old inside-right position and filled the right-half role by recalling Harold Davis to the colours. With the Iron Man back for his first appearance of the season and the Old Warhorse working with a will, Scot Symon had once again shown how shrewd his judgment of men could be.

There was also a recall for someone who was one of his harshest critics, Eric Caldow, playing his first game since suffering that horrific leg break at Wembley nine months before. Davie Provan moved to right-back, with Caldow restored to his favourite left-back berth and asked to cope with Dundee's ageing, but still skilful and subtle, Gordon Smith. There was another surprise as Symon slotted centre-forward Forrest in at outside-left in a bid to cover for the missing Baxter's brilliance on that side of the field with the young player's speed. It all worked a treat, with Forrest netting after half an hour, followed by a Provan penalty. Andy Penman got one back, also from the spot, but Symon's side dug in and found the extra reserves needed.

Rangers went to Parkhead on New Year's Day 1964 trailing Kilmarnock by a point and needed the grit and strength of Greig, along with a string of super saves from Billy Ritchie, to help them withstand a barrage from Celtic in the first half before the team started to get the measure of their opponents. Millar showed his sharpness when he pounced on a Brand shot which had been blocked and hooked the only goal of the game. Twenty-four hours later when Partick Thistle arrived at Ibrox, Davis lived up to that Iron Man tag by playing his third game in five days, as

Brand got two, with Greig and Millar the other marksmen in a thrilling 4-3 win. Shearer watched all of those games from the stand and remembered, 'We all felt that if we could win away to Hibs two days after we beat Thistle, then we could go on to take the title. Jimmy Millar got the only goal of the game.'

Shearer returned and I well recall that match at Easter Road, which I had gone to watch with my wee pal, Neil. It was another of the many matches played on a muddy pitch which were so common back then, and there was a real feeling that Rangers would be champions again. Kilmarnock's spirit must have been broken by watching how Symon juggled his pack, recalling old favourites and sending out a rallying cry. It was a master class in old-fashioned management. And by old-fashioned, I mean exactly the same sort of managerial trick Sir Alex Ferguson has so successfully pulled off in the twenty-first century.

Rangers were back on top of the table after beating Airdrie 4-1 on 29 February, and when Kilmarnock arrived at Ibrox on 14 March with only half a dozen matches left after that encounter, they knew they had to win. Rangers recalled the Wee Prime Minister, and McMillan had one final, final fling, influencing the pattern of a game in which Millar scaled the heights. George McLean and the fit-again Wilson were the scorers in a 2-0 triumph. The league was in the bag and Rangers were able to turn their attention to completing the last leg of the Treble by lifting the Scottish Cup for a third successive season to round off a Cup campaign which started in such spectacular style. Rangers had beaten Stenhousemuir 5-1 and then Duns 9-0 before seeing off Partick Thistle at Ibrox 3-0. Next up were Celtic, due at Ibrox on 7 March. Shearer remembered, 'We had already beaten Celtic four times, but they had given us a fright at Parkhead in January and Symon impressed upon us just how determined they would be to avoid losing five out of five to us in the one season. He was sure they would play for a draw. As it was, it didn't matter what they did.'

Rangers got the break needed just before the interval, when Celtic keeper John Fallon let a corner bounce off his chest and Forrest snatched a rare headed goal. If there was a touch of good luck about that then the second, sixty seconds into the second half, was sensational. Wee Willie Henderson scampered on the right, cut in, avoiding tackles, and as he entered the penalty area at full pelt scorched a shot that flew into the net. Scot Symon had a perfect five out of five against Celtic in a single season.

Shearer's part in a 1-0 scrambled semi-final win over Dunfermline was to clear off the line twice in the latter stages after Wilson had poked a Baxter free-kick into the net. Symon was just ninety minutes away from his most magnificent managerial achievement. And what a ninety minutes it was when Rangers faced Dundee on 25 April in the Scottish Cup final at Hampden.

The first half was a battle of wills and Rangers prevailed to take the lead in seventy-one minutes, when a Henderson corner picked out Millar, who floated his header perfectly back across the previously unbeatable Bert Slater and into the net. Sixty seconds later, all Rangers' good work was undone as Kenny Cameron fired an equaliser. And so into the closing two minutes, the teams locked together with a mere ninety seconds remaining. Then destiny knocked at Symon's door, thanks to quick thinking from the two players with the wit and skill to do something different. Rangers got a free-kick and Baxter, always alert to every nuance in a match, spotted that Henderson had suddenly switched to the left wing. Without further thought, Baxter slipped him the ball, Henderson accelerated into the box defying the strong-tackling Alex Hamilton to challenge him and lofted a cross for Millar to find the space for another scoring header.

As the seconds ticked away, Rangers put the icing on their Treble cake when Henderson set up Wilson for a shot which Slater could only parry, and Brand's scoring instincts saw him in the perfect position to turn the rebound into the net for a 3-1 triumph and the Treble.

Of course, there was no sign of Symon as the players cavorted with the trophy. Davie Wilson did the lap of honour wearing director John Wilson's bowler. He had promised it to Wilson if the team won the Treble. Note that it was a director's bowler and not manager Scot Symon's customary soft hat that was the subject at the centre of the banter, which once again showed just how quiet and reserved the manager was and how he kept the players at arm's length.

But as Rangers celebrated on that late April day at Hampden in 1964, with the rest of Scottish football at their feet, if anyone had suggested the slippery slope for the club and Scot Symon was only months away from starting, they would probably have been told to eat the manager's hat.

29

TEN YEARS IN CHARGE

WHEN Scot Symon took his annual holiday on the Isle of Arran in the summer of 1964 he must surely have felt a contented man. He was certainly entitled to, having delivered the clean sweep of Scottish honours to Rangers. That summer also saw Symon celebrate his tenth anniversary as Rangers manager. And that decade had been a trophy-laden one for the Ibrox club, thanks to his astute eye for a player and his team-blending skills.

Symon's talents as a manager had seen Rangers crowned as champions six times, with the Scottish Cup lifted four times and the Scottish League Cup won three times. There had also been inroads made on the new challenge presented by European football with Rangers reaching the semi-final of the European Cup in 1960 and the final of the Cup Winners' Cup in 1961. He had celebrated his fifty-third birthday just weeks after Rangers completed the Treble and must have thought he was good for at least another ten years of ruling the roost inside Ibrox while making sure Rangers did the same in Scottish football. For, as Symon's Treble-winning captain Bobby Shearer observed, the team was a nice blend of youth and experience, with those players at the younger end of the age scale, such as Willie Henderson and John Greig, already well blooded, while, at the other end, even old hands, such as Jimmy Millar and Shearer himself, still looked to have a few more seasons left.

As he and his wife Doreen tramped the Arran hills, Symon could also look forward to the emergence of others who he had started to promote to the top team. Players such as Jim Forrest, already looking like a successor to Old Warhorse; Millar at centre-forward; Alex Willoughby, whose inside-forward scheming skills were much admired; plus someone who few had heard of but who was to go on to become one of the best of the many Rangers legends first discovered and promoted by Scot Symon, none other than Willie Johnston. There was also, at the back of Symon's mind, the hope that the months ahead would see Eric Caldow return to his best following his long fight for fitness after suffering a horrific leg break playing for Scotland against England at Wembley in the spring of 1963.

Caldow's re-emergence had begun halfway through the Treble campaign, but he had suffered a setback and played only three times in the championship and once in the Scottish Cup. There were, however, high hopes that Caldow, who was still only thirty years old and the finest left-back I have ever seen, would regain the speed and balance which made him such a classy defender. As Shearer said, 'There was nothing we felt we should fear in Scotland. Kilmarnock had a very good team and we expected them to provide the big challenge again, but that summer I believed that with a wee bit of luck in the Cups we could lift the lot again. The idea that we would not win a third successive title just never entered my head.'

Of Symon's long-standing stalwarts, Shearer was thirty-two, Millar actually only twenty-nine, Ralph Brand twenty-seven and Davie Wilson twenty-five, while Willie Henderson at a mere twenty must surely get even better and John Greig, twenty-one when the Treble was won, already had the look of a future Rangers captain. And Jim Baxter? Baxter was due to celebrate his twenty-fifth birthday within weeks of season 1964-65 and, unlike the previous summer, he had given Symon no cause for concern. The £45 per week he collected as his Rangers wages, added to the £40 he got for being a guest columnist in the *Sunday Mirror*, meant that his wages were, in today's terms, around £1,400 a week. That may not sound like a lot compared to the money trousered by some of the players around today who couldn't lace Baxter's boots, but he once told me that he was happy enough with it at the time.

Baxter said, 'A year earlier I was fed up with hearing how much more than me some of the guys I played with for Scotland were getting and I dug in my heels. I knew what Scot had done for me and I was happy enough. I had enjoyed the season and felt sure the next one was going to be just as good, if not better. I have never kidded anyone about how good I thought I was and I had a hankering to show the rest of the world, too. That meant Europe, and after what had happened against Real Madrid, I felt I owed Symon at least one last shot at doing better in Europe. I also knew that if I moved to England then there was no guarantee I would sign for a club that played in Europe, so I decided to have another season and another go at Europe. At the time I didn't say anything to anyone, but my plan was that if we did really well in Europe, I might have been able to get a rise from Rangers. I didn't really want to leave.'

Shearer was confident and Baxter was confident. And although, as was his way, Symon kept his own counsel, what he did – or rather did not do – in the late summer of 1964 showed that he had supreme confidence in the players who had secured the Championship, Scottish Cup and League Cup for the Ibrox trophy room. For Symon made not a single signing that summer.

When the defence of the League Cup kicked off, it looked as though Rangers were picking up where they left off when they paraded the Scottish Cup around Hampden. Aberdeen were swept aside 4-0 at Ibrox, and although a goalless draw away to St Mirren followed, Rangers hit top gear when they went to Perth and swamped St Johnstone 9-1.

I recall travelling to Aberdeen three days later with my wee pal Neil. Both our dads worked for British Railways and we got cheap tickets. The train that pulled out of the old Buchanan Street Station also carried Symon and his stars. It is a sign of what the times were like that I recall staring in awe at Davie Wilson and Billy Ritchie and being disappointed there was no sign of Baxter, who was travelling via Edinburgh, but cannot recall even looking for the manager.

Baxter was waiting in the station in Aberdeen, and Neil and I were rewarded for our patience when we saw he was wearing a natty leather hat. It's a small detail, but perhaps helps to paint a picture of a long-ago era. The match was a humdinger, Greig was injured and Bobby Watson took his place. Watson was a forceful, driving wing-half and another young player who was handed his chance by the manager. The match was like so many Neil and I had watched Rangers take part in – tough, tight and thrilling – but with Rangers emerging victorious 4-3.

The trouble was that by the time Rangers won their League Cup section, saw off Dunfermline in the quarter-finals and edged through a semi against Dundee United to book a place in the final against Celtic, things had started to go wrong. League form was patchy, Shearer was injured and then Henderson developed a bunion problem which sidelined him from 26 September until 30 January, leading to the balance of the side being affected. Willie Johnston got his chance on the left as Symon tried Davie Wilson on the right, even moving Ralph Brand to outside-right, the position he played when he first signed for Rangers.

Suddenly, from having a settled side, a balanced team and a consistency of performance, Rangers were all over the place. It had taken only a couple of months of the season for Rangers to go from being unassailable to going into a Hampden Cup final in October 1964 against Celtic as underdogs for the first time in living memory, after having lost to Celtic at Parkhead in the league a few weeks before.

Caldow returned at left-back, but with Shearer out, it was Baxter who Scot Symon turned to to become the Rangers captain. Now, for all his many merits, one thing that Baxter had never struck anyone as being was a Rangers captain. Once again, though, Symon's astute judgment of men and what made individuals tick proved to be the masterstroke. Celtic fielded a strong side and on the right wing Jimmy Johnstone was being spoken of by some as being better than Henderson. Certainly there were many who had feared his twisting and turning would have caused Davie Provan problems and Rangers supporters were glad to see the tall Provan switched to the right to face John Hughes, with Caldow charged with rolling back the years and taming Johnstone.

That's what happened as Celtic tried to capitalise on a Rangers side which, with Baxter wearing the number ten shirt and Wilson Wood at left-half, looked hesitant. Johnstone could make no headway against Caldow. Celtic's wingers switched flanks, so Symon's captain Baxter simply ordered the Rangers full-backs to do the same. Every time Celtic tried the tactic, Baxter barked his order and the threat was negated. Baxter recalled, 'Old Scot never gave me any special instructions about what I should do as a captain, but switching the full-backs was hardly rocket science. Hughes was tall and powerful and big Davie could handle that, while Johnstone was a wee dribbler who tried to tempt you into a tackle. Eric was too good to fall for that. And we were lucky because Provan and Caldow could play right-back or left-back just as well, while Hughes and Johnstone were not nearly as adaptable.'

It took until early in the second half for Rangers to start to impose themselves, and then it was Celtic's turn to be hesitant and a defensive mistake was meat and drink to the always-eager Jim Forrest, and Rangers were a goal in the lead. Five minutes later Baxter put his mark on the final. He made room for himself, looked up and slid a precision pass which spread-eagled the Celtic defence. Forrest had been on the move as soon as Baxter looked up, and the striker buried a second goal. Johnstone got one back for Celtic, but it was Baxter who collected the trophy and tossed it high in the air as he led the team on yet another silverware lap of honour, with Celtic beaten yet again. I watched that afternoon unfold standing with my dad and granddad in the old North Enclosure at Hampden and the general feeling was that the worries and problems of the past few weeks had been put behind by a Rangers win which would surely restore confidence and consistency.

Whatever worries Scot Symon may have been feeling and may have carried into that League Cup final against Celtic at Hampden in October 1964, he too must have felt a huge wave of relief. After all, form is temporary, but Baxter was the class that was permanent. All seemed well again in Scot Symon's world. As we left Hampden, my dad cracked his old joke about having seen that movie before. Little did I know it would be the last time I would hear the gag.

30

BAXTER BREAKS HIS LEG

THE big difference between football during Bill Struth's era and the game in the Scot Symon years was the arrival of European football and, under Symon, Rangers had at times risen magnificently to the extra challenges and demands of facing the best the continent had to offer. There had been the trailblaze to the semi-final of the European Cup in season 1959-60 and the even greater heights scaled the following campaign which saw Rangers become the first British club to reach a European final when they made it through to the ultimate stage of the first-ever European Cup Winners' Cup.

There had also, of course, been low points, such as the two-legged drubbings in the Cup Winners' Cup by Tottenham Hotspur in 1962, followed a year later by being overwhelmed by the legendary Real Madrid, all of which left Symon craving more success for Rangers in this exciting arena. And there are many who were around at the time who fancied the Treble team of 1963-64 capable of going on to bigger and better things in the European Cup campaign which began in the early autumn of 1964.

Bobby Shearer was one and, years later, after watching Rangers fall at the final hurdle when attempting to gain a place in the final of the first-ever European Champions League in the spring of 1993, the former captain recalled the belief with which Rangers had gone in search of even greater European glory. Shearer said, 'The truth was that we had not been lucky as far as who we were drawn against. Tottenham Hotspur were the outstanding side of the early Sixties in England and Real Madrid had been the masters of Europe for so long that they seemed invincible. What we all hoped for was the chance to get a run going in the European Cup. We felt that if we could get into our stride then we could be a match for whatever the best in Europe had to offer.'

The evidence of what Shearer believed was there to see when Rangers were paired with Red Star Belgrade in the first round, with the first leg played at Ibrox in front of 80,000 screaming, singing supporters, even though Captain Cutlass had to watch from the sidelines, out with a rare injury. Symon, as was his way, turned to youth to fill the right-back slot, in the shape of the powerfully athletic Roger Hynd.

Rangers were sparkling that evening, especially in the game's opening phase, with Ralph Brand finishing off a move started by Jim Baxter and carried on by Davie Wilson to give them a tenth-minute lead. There was an even more barnstorming start to the second half when Baxter, so suited to this style of football, found another pass to release Wilson for a dash and a cut back which was finished by Jim Forrest. It was at that point things stuttered, as Red Star scored then hit the post, and all the confidence of the opening spell seeped away from Rangers. Baxter, though, was not finished and in the last minute his artistry and eye for an opening released a pass for Brand to swoop on to give Rangers a decent, if not unassailable, 3-1 lead to take to Belgrade.

Shearer was restored for the action seven days later, as Symon showed he was no slouch tactically, bringing Jimmy Millar in at inside-right for George McLean, trusting to Millar's greater ability to read the game and far greater work ethic, geared to help John Greig attempt to deny Red Star the chance to get the boost of an early goal. The plan worked for just over half an hour before Billy Ritchie looked hesitant and the Rangers aggregate lead was cut to a single goal. However, on the forty-minute mark, Greig lobbed Rangers level on the night and put them back into the position they had been in at the start of the second leg.

Once again Millar and Greig were magnificent in the second half, and once again it appeared that Symon had chosen the right team and that Rangers would survive a formidable challenge. Rangers held out for twenty minutes and then in a horrific two-minute spell their aggregate lead vanished as Red Star struck twice. Another followed with thirteen minutes remaining and Rangers looked on their way to making a second successive exit at the first round of the European Cup.

Symon's side, however, had spirit and nobody embodied that more than wee Davie Wilson, to this day one of the most ebullient and likeable characters anyone could wish to meet anywhere. Wilson made a run on the left wing and won a corner-kick. Wilson flighted an out-swinger which fooled the keeper and Forrest rose to power a header. The ball smacked against the crossbar, but in a last desperate throw of the dice, Ronnie McKinnon – unusually for a centre-half in those days – had come up for the corner and he threw himself at the ball and headed the equaliser which sent the tie to a play-off.

The toss of a coin sent the play-off to Highbury, ensuring a big following for Rangers, who were by the time of the match in London without Willie Henderson but buoyed with the confidence gained from beating Celtic in the final of the Scottish League Cup. Once again it was a night which belonged to Jim Baxter as he strolled his skills, prompting, probing and passing with perfect precision, turning Red Star one way and then the other and finding the way through for two goals from Forrest and another by Brand. Red Star did get one back, but Baxter had worked his magic by then and Rangers had more than earned the right to meet Rapid Vienna in the first leg of the next round at Ibrox just two weeks later.

After the thrills and spills of those three epics against Red Star, Rangers faced a very different challenge from Rapid. Symon was well aware of the stifling tactics the Austrians would resort to and put his faith in breaking them down in wing play, plus, of course, Baxter's ability to send them scampering in behind a blanket defence. With Henderson still missing, Symon trusted Willie Johnston, still only eighteen years of age, on the left, allowing him to switch Wilson to the right. Symon called it right again, for it took the best part of an hour for Rangers to get a vital goal and it came when Baxter released a pass for Wilson to read, cutting inside to get on the end of it and score.

It was what happened in the second leg that caused hopes to soar that this was going to be Rangers' year in Europe, even taking into account who they were to face in the next round. And it was what happened in the very last minute of what is still often described as Rangers' best away performance in Europe which put a question mark over those hopes. There are those who still insist that the afternoon of 8 December 1964 at the Praeter Stadium in Vienna against Rapid Vienna Jim Baxter produced the greatest performance of a career littered with memorable matches. Certainly Davie Wilson believes Baxter was at his best that day and he played in the same Rangers teams as Baxter during the spell when Celtic were routinely seen off, plus Wilson vied with Baxter for star billing at Wembley in 1963 when ten-man Scotland beat England 2-1, with Baxter scoring twice.

Wilson said, 'Rapid tried to play the offside trap and they were very good at it. But Baxter just waited them out. He refused to pass the ball until he knew we could beat the offside trap and no matter what Rapid did, they could not get the ball away from him. We had some pace up front with Jim Forrest, myself and Willie Johnston too.'

It was as though Baxter had decided this was to be a rehearsal for bigger and better things. A try-out for when Rangers would come up against the even more sophisticated defensive methods of those Italian masters of the negative. He did the main damage just nineteen minutes in with just such a pass to let Forrest double Rangers' aggregate lead before Johnston left three Rapid players in his wake with a youthful jet-paced run and cut the ball back for Wilson to finish the tie before an hour had been played.

That was the signal for Baxter to tease and torment the Austrians, trying tricks to see if they would be good enough to fool even bigger and better teams. In the end his mastery was his undoing as, with a mere twenty seconds left, a terrible tackle from behind by the Rapid thug, Skocik, thudded into Baxter, leaving him writhing with the pain of a break, two inches above the ankle of his right leg.

That was the night veteran reporter Rodger Baillie recalled that Scot Symon broke with tradition and joined the press pack for a few drinks in the hotel after the post-match banquet. Baillie recalled, 'You could see at the banquet that Symon was a bit shaken. He never said anything to us about his hopes for Rangers in Europe that season, but you could just sense that his team was coming to the boil in the European Cup and that they may just have managed to go all the way with a following wind and some good luck. And, of course, with Baxter.'

Rangers were drawn to play the European Cup holders and world champions Inter Milan in the next round and Helenio

Herrera's men were hot favourites to hold on to the European Cup. They were a fascinating mixture of the brilliant and the cynical, laced with attacking flair, but with a game plan based on the notorious *catenaccio* system of defence. Could Rangers cope with what Inter had as an attacking force? Most critics agreed that with Eric Caldow's class and speed back at left-back, with the growing maturity of John Greig in midfield and with a centre-half who covered the ground with the speed of Ronnie McKinnon, Rangers had a chance of doing just that. But could Rangers find a way through the carefully planned Inter defensive system, plus be able to cope with their cynical approach? With Jim Baxter they had a chance. Without him? Not a snowball's chance in hell.

So Scot Symon's race began to have Baxter fit for the tie against Inter Milan, due to be played in February and March 1965, the first in Milan, which was seen as a slice of good luck. If Rangers could emerge from the San Siro with the tie still in the balance, and if Baxter was back for the game at Ibrox? Well, said Rangers supporters, with Slim Jim in the team the sky's the limit. Symon, therefore, had to come up with a plan to keep Inter Milan at bay in the San Siro – no mean feat, for this was Inter at their very peak, and in front of their own noisy Italian supporters they were unstoppable.

It is often said that Symon was no tactician, but that judgment is a hasty one which flies in the face of the way he fashioned his teams. True, as Ian McMillan remarked about his reluctance to say anything at half time in the 1960 European Cup semi-final in Frankfurt with the score still 1-1, he tended to trust his players when the action was under way. But Scot Symon was a long way from being anywhere near as tactically naïve as some folk who have never truly studied him and his teams would have us believe. The Rangers line-up he sent out to face Inter Milan in the cauldron of the San Siro gives lie to the way some seek to denigrate Symon. In fact, the team he chose and the shape and tactics he fashioned were not all that far removed from the set-up Walter Smith used to take Rangers to the UEFA Cup final in Manchester more than forty years later.

Symon handed Old Warhorse Jimmy Millar the number eight shirt but asked him to stay deep, to join John Greig and Wilson Wood in positioning themselves as a shield in front of the Rangers defence. He knew that it was a risk, as his players were used to the opposition in Scotland adapting their tactics to try and thwart Rangers, but he had great trust in Millar, as stout, stalwart and mature a player as ever played for Symon. Millar didn't let his manager down and when the teams emerged for the second half the game was still goalless and Symon's tactics were working a treat. When disaster struck it was nothing to do with the way the team was set up or the ability of the players. It was pure bad luck, made all the more unfortunate by the fact Millar, so strong, so brave and so brilliant in the first half, was involved.

Three minutes into the second half the ball ricocheted off Millar's head towards the most dangerous player in the Inter team, the great Louis Suarez, who lashed an unstoppable volley into the net. As if that was not bad enough, Lady Luck curled her cruel lip at Rangers just sixty seconds later when a shot from Inter captain Corso, which was flying wide of the target, struck Peiro on the head and was deflected beyond the stranded Billy Ritchie. Two minutes later the same Peiro needed no luck with a smashing shot to give Inter a 3-0 lead. Even then Rangers were not finished, and Jim Forrest got one back with just under half an hour left. It is a measure of how respectful of Scot Symon's Rangers, European Cup holders and world champions, Inter Milan had become that they were content to play out that time protecting their lead. And it was a measure of how more sophisticated Symon had made Rangers, they were too streetwise to be tempted into opening out in search of a second, inviting the danger of losing a fourth.

Baxter had known he would never make that match, but he did his best to be ready for the second leg, due at Ibrox a fortnight later. He recalled, 'I thought I might have made it, but the truth is when I look back, I was still a bit away from being able to go out and take on Inter Milan.' Even without their hero, the 80,000 who packed into Ibrox that night – me included – believed that with Henderson on the right, Johnston on the left and Forrest through the middle, Rangers had a chance. A good chance, too. Especially if they could get an early goal. That boost came in six minutes when Wilson Wood unleashed a fierce drive which bounced off the chest of Inter keeper Sarti. Forrest, as ever, had been following the ball in and pounced with the perfect poacher's finish. Inter, who had started cagily, went further into their shell. Symon had hoped that the speed of his two wingers would get behind a defence containing a sweeper which was then alien to Scottish clubs. But there was no Baxter to release the passes to tease a defender out of position, giving either winger a clear run. And the game had been changing since Henderson had first burst onto the scene electrifying crowds with his directness. That didn't work as well, especially against the Italians. For if Henderson went beyond his full-back, the great Facchetti, before he could deliver the ball into the box, he faced another defender. That was a lesson the then teenage Johnston learned that night. Years later, sitting in Baxter's bar in the Paisley Road, Johnston remembered almost every kick of that night.

Johnston said, 'Even at that age I had plenty of confidence in my own ability. I was very fast and in Scotland when I got away from the full-back, that was me away. Nobody could catch me and I had a run to see whether to stay out wide and cross, get to the by-line and cut back, or even cut in and shoot. I thought I knew the game. That night taught me I knew nothing. Those Italians were just too good and too clever. I don't think I got away once to get a cross in. It was an education.'

Johnston's memories of the match tally with mine, but even at that the tie was still finely balanced going into the closing stages. One break, one deflection, such as the two which had favoured Inter in Milan, or even another fumble by keeper Sarti. That was all that was needed and the tie would need to be decided by a play-off. And Rangers were dab hands when it came to play-offs.

The moment appeared to have arrived as the game moved into its last ten minutes and George McLean, out-thought and outplayed all night by the Italians, looked up. He had the ball and some room and was twenty yards from the target. McLean resisted the temptation to lash a shot and instead tried to steer it over the smallish Sarti's head. The keeper leapt and missed it. The crowd rose. And the sound died in 80,000 throats as the ball hit the crossbar. Rangers, without not just their best player, but the best player Scotland has produced in over half a century, Jim Baxter, had gone within a whisker of beating one of the truly great teams in the history of the European Cup, Inter Milan. And before their decline set in. But what if Baxter had not suffered that broken leg in Vienna? Baxter was the best person to ask.

When I did, one afternoon in his Paisley Road pub, Baxter did not start off by giving me the gallus grin and answer I fully expected. He was more thoughtful. He said, 'You have to remember how unlucky Old Scot was in the first leg. He called everything just right and had the sort of defensive look that gave Rangers a chance. But could he have tried to do the same thing if I had been playing? Would he have tried it? I know that when I was in the tactic was to give the ball to me and then run into space. That worked against Red Star and Rapid Vienna, but Inter were better and also much better organised. Of course, if I had been as close to making the first leg and had a couple of matches before the game at Ibrox, then it might have been different. But I do remember watching the match and thinking how good Inter were. They never let Henderson or Johnston get away, and they were two terrific wingers.

'Maybe I would need to have stayed fit and not broken the leg for me to have been able to do it against Inter. I do know that during the match in Vienna I started thinking ahead. Maybe I lost my concentration at the end and maybe that cost me. But I did believe that, as far as Europe was concerned, Old Scot had the right team and that this was my best chance.'

Whatever the ifs, buts and maybes, two facts from that era stand out. The Real Madrid team that beat Rangers in season 1963-64, went on to reach the European Cup final, losing 3-1 to Inter Milan. And the reigning world champions and European Cup holders, Inter Milan, who narrowly beat a Baxterless Rangers in 1965 went on to retain the European Cup by beating Benfica 1-0 in the final.

Events unfolding on the home front, however, meant that night when Rangers went so close against Inter Milan at Ibrox in March 1965 was the last time Scot Symon was to get a crack at the European Cup.

31

SYMON'S PAIN

IN a career that has stretched over six decades, journalist Rodger Baillie has conjured many memorable phrases to describe what he has witnessed on football fields all over the world. But there have been none more eloquent than the words he used to me to describe the look on Scot Symon's face the day Jim Baxter signed for Sunderland. Baillie recalled that day in May 1965 and how the picture of the Baxter signing, watched by former Rangers man Ian McColl – then the Sunderland manager – and Symon was one of the most revealing insights ever into Symon's deepest thoughts. Painting an even more vivid word picture, Baillie said, 'When you looked at Symon's face you were reminded of those pictures at the end of the war when you could see the pain etched on the faces of German generals as they witnessed Montgomery accepting their signatures on the surrender document. You could see from the way Symon looked that he knew things would never be the same again. Goodness knows what sort of thoughts went through his mind.'

Symon had survived the premature loss of Willie Woodburn, the man around whom he expected to build a new team. It had only been weeks into his appointment as team boss, yet somehow he managed to muddle through with a succession of centre-halves, keeping Rangers at the top as often as not, until Ronnie McKinnon emerged. He had been able to replace Willie Waddell when the legendary right-winger's hamstrings finally gave out by unearthing Alex Scott. And when Iron Man Harold Davis started to show understandable signs of wear and tear, Symon had handed the task of replacing him to an even better player, John Greig. True, there had been no obvious replacement for Ian McMillan at inside-right, though Jimmy Millar had often made a good fist of it as a schemer. And when Millar could no longer cut it as a centre-forward, Jim Forrest burst on the scene to create new goalscoring records.

But Baxter was different. He was the pivot on which all of Symon's plans, hopes and secret dreams rested. The player whose teasing and tormenting could reduce opposition to incoherent and eventually disastrous rage, whose magical left foot and slim swivelling hips could twist himself into space for that magic wand of a left foot to put a killer pass through any defensive system any coach could dream up.

At any other time, Scot Symon may have been relied upon to do what he had done so often during eleven years as Rangers manager: conjure a replacement who, if he wasn't quite on the same level of excellence as the previous player, was at least good enough to keep Rangers among the honours domestically. However, the landscape of Scottish football was changing and perhaps that haunted, defeated look on Symon's face the day his most prized and pleasing asset, Slim Jim Baxter, put pen to paper and left Ibrox summed it up. And the most sweeping change which had taken place was across the city from Ibrox, where Jock Stein had returned to Celtic to take over as manager from Jimmy McGrory and, within weeks, steer Celtic to a Scottish Cup final triumph, beating Dunfermline 3-2.

To his dying day, Baxter insisted that he never really wanted to leave Rangers and he believed that if Symon had been given the final say, a financial deal could have been struck to keep him happy. Baxter said, 'I was still on £45 a week and told Scot that I wanted a new deal to take me to £75 a week. I knew it was a stretch and that everybody in the first team was on the same wages. But I said to him that I knew how important I was to his team and that I knew he knew that too, so it was only right that I should get more.

'The fact I had broken a leg was something else that was in my mind. I had never been bothered with injuries before, but suddenly I had been made to realise how easily a career could be ended. I looked at Eric Caldow, who was as fit as a flea and looked good for another six or seven years as Scotland captain until he broke a leg at Wembley, and even though he had been back in the Rangers team, he had lost something and was not the same player.

'Even at that, I was willing to meet Rangers somewhere if the club had made me some sort of decent offer. If they had said we can make it £70 a week that would have done me. Even £65 or £60 and I would have stayed. Symon said he would speak to the board and then came back and told me their answer was no. So I left. I didn't really have a choice. I signed for Sunderland for £90 a week, but would have stayed at Ibrox for £60.'

Baxter's recall of those days throws into the daylight the way Scot Symon's wishes were beginning to be overruled and his advice increasingly ignored by the new board. Chairman John Lawrence was like an absentee landlord, more often away at his holiday home in Morocco where he had retired to escape the harsh Scottish winters, which left his pal, Matt Taylor, soon to oust John Wilson, the Baillie's son, as vice chairman. Taylor was close to Willie Allison, whose job description of public relations officer belied the power and influence he exerted. Every description of Allison I have heard or read – from reporters who were around at the time to Sir Alex Ferguson's autobiography – reveal a staid, autocratic, self-important man with no sense of himself and even less of a sense of humour. His idea of Rangers was not how the club really was, or indeed had been when Bill Struth ruled the roost. And certainly not the way Scot Symon saw Rangers.

In short, Willie Allison was everything Jim Baxter was not, and it is extremely likely that Baxter found no favour with the influential Allison. If Matt Taylor had asked Allison advice on how to react to Baxter's wages demands before in turn advising chairman John Lawrence, it is odds-on Allison would have done everything in his power to see Rangers rid of Baxter.

This scenario also helps illustrate the changing of the guard at Ibrox and Parkhead. During his twenty years as Celtic manager, Jimmy McGrory had to defer to the owning White–Kelly dynasty, with chairman Bob Kelly the man who made the major decisions regarding signings and team selection. At Ibrox, during his first ten years as manager, Scot Symon was in charge of all team matters, including signings and picking the team.

When Bob Kelly first tried to entice Jock Stein to leave Hibernian, where he had been for less than a year, and become Celtic manager, Stein insisted on full control. Over signings, over team selections and also how much Celtic would pay their players. It is interesting that, just as Stein was gaining full control of football matters at Celtic, placing these things in the hands of a professional at Parkhead for the first time for twenty years, at Ibrox the power was gradually slipping through Scot Symon's fingers and, after the summer of 1965, he was never again allowed to manage fully in the way he wanted – the way that had given Rangers so much success since he took over in 1954.

In effect, what had happened to Rangers in season 1964-65 was not as bad as it seemed on the surface. The Scottish League Cup had been retained, with Celtic beaten in the final, and there had been an exciting run in Europe, halted by such a narrow 3-2 defeat by the holders, Inter Milan, who went on to retain the European Cup. In the Scottish Cup, Rangers started their defence of the trophy by easing through 3-0 against Hamilton Accies and then went to Dens Park, home of the Dundee side they had beaten in the previous year's final. They won again, this time 2-0. A Scottish Cup undefeated run which went back to March 1961 finally ended when Hibernian triumphed 2-1 at Easter Road. After winning three Scottish Cups in a row, nobody could complain too much about that.

The defence of their title, won in 1963 and then again in 1964, though, was what brought the howls of complaint from Rangers supporters, who refused to countenance their team being so far out of the championship chase so soon, especially when that early season poor form and shocking results included a 3-1 defeat at Parkhead in September. By the time the campaign had gone eight games – at a time of two points for a win – Rangers were slumped in a lowly tenth position, and their seven points from a mere two wins, three draws and three defeats, saw them trail leaders Kilmarnock by eight points. And all that in October, before Jim Baxter suffered a broken leg.

True to his nature, Scot Symon had refused to press the panic button and plunge into the transfer market at a time which predated the January transfer window. His only signings were Findlay McGillivray, a right-back seen as a replacement for Bobby Shearer, who arrived from Third Lanark in exchange for Doug Baillie and £12,000 in September. It didn't work out for the defender, who never even played in the first team. The robust St Mirren Icelandic inside-left Thorolf Beck arrived for £20,000 in November. He was another who found the step up too much. By the end of the season Rangers were in fifth position, the second-worst in the club's history, having won only eighteen of the thirty-four-game championship programme, losing eight times. However, worse had happened when Bill Struth was the manager. Back then, Rangers had won the title on the three previous seasons, but managed to finish in a shameful sixth spot, with matters made worse by the fact the champions were Celtic. In 1965 the title was at last taken by Willie Waddell's fine Kilmarnock side, which had been threatening to become champions for five years.

Yet, after their bad start and even taking into account the loss of Baxter and Willie Henderson, Symon's quiet patience and steady nerve appeared to be bearing fruit, for Rangers did not go into the New Year programme without a hope. They were given a boost when Celtic visited Ibrox on New Year's Day 1965 and Jimmy Johnstone scuppered any chance his team had when he launched a red-mist assault on Beck, which saw him sent off, with Jim Forrest's goal winning the match for Rangers.

Twenty-four hours later, a draw at Firhill, Eric Caldow netting the equaliser with a late penalty was a decent result, especially when it was followed by the 4-0 drubbing of Dundee at Ibrox and another 4-0 win when Symon took his team to Airdrie. Therefore, by the time Rangers went to face Hibernian at Easter Road on 30 January, Scot Symon could have been forgiven for starting to believe another great Rangers fightback was under way, especially as Henderson had made an unexpectedly quick recovery from a serious bunion operation and returned to action.

The day was cold and my dad and I joined the nation in watching the funeral of Sir Winston Churchill on television before travelling to Edinburgh. Henderson was subdued, Beck was no real replacement for Brand at inside-left, while Wilson Wood was certainly no Baxter. Just over half an hour had gone when the tall Hibs striker Neil Martin found space to get on the end of a cross and power a header behind Billy Ritchie from close range.

It was the only goal of the game. Though when Rangers could only manage a draw with Hearts at Ibrox the following week and then sneak a 1-0 win over St Mirren, they were still just six points behind leaders Hearts, with three games in hand.

However, it was the news about Jock Stein which hit the headlines fewer than forty-eight hours after his Hibernian side had beaten Rangers 1-0 at Easter Road, on the day of Churchill's funeral, that filled the back pages. Stein was to become the new Celtic manager, but had agreed to stay at Hibs until a replacement was found. Bob Shankly was tempted away from Dundee, allowing Stein to take over at Parkhead on 9 March.

Symon's side's first outing after Stein became Celtic manager was a trip to Aberdeen on 13 March. Rangers lost 2-0. Whether or not the date was exact, it was certainly near enough for the Ides of March to have blasted their chill warning in Scot Symon's direction.

32

THE NEW CHALLENGE

THE new challenge which Scot Symon had to face up to and work out in the summer of 1965 was one which was entirely different from anything which had confronted him before in his managerial career, not only at Rangers but when he began at East Fife and then when he moved to England to take charge of Preston North End. One of the recurring themes in Scot Symon's life was the memory he left behind among his players and so many others who came into contact with him that he was a gentleman. He could be gruff, he could be infuriatingly self-contained, but the common decencies always appeared to be important to the way he not only lived his own personal life, but also how he went about his business as a manager. This was especially true of his vision of himself as being manager of Rangers. The clear impression of Scot Symon was that he believed in the dignity of his position and that he cared for the image of Rangers.

Facing him across the city now was Jock Stein, who was an entirely different type of man. He did have certain things in common with Symon, among them a passion for the way Celtic were viewed, of people's perceptions of the club, plus, like Symon, Stein held no great love for the press. However, Stein was more adept at bending and manipulating newspapers to his will, using a combination of the force of his more outgoing personality, plus a hefty dose of bullying tactics.

For unlike his predecessor at Celtic, Jimmy McGrory, and completely opposite to Symon, Jock Stein was not a gentleman. Far from it. Perhaps it was that, more than any of the great tactical acumen he has been credited with and which has grown into a myth, which allowed him to get the upper hand over Symon's Rangers over the two and a bit years when they were in direct conflict. It was not so much Stein's tactics that Symon found so hard to understand and meet with his own football knowledge that proved to be the problem, as much as that Symon could not quite read the way Stein's mind worked in other ways. Ways that were alien to the Scot Symon character.

When it came to dealings with the press, Symon remained true to his own feelings and kept them to the minimum. He was not entirely comfortable in the company of reporters. That much was made clear by journalist Rodger Baillie's story about one of the few times Symon socialised with the hack pack that night in Vienna after Jim Baxter suffered a broken leg. One of the things Baillie recalled was a small detail, but a far from insignificant one. When he sat down for a drink with the reporters his tipple was Dubonnet and lemonade. In those days, sportswriters were a hard-drinking bunch and hard liquor was the order of the day, with whisky in the traditional hauf-'n'-half pint style, the favourite. Symon must have felt he had to be seen joining in, but his choice of refreshment revealed his unease at being in such company in the first place.

Stein was teetotal, but he could sit sipping tea in the company of reporters he despised for hours, watching who spoke to whom, who drank what and how much, and listening intently for any sign of any reporter revealing any natural bias. He was also a great stirrer, often dropping a verbal hand grenade into a conversation and then withdrawing, leaving reporters to squabble among themselves, while he waited to see what the result would be in various newspapers. Nowadays, it is run of the mill for reporters to be able to quiz managers after a match, but back then post-match press conferences were unheard of. Journalists could lurk on the pavements outside Ibrox and Parkhead and try to buttonhole a player, but managers were off limits. Stein had his own ideas. It was not long after he took over at Celtic that he instituted something cute and clever which put reporters on the back foot.

Stein's cunning move was not to speak to reporters immediately after the game, as has become the norm now, but to summon them to Parkhead for an early morning briefing each Sunday. Miss it or be late and Stein was on your case. This was Stein at his manipulative best and it was something Scot Symon had no way of countering. Had he done the same he would have been accused of simply pandering to Stein's ways.

Reporters, therefore, left Celtic's game on a Saturday afternoon with certain thoughts about what they had seen and certain ideas of what they would write in their match reports – just as they did when they had watched Rangers. Stein's shrewd eye spotted an opportunity. In those days, newspapers were smaller, printed by the old hot metal method, and there was no room for the huge quotes-based pieces that fill papers today and reduce the role of the sportswriter to stenographer. Back then, giants filled the sports pages: Alex Cameron, Hugh Taylor, Willie Waddell, John McKenzie and John Fairgrieve were men whose Monday morning verdicts were eagerly anticipated. Stein's mission was to influence those views.

Whatever the sportswriter who had watched Rangers at the weekend thought about the game were the views which appeared in Monday's papers and which set the agenda for the week. Not so with Celtic. By the time even the biggest sports-writing names in Scotland had completed their Sunday morning audience with Stein, their views were coloured. Stein subtly let them know what he thought, not by argument but by subtle suggestion, pointing reporters in another direction, revealing a tidbit, or by outrageously diverting attention away from either a misdeed by a Celtic player or a poor team performance, by suggesting so-and-so may be a transfer target. Much of the time these briefings were not as today's immediate post-match press conferences, up front, out in the open and on the record, but given on lobby terms with no quotes and nothing attributable.

Reporters soon learned to play the game. They knew that to step out of line would see them incur Stein's displeasure and see them exiled from the many tip-off phone calls Stein was wont to make, many of them to upstage Scot Symon and Rangers in the publicity stakes. It was a well-known Stein tactic to remove Rangers from the back pages as they prepared for a big game by tipping off press pals that he was about to make a signing, again off the record. Sometimes he even managed to time the actual signing to do the job for him.

These were games the gentlemanly and old-school Scot Symon could not begin to understand, never mind start playing in any effort to beat Stein at his own game. Reporters, all of whom knew there were no favours to be had from Symon, were then buried deeper and deeper inside Stein's pocket. Stein also played on the belief that Rangers had been given the lion's share of publicity in newspapers, were secretly favoured by many sports-writers and were part of the Establishment which had it in for Celtic. The conspiracy theory is far from new, but nobody played it more skilfully and turned it in his favour more cleverly than Stein. This was again Jock Stein at his streetwise best. Like Robert Redford and Paul Newman in *The Sting*, Stein could read his 'mark' and pull off the con with supreme skill simply by turning someone's weaknesses into his strength.

Reporters always strive to be fair, regardless of any affiliation they may have grown up with. Of course, for instance, the *Scottish Daily Express* man main, Willie Waddell, was Rangers through and through, but he was a professional journalist, as proud of that as he was of his playing career at Ibrox, and determined to be fair. Among some of the other big sports-writing names of the era, Alex Cameron, who later became my great and still much-missed friend, grew up supporting Stirling Albion, while someone else I was lucky enough to get to know, the legendary Hughie Taylor, was a Kilmarnock supporter and John Fairgrieve wore his passion for Hearts on his sleeve.

These were not the sort of guys who would be unfair to Celtic as a matter of course. But since the Parkhead club had won the League and Scottish Cup Double in 1954, and until Stein's first trophy, the 1965 Scottish Cup, the 1957 League Cup was the only trophy Celtic had won. In that time Rangers had won title after title, Cup upon Cup, and blazed a thrill-a-minute trail of adventure in Europe and produced what Rodger Baillie believes was as good a team to have come out of Ibrox before or since, the 1963-64 Treble winners. No wonder Rangers got all the praise and Celtic the brickbats. But Stein's tactics – perhaps he was a better tactician off the field than on it – made the Camerons, Taylors, Waddells, McKenzies and Fairgrieves stop and think. There must have been times when Stein's incessant propaganda in their ears made them pause, fingers frozen above those wonderful Royal and Imperial typewriters, pondering whether what they were about to write would be seen by Stein as an example of what he believed to be an institutional bias against Celtic.

There is no doubt in my mind that Jock Stein knew exactly what he was doing. His greatest strength was being a good judge of men, of their character (or lack of it), and he knew Scot Symon was too much of a gentleman to get down and dirty the way he could. Just a glance at their different backgrounds tells the story. Symon the Perthshire country boy. Stein the toughie from Lanarkshire. Symon the junior footballer with Dundee Violet, going on to a stellar playing career with Dundee, Portsmouth and Rangers, who was good enough to play for his country; a cricketer, capable enough at that sport, too, to play for Scotland, Stein a miner who played part-time with lowly Albion Rovers, whose idea of another sport was pitch and toss. In Coatbridge, where my dad was born and grew up and where he continued to work as a fitter engineer until the mid-Sixties, Stein's reputation among his contemporaries was that of a fly man.

Stein's only brief flirtation with a playing career at the top came when Celtic rescued him from the obscurity of non-league football in Wales where he played for Llanelli. His success as a captain and centre-half in the Celtic team which won the 1954 Double was based on a skill at kneeing the ball clear and organising others. When injury ended his playing career he moved on to the Celtic coaching staff before becoming manager of Dunfermline, where he won the 1961 Scottish Cup, beating Celtic in a replay, before a ten-month spell at Hibs, where he managed them to the short-lived Summer Cup.

Even at that stage of Stein's still-fledgling managerial career, in the summer of 1964, there was little to suggest that the Parkhead decision-makers, in particular chairman Bob Kelly, were willing to give up any of that power by bringing in a new manager, especially a man such as Stein, who would clearly insist on full control. Of course, there were many close to Celtic in many different walks of life – including the media – who argued the case for Stein being the only man to save Celtic from twenty years of mediocrity, just as a few years later those whose noses were blue championed the cause of a reluctant Willie Waddell as the only man to take on Stein.

As season 1964-65 got under way and even after Rangers beat them in a League Cup final, Kelly and Celtic held out. But, as events early in 1965 unfolded, it became clear, even to the autocratic Kelly, that things had to change and the streetwise Stein and the gentlemanly Symon became fated to be pitched into direct conflict.

33

FIRST CHALLENGE FROM CELTIC

TO prepare for what seemed certain to be the first challenge from Celtic for more than a decade, Scot Symon made changes which he hoped would not only add freshness, but would also re-introduce more guile. Without Jim Baxter, guile and invention were qualities he knew Rangers lacked.

In the summer he had gone to Morton and signed the man he saw as a long-term replacement for the now departed Bobby Shearer, Danish defender Kai Johansen. In doing so Symon laid waste to the notion that he was stuck in a time warp where football was still played the way it had been when he was such a key member of Bill Struth's team in the 1940s. Only a fool would believe his team did not need to change and evolve to cope with the modern ways, and Scot Symon was far from being a fool. His repeated exposure to the ways and moves of how the continentals played the game sharpened Symon's appetite to learn. Two years earlier, after the Real Madrid defeat, Symon, in a rare public utterance, said, 'There is much for Rangers to learn from Real Madrid.'

Contrast and compare that to Sir Alf Ramsey's reaction after his England were beaten by Brazil in the initial section of the 1970 World Cup finals in Mexico before going out to West Germany in the quarter-finals. The Brazil of Pelé, Gerson and

Tostao – the greatest-ever international team – went on to win the Jules Rimet trophy for a third time, claiming outright owner-ship of it. But Ramsey did not hang around to watch and study them, declaring that there was nothing for him to learn from Brazil.

Symon was neither so arrogant, nor insular nor just down-right silly, and the arrival from Morton of Johansen for £20,000 – a lot of money then for a full-back – is the perfect example of the way his mind was working in the summer as he pondered how best to change things. Up to that point, Symon remained true to the tradition of full-backs as defenders who could either tackle fiercely, the way Shearer did, or were fast and classy and could send their opponent up a cul-de-sac in the manner of Eric Caldow at his best. Europe, in particular Inter Milan and their left-back Facchetti, had caught his shrewd eye when Rangers had gone so close to beating the two-in-a-row European Cup holders and world champions.

Symon remembered the two games Rangers had played against a newly-promoted Morton side, which had finished a creditable tenth, and he recalled the Greenock side's right-back, Kai Johansen, whose forays forward marked him as the perfect example of what Symon was looking for. I first encountered Johansen when he ran a pub in Govan and later in the cabaret restaurant that bore his name in Howard Street, just behind St Enoch Square in the city centre of Glasgow. But it was not until the 1990s when I interviewed him for a Scottish Cup memory lane-type of feature that we started to really get to know each other. We became friends and shared many a glass. He also shared many a memory of his time under Symon and was a talkative, indeed garrulous, character.

It was Johansen who put to bed the notion that he took time to settle at Ibrox because Symon insisted on putting the shackles on the Danish player's natural attacking instincts. In fact, nothing could have been further from the truth. Johansen remembered, 'I know I took time to settle and I know I was not the same player that I had been with Morton, but none of that had anything to do with Scot Symon. It was my fault. It is not easy for a player to play for Rangers and, even though I was in my mid-twenties, I had gone to Morton from Denmark where football was still amateur and Scottish football was much faster and tougher. And more was expected of me at Rangers than had been at Morton.

'I also knew that Rangers had preferred their full-backs to be defenders and not wingers, so I kept my natural instincts under control and my game suffered, and the more it suffered the more nervous I became and the more nervous I became the more I struggled.'

The initial settling-in period came to a head on 3 January 1966 at Parkhead where, in a foggy atmosphere and on a cold day which left the pitch icy and bone hard, Johansen was ripped apart by John Hughes as Celtic won 5-1. However, that is skipping ahead in a season in which Symon's steadfastness, courage and football intelligence were the subject of scrutiny as never before. And all the time, across the city, Jock Stein was pouring his poison into the ears of reporters and anyone else who would listen, setting the agenda and showing that whatever he lacked as a football tactician – and we shall examine his limitations in this area later – he was a master off-the-field strategist. Symon had spotted that Ralph Brand's pace had gone. The sharpness which made him the perfect foil for Jimmy Millar – whose race as a centre-forward was run, though not his worth to Rangers – had gone. He sold Brand to Manchester City for the then sizeable sum of £30,000. Clearly even that wily old fox of a manager, City's Joe Mercer, had not seen what Symon had spotted.

Brand too did not agree with the Rangers manager and sold his story to a now-defunct Sunday newspaper, in which he made a forthright attack on Scot Symon and Rangers. Brand has since returned to the Ibrox fold as one of the legends who act as match-day hosts in the hospitality suites. However, there are still many Rangers supporters of a certain vintage who refuse to forgive him for what they still see as an act of bitter betrayal. I belong to that generation, but prefer to take a more charitable view. Brand truly believed Symon got rid of him too soon. He loved playing for Rangers and was understandably angry at being denied that. He lashed out in a fit of pique. It was a long time ago, and whatever Ralph Brand said must be balanced against what he gave to Rangers with his contribution to the Ibrox cause heavier on the scales of justice. When he said what he did, Ralph Brand was just having a bad day.

Brand left weeks after Shearer departed and his exit followed that of Ian McMillan, who returned to Airdrie. Symon got £5,000 for the Wee Prime Minister, exactly half of what he paid for him in 1958, proving once again what an astute judge and shrewd businessman on behalf of Rangers the Ibrox manager was. He had also persuaded McMillan to stay on for a season beyond when he could reasonably be expected to perform at the top level, playing in the reserves and helping to tutor emerging talents such as Alex Willoughby, Jim Forrest and Willie Johnston.

Willoughby once told me that the greatest learning experience of all his years in football was playing in the same team as the essentially shy and modest, yet shrewd, brilliant and extraordinary McMillan. Symon actually tried to repeat his feat in signing McMillan when he went back to Morton in the August of 1965, on the eve of the league season kicking off, and signed another Dane, inside-forward Jorn Sorenson, a balding playmaker who claimed to be twenty-nine at the time, but looked older and, according to his fellow-countryman and Morton and Rangers team-mate, the deliciously indiscreet Kai Johansen, was indeed considerably older. Once again, though, by signing Sorenson, Symon showed his continuing lack of faith in McMillan's prodigy, Alex Willoughby, who many, myself included, firmly believe was the Rangers player lost to legendary status because Symon refused to trust him to replace the Wee Prime Minister, a task to which Willoughby was supremely suited. Sorenson managed just one season with Rangers, playing sixteen times, the most memorable of those being the first Old Firm game of the season, at Ibrox on 18 September at the end of a week of incessant rain.

I recall the conditions vividly because on the morning of the game the maths teacher who ran the Woodside Senior Secondary School team needed a left-back, and I was the victim. I say victim because my left foot was for standing on and on a grass pitch – I was more used to black ash – which was heavy and muddy, we lost 9-0 in East Kilbride, with their outside-right, too fast and slippery for me to even kick, laying on . . . oh at least seven of them. In the afternoon Willie Henderson did much the same to Celtic's Tommy Gemmell, courtesy of the sort of service he used to rely on from McMillan, now provided by Jorn Sorenson. It was the first Old Firm match of the Jock Stein era as Celtic manager, and Scot Symon drew first blood. Kai Johansen remembered in much the same way as I did, though he recalled he was in direct opposition to Bertie Auld, before Stein finally wised up to inside-left, as a schemer, as Auld's best position. My memory had him up against John Hughes. The record books proved Kai correct.

Johansen said, 'Auld had no real pace and did not give me any problems, and I was pleased with the way I played. I was also pleased for Jorn. Sorenson was a very good player and he was at his best for about an hour. Celtic could not figure out what he was going to do and in the end somebody kicked him and he had to limp along at outside-left. We were leading 2-1 by then and Celtic naturally came at us with everything, but Auld could not get away from me, and although Jimmy Johnstone caused problems, we held on.'

The heroes of Scot Symon's first encounter with Jock Stein in an Old Firm match were goalkeeper Billy Ritchie and the man the manager had converted from being a ball-playing, attacking right-half to a classy and composed centre-half, Ronnie McKinnon. The burly John Hughes was at centre-forward, but even his bulk could not unsettle the slim McKinnon, while the lightning thrusts of Hughes' strike partner Bobby Lennox failed to shake off the extremely mobile centre-half. And behind McKinnon was Ritchie, in inspired form. One of the saves the keeper made was from a Hughes effort which had been so fierce it saw the unflashy Ritchie land on his head, an image captured in a wonderful newspaper picture of the time.

The goals were all scored in the opening twenty minutes, with George McLean coming in from the left in the seventh minute and cutting the ball back for Jim Forrest to get there first and score. Celtic equalised in eighteen minutes when Lennox went down when challenged by John Greig, Hughes scored from the spot. Two minutes later the fleet-footed Forrest was too fast for Billy McNeill who hauled him down in the box. McLean tucked the penalty beyond John Fallon.

Scot Symon may have lost Jim Baxter as well as Ian McMillan, Bobby Shearer and Ralph Brand, while Jimmy Millar was growing too battle-scarred to continue as a centre-forward, and Jock Stein may have arrived to take over as Celtic manager, but on that September afternoon in 1965 my pal Neil and I left Ibrox thinking it was going to be a case of business as usual. We were wrong!

34

STEIN'S PRESENCE

NOT since just before Scot Symon had joined the ranks as a player in 1938 had Rangers had to face up to anything other than the odd flash-in-the-pan challenge from Celtic. But by the autumn of 1965 it was becoming obvious that the Scottish Cup Celtic had lifted in the spring just a few weeks after Jock Stein had taken over would not be the only silverware heading towards Parkhead.

That much became obvious when the two old foes met in the League Cup final for the second time in successive seasons. Twelve months earlier, even as Rangers stuttered in the start of their defence of the league, there was still a supreme belief inside Ibrox that nothing coming out of the east end of Glasgow would upset the balance of power, a belief that was justified by the fact Rangers retained the League Cup. A year down the line and once again there was confidence inside Ibrox that following the inconsistencies of the previous campaign, and even without Jim Baxter, the old order would re-assert itself, something given credence by the fact Rangers won the first Old Firm game of the season. Billy Ritchie had missed the opening matches of the season as Scot Symon's side began their defence of the League Cup, a trophy they had captured in the two previous seasons, with Norrie Martin taking over in goal. That and the absence of

Willie Henderson upset the rhythm of the side in the opening match of the qualifying section, which ended in a 4-2 defeat by Hearts at Tynecastle, and even after Rangers beat Clyde 3-0 in the next game there was another shock when Aberdeen came out on top, 2-0 at Pittodrie.

At that stage, there was a real prospect that Rangers would fail to progress to the knockout stages. But a Willie Johnston strike beat Hearts at Ibrox, Clyde were seen off 3-1 at Shawfield and Aberdeen trounced 4-0 at Ibrox to take Rangers into a two-legged quarter-final tie against Airdrie, which they won on aggregate 9-1. Kai Johansen remembered the semi-final as one of the most extraordinary matches of his career. I was at Hampden for the match against Kilmarnock and can vouch for what a strange evening it turned out to be as Rangers went from one extreme to the other. Johansen told me, 'We were brilliant for just over an hour. In that time it was as well as I can remember Rangers playing in a domestic Cup match in all my time there. George McLean was at his best and scored a hat-trick and Alex Willoughby was also brilliant as he scored one, too. We really did play some sensational football.'

Johansen's memory did not let him down. Rangers were 6-1 in front after Jim Forrest and Willie Henderson scored, and there were just over twenty minutes left for Symon's team to play out. Things went wrong after Tommy McLean, later to become a Rangers legend, got one back in seventy-one minutes and then netted a penalty in eighty-three minutes. Had McLean completed his hat-trick, as he did in the last minute, two or three minutes earlier, things could have turned out different.

As it was, there was little fear among the Rangers supporters who made their way to Hampden for the League Cup final against Celtic on 23 October 1965, and it looked as though their confidence was well founded as Rangers started in a whirlwind of attacks which saw Jim Forrest presented with two great chances. Twelve months earlier, Forrest had made the most of the couple of opportunities that came his way; this time he squandered them. At the other end, there were other inexplicable things happening. Contrary to popular myth, one of them was not that John Hughes, by then switched to the left wing in place of Bertie Auld, who did not play, terrorised Johansen. That nightmare ninety minutes was to come later for the Danish defender.

What happened was that after eighteen minutes, Ronnie McKinnon, normally so cool at centre-half, stuck up his hand when a harmless free-kick was lofted into the area, to concede a clear penalty, allowing Hughes to give Celtic the confidence of an early lead. Ten minutes later, as Jimmy Johnstone wriggled in from the right, but with no danger signals flashing, left-back Davie Provan was tempted to attempt a tackle from behind, at that time not illegal, as it is today. Johnstone went tumbling and referee Hugh Phillips was quick to point to the spot. Hughes stepped up again and, although Ritchie made a brave effort getting a hand to the shot, he couldn't keep it out. From that moment until the end, the outcome was never in doubt, even when Celtic defender Ian Young, under pressure from John Greig, put the ball into his own net. There is no doubt in my mind that from that day, Scot Symon knew a whole new ball game was starting to unfold and that no longer would the challenge to his Rangers come from either Aberdeen, or Hibs, or Hearts, or Dundee or Kilmarnock, but from Celtic . . . and that upped the ante considerably.

Rangers supporters are notorious for their lack of tolerance with their team during any lean season, but Symon knew their demands would increase if it wasn't Aberdeen, or Hibs, or Hearts, or Dundee, or Kilmarnock who were stealing their club's thunder, but Celtic, instead. Symon was a clever enough man, as well as being a shrewd enough manager, to be aware of the growing threat from this new Celtic, managed by Stein, which had won the Scottish Cup at the end of the previous campaign. One of the things he had to address at the start of season 1965-66 was, therefore, finding a new leader to inspire his team on the park. After Bobby Shearer, Jim Baxter had been captain for a spell before his departure. But now Symon knew he needed a skipper in the Shearer mould. The decision he made in the summer of 1965 was one of his finest and ensured that in the coming years, for as long as Symon remained manager and well beyond, Rangers would have an inspirational giant of a captain.

As his new captain, Symon chose John Greig. The man Symon had once called 'Wee John Greig' was to go on and become a giant, not just in the history of Rangers but in the annals of Scottish football. Not surprisingly, Greig's elevation to the captaincy of Rangers was carried out by Symon in a quiet, matter-of-fact way with no fanfares or stirring speeches, from the manager to his new skipper. Greig remembered the moment. 'He simply took me to the side one day after training and told me that he wanted me to be captain, and that was all there was to it, as he clearly did not believe that any other words were necessary while bestowing this honour on me.'

If the manner of the way Symon appointed Greig as Rangers captain was so very typical of him, then the manager's choice also spoke volumes. Not just for his eye for a player and ability to nurse and nurture a talent, but also for something else he had in common with the man he succeeded, Bill Struth. Symon was as fine a judge of character as we have seen in Scottish football. Greig was to go on to captain Rangers under three successive managers after Symon – Davie White, Willie Waddell and Jock Wallace – and pick up trophy after trophy, including two Trebles and the European Cup Winners' Cup, before occupying the manager's office at the head of the marble stairs, once the seat of Symon's power and from where so much Ibrox glory had flowed.

35

CHANGING TACTICS

WHEN Rangers played Celtic five times in season 1963-64 and beat them five times, it was unusual. On two counts. This was the era of each side only playing each other twice during a league campaign, so the chances of so many Old Firm encounters, even taking Cup clashes into account, were much rarer than they are nowadays. The fact that Rangers had completed such a spectacular whitewash of their most bitter rivals was also out of the ordinary, as no matter how far down Celtic had been in comparison to the Ibrox outfit for close to thirty years, they had often been able to raise their game for the odd win or draw. During the Ibrox Treble campaign of 1963-64, though, Rangers had been unstoppable.

However, despite the unusual nature of Rangers and Celtic meeting so often, just two seasons later, in 1965-66, the Glasgow foes were thrown together five times once more. This time Celtic had made up a great deal of ground, though they were still a long way short of holding the same sort of whip hand over Scot Symon's team, even with Jock Stein in charge, as the Rangers manager had guided his team over Celtic two campaigns previously. Of the five meetings, Rangers won two, Celtic came out on top twice and one was drawn.

Those figures effectively put to bed the old myth that Stein breezed into Parkhead with a whirlwind of bright new tactical ideas and simply blew the supposed old-fashioned Symon away. Not only did it not happen that way, but the supposedly tactically inept Symon produced a new look and a different shape for the Rangers team, which meant a much more modern approach. Over the course of a thrilling and rollercoaster campaign, Symon ensured that Rangers evolved into a much more sophisticated side. He knew that he must do this to respond to a Celtic challenge, the like of which Rangers had not had to cope with for the best part of forty years. Celtic titles since just after the First World War had come rarely and there had been no sustained period at the top for the Parkhead club.

Celtic won the championship only twice in the 1930s, in seasons 1935-36 and 1937-38. During the years of the Second World War, Rangers had been champions of the re-organised regional league every year and Celtic's only post-war title had been in 1954. Therefore, an Old Firm title tussle was something new to more than one generation of Rangers supporters. They found it hard to accept, but Symon was not so blinkered and he responded well to the fresh challenge. Or at least he did on the park, for he never sought to match the shadowy off-the-field shenanigans Stein used to put pressure on the press as he created a brilliant and still-believed illusion.

One alteration to the team which Symon made that season, but which is seldom acknowledged, was a positional switch for his new captain John Greig. Greig had started as an old-fashioned powerful inside-forward in the mould of someone Symon had played with at Ibrox, the legendary Bob McPhail. He had then been converted to a strong-tackling, shrewd-passing wing-half, much the same as the manager himself when he had played, though with a much greater ability to score than Symon had

had. Now he was to drop back again, this time to the middle of the defence, standing shoulder to shoulder with centre-half Ronnie McKinnon. It was a tactic Stein soon switched Celtic on to, with John Clark providing on-the-deck cover for Billy McNeill, whose ground skills no way matched his ability in the air. This is something that is often forgotten, as Stein is almost exclusively revered for his so-called attacking principles. Yet one of his first major decisions as he reshaped Celtic was to shore up the defence by increasing its numbers.

A four-man back line was the norm on the continent and Symon had watched his favourite attacking weapon, fast-raiding direct wing play, stymied by the so-called sweeper who could leave his central beat, covering across to provide another barrier for any winger who got beyond the full-back. In effect, it was an insurance blanket Celtic needed more than Rangers for, while the taller McNeill had the edge over McKinnon for command in the air, the Ibrox centre-half was quicker and, as a former play-making wing-half, considerably more accomplished on the deck. It was not until the second half of the season that Celtic made the two other changes, switches which gave them a more formidable midfield than Symon could muster. Jim Baxter was gone and also Greig had been removed from midfield. Celtic's Bobby Murdoch, previously an inside-right of limited range, was moved back to right-half by Stein and, from the deeper position, was able to deploy a range of passing which had not been hinted at previously.

Murdoch formed a midfield duo with Bertie Auld. Auld had been a fiery-tempered winger through the late 1950s, who had left Parkhead for an unremarkable spell with the equally unre-markable Birmingham City, before Jimmy McGrory re-signed him. Under Stein, Auld had remained out on the left and seemed destined to slip into a support role as, with new signing Joe

McBride at centre-forward, John Hughes was increasingly preferred on the left wing. Stein, though, spotted something about Auld's style which convinced him he had the hardness and vision to pull the strings in midfield in tandem with the more powerful, more mobile and rampaging Murdoch. It was a ploy which worked and handed Symon a problem. How to match them? By the end of the season he came up with an answer, which even though it was only a stop-gap measure, landed the Scottish Cup, ensuring Celtic were halted in their tracks.

Season 1965-66 was important in Scot Symon's career because it was the one in which many of the myths that attached themselves to him started to be perpetrated. As the way he changed the shape of the Rangers team showed, they do not bear out much of the criticism the Rangers manager had to suffer at the time and which has endured down through the years. For a start, Rangers won the first Old Firm game of Celtic's Stein era. They lost the second, the League Cup final, only 2-1, after squandering two great early chances, with Celtic needing two penalties, one an aberration from McKinnon and the other hotly disputed. The third meeting came at Parkhead on 3 January 1966 and resulted in an overwhelming 5-1 win for Celtic. That, though, was not as clear-cut as it may look as a stark statistic.

Rangers' Danish right-back, Kai Johansen had cause to remember the bitterly cold, frosty afternoon, as it provided him with what he later recalled were the worst forty-five minutes of his entire career. That time came in the second half of a game, which had seen Rangers streak into a ninety-second lead when a John Greig shot took a deflection and broke to the always alert Davie Wilson for him to squeeze a shot past Ronnie Simpson. Johanson remembered, 'The pitch was rock solid and icy, and both teams could not keep their feet and for the rest of the first half it was a case of just trying not to make a mistake. At half time Symon told us to be careful and not to try and play too much football, but just to get the ball up the field as quickly as we could. We had Davie Wilson, Jim Forrest and Willie Johnston, who were all small and had good balance, and they were quick. Symon's idea was that they were the kind of players who could cope with the conditions.'

As it was, a switch of footwear inside the Celtic dressing room at half time turned John Hughes, one of the biggest, least elegant players on the park, into the day's most unlikely hero and provided Johansen with an experience he was to remember for the rest of his life, even though he told me he often tried to forget it. He said, 'Hughes changed into a pair of the old-fashioned baseball boots we sometimes used in training in those days. They had a rubber sole and gave him a grip nobody else had. He could bodyswerve and change pace and I kept slipping and sliding and could not get near him to make a tackle. Hughes tore us apart in that second half.'

Hughes caused havoc, with Steve Chalmers cashing in with a hat-trick, the last, which made the final scoreline a damaging-looking five for Celtic, arriving in the ninetieth minute. Charlie Gallagher and Bobby Murdoch were the other Celtic scorers. It is often claimed that was the result which started Scot Symon's downfall and put Jock Stein in command of the Old Firm battle for years to come. That is simply not the case. Certainly Celtic emerged from the match as league leaders, the pair having gone into the encounter level on points, but what happened in the second half of the season in no way sustains any belief that the Celtic march to the club's first title for twelve years, and only its second in twenty-eight years, was a mere stroll.

Symon's side buckled down and won their next five games. By the end of February, Rangers were once again level on points with Celtic, but back at the top thanks to a better goal average.

If there was a point in the campaign when Ibrox's hopes of regaining their crown and shutting out Celtic began to fade, it was in March. A defeat to Falkirk at Brockville was followed by an Ibrox draw against Hearts and then another stalemate, this time away to Kilmarnock, and a defeat to Dundee United at Tannadice.

The Ides had seemed to stretch through the whole month for Scot Symon. Hopes were rekindled when a win over Aberdeen at Ibrox was followed by the 5-0 crushing of Morton at Cappielow and a 2-1 win at home to Motherwell. However, Celtic had got their nose in front and did not slip up in the last fortnight of the season, finishing at the top, but a mere two points clear of Rangers, who had responded well to Symon's new strategies, with the bleak month of March the exception and the period which cost them dearly. But Rangers under Symon – and indeed under Struth, too – had performed much worse in the past and finished much further behind the champions. But as Struth had before him, Symon had always managed to respond to the challenge.

Events right at the end of that season gave Rangers supporters reasons to believe they could still trust their manager to rise to the challenge in the season which would follow, for it was Scot Symon and Rangers, not Jock Stein and Celtic, who had the last laugh in the spring of 1966.

36

SYMON OUTWITS STEIN

MARCH 1966 was the month that almost blew the whole season for Rangers. They did not win a single League match, losing two and drawing two as the team's form slumped.

Rangers also had to face up to three Scottish Cup ties during a four-week period in that key month, which stretched their resources to the limit in the days before squads and rotation. Had they lost one of those games then who knows what sort of knee-jerk reaction would have come from chairman John Lawrence and his sidekick, Matt Taylor, both of them having their strings pulled by Willie Allison.

Perhaps Symon would have been out before the end of the season. There were certainly straws in the wind at the time that Willie Waddell was being sounded out to quit his job as chief football writer on the *Scottish Daily Express* and return to front-line management with Rangers.

There was never any chance of this happening, as Waddell and Symon were friends, a relationship which stretched back to the 1930s when they shared a flat for a spell after they both signed for Rangers. It is more likely that any backdoor approach to Waddell would immediately have been passed on by him to Symon, making the already hard-pressed Rangers manager acutely aware that there were those within Ibrox who may smile to his face, while at the same time try to wield the dagger behind his back. For a man who lived his life by a clear set of honest and open rules and who did not appear to have a devious bone in his body, this information must have been hard for Symon to understand.

By this time I had started out in newspapers and joined the *Evening Times* in Glasgow, and even as a lowly copy boy I was privy to much of the inside gossip as I listened to chief football writer Gair Henderson and sports editor Bill Stewart discuss what they knew. It was as early in my career as that that I learned the best stories were not the ones which necessarily appear in the paper, but the ones journalists tell each other.

However, push did not come to shove for Symon, as his team, even if only by the skin of its teeth, survived three tough tests in the Scottish Cup during the mad month of March.

Airdie had been beaten 5-1 in the opening round of the Cup in January, and that was followed by a 2-0 February win away to then Highland League outfit, Ross County. But the March sequence began with a trip to Perth on 5 March to face a fine St Johnstone side. Saints were a pretty decent footballing outfit, and Symon decided that despite the extra cut and thrust of a Cup tie, his team should put the accent on skill, passing and guile. Alex Willoughby was at inside right with Jorn Sorenson, who had played well in the 4-0 win over Hamilton the previous week, at inside left. Steel was added in the shape of right-half Bobby Watson. Things came very close to not working out, but Willoughby struck in seventy-two minutes for the only goal of the game to earn a semi-final appearance against Aberdeen.

The game at Hampden on 26 March was played in a blizzard, which neither team coped with and ended goalless. Three days later in an edgy game, Jim Forrest put Rangers ahead in eight minutes, only for Aberdeen to level just before half time. Symon must have sighed with relief when, ten minutes from time, George McLean got the winner.

There was not much of a feeling of relief among Rangers supporters though, for Jock Stein and Celtic awaited them in the final, with the Parkhead side, who had already beaten Rangers in the League Cup final and edged them out in the Championship, odds-on favourites to win the third of Scotland's Honours Three, and annex the club's first-ever Treble. At the time Rangers had already won two Trebles, one under Struth and the second with Symon as manager.

As the big day approached, it was hard to find any of the football writers who thought Rangers could win. This was difficult for Rangers supporters to understand. You had to go back to the 1920s to find a time when Celtic went into a crunch Old Firm match as favourites. Only the greybeards could recall it.

One of the biggest talking points during the countdown to 23 April and the Hampden showdown was what Celtic left-winger John Hughes was going to do to Rangers' right-back Kai Johansen. Celtic supporters had gloated with much joy over the way the burly Hughes had sand-danced on ice in January, reducing Johansen to a wreck as Celtic won 5-1. Rangers supporters, though, were worried. They feared that if Jimmy Johnstone, tiny and tricky on the right, could pose problems for tall left-back David Provan, then there would be no cover to help Johansen cope with Hughes. Johansen however, thanks to a quiet word from Scot Symon, was completely unfazed at the prospect of once again facing Hughes, his tormentor on that ice-bound Parkhead pitch.

The last time I saw Johansen was when we sat together for a meal after the funeral of that great *Daily Record* sportswriter, Alex Cameron, and the Dane, as is often the way after homage has been paid to a departed friend, was in the mood to reminisce and to talk even more than usual. Johansen said, 'Symon called me up to his office nearly two weeks before the final and he told me what to expect to read in the newspapers, but to pay no attention to what was being said. He said he had every confidence in me and knew what had happened against Hughes at Parkhead had been a freak of nature and that on a decent pitch he knew I could handle Hughes.

'I was pretty confident that I could, but being told that by the manager made me doubly confident. And for the rest of the time before we played Celtic I let all the predictions about what John Hughes was going to do to me wash over my head. I knew better.'

Of course, Alex Cameron, back then working in the front line for the *Scottish Daily Mail* as well as fronting *Scotsport* with Arthur Montford and commentating on big games, was one of the experts who predicted a torrid time for Johansen against Hughes. It is a measure of the man that after proving him and everyone else wrong, Johansen carried no grudge and nearly forty years later was there to pay his last respects to Cameron.

However, and despite Johansen's confidence, it is worth examining the way Symon went about making sure his player was aware his manager had faith in him. Symon did not wait until the weight of the expectation of it being a disastrous day for Johansen built up in the week before the final. He anticipated what was coming and took steps to ensure his player knew what he thought. That was hardly the action of a manager losing touch with the modern game.

Nor were Scot Symon's tactics and team selection for the Scottish Cup final a sign that he had failed to grasp the way the game was changing. He had already withdrawn his captain John Greig from midfield to partner Ronnie McKinnon at the heart of the defence, as was the style among the best teams throughout

Europe. His efforts at finding guile in the midfield area centred on the by now slow Old Warhorse, Jimmy Millar, past it not only as a centre-forward, but also unable to cope at inside-right. Symon still saw a role for the astute Millar, whose vision and passing skills were – and indeed continue to be – overlooked in favour of his toughness, power in the air and goal-scoring touch. That role was in Jim Baxter's old number six shirt, lying deep and trying to dictate the pace and the play.

But Symon knew that to allow Millar to do that he needed an energetic tough-tackling partner in midfield. Which meant, once again when it came to the big day, there was no place in Symon's plans for the delicate playmaking skills of Alex Willoughby. Symon was not always right in leaving Willoughby out, but this time he was absolutely correct. Willoughby and the ageing Millar would just not have worked. Symon handed the number eight shirt to the combative Bobby Watson.

Once again, as he had done throughout his managerial career, Scot Symon defied the lemmings who branded him both old-fashioned and conservative. For, and it has been a recurring theme of this story, Symon promoted youth, handing a vital role to Watson, who was still only nineteen. He told Watson he had to go head-to-head with not only Charlie Gallagher, a skilful ball-playing artist who replaced the suspended Bertie Auld, but also Bobby Murdoch, who had emerged that season as a power-house who was built like a battleship, could run like a tank, tackle like one too, and shoot like a bazooka.

Watson did not let Symon down in front of a Hampden crowd of 129,599, which included me and my wee pal Neil behind the goal. My dad and granddad were among the few Rangers supporters who felt Symon's men could overcome the odds and Neil and I took heart from their wise old heads as we parted outside Hampden. The newly-working me had treated them to tickets for the North Enclosure. The game ended in stalemate. Billy Ritchie saved an early effort from Joe McBride, the only time Celtic's top scorer threatened, and Billy McNeill hit the crossbar with a header.

As for what John Hughes was going to do to Kai Johansen? The Rangers right-back clattered him with a perfectly-timed tackle early in the game, came away with the ball at his feet, the Rangers end sent a roar of approval into the air and Hughes was never seen again.

And so it was back to Hampden for a replay just four days later. No messing about with tickets and no namby-pamby police demands. The 96,862 who paid at the gate and stood on the old Hampden slopes, witnessed an epic Old Firm Scottish Cup final with all of Scot Symon's faith in his players and belief in his own ability to outwit Jock Stein vindicated.

Celtic had the meaner but even more skilful Bertie Auld in for Gallagher to partner Murdoch, as Symon kept faith with the combination of Watson's youthful vigour and Millar's experience to ensure the Celtic engine room never got the chance to operate at full throttle. The only change was George McLean in at centre-forward for the injured Jim Forrest.

For Celtic, Jimmy Johnstone found the form which had eluded him in the first game and gave Provan a tough time, but Greig was always there to cover as he knew the other side of the park had been sewn up by Johansen, who once again, to the great delight of the Ibrox support, reduced Hughes to a cipher. There was even greater joy for them when the final's decisive moment fell to Johansen who forever more for that generation of Rangers followers became the Great Dane.

Though what is often forgotten is the way Symon's pairing of Watson and Millar worked, even with Auld back for the replay. For Celtic went into the match as red-hot favourites once again, the favoured view among sportswriters – Gair Henderson of the paper where I was a very junior member of the editorial staff, the *Evening Times*, among them – was that Rangers had only escaped on the Saturday because Auld was missing. With his steel and skill back to partner Murdoch, Celtic, Henderson and the rest of the experts in the ranks of the sports writers insisted, would be too strong in midfield for the young Watson and the ageing Millar, who they all declared could not possibly cope with the inferno and blistering pace of a second Old Firm Cup final in four days.

Symon too must have been concerned. Not so much at Watson's ability to run as two men and tackle like a duo of demons as with Millar's legs being able to cope. But Symon, more than anyone else, knew the Old Warhorse was made of the same stern stuff as the manager himself had been as a player. Symon knew he came from a long line from the past Bill Struth had built for the club. Millar's pedigree stretched back from Davie Meiklejohn, through Willie Woodburn and Tiger Shaw.

The match is remembered as Johansen's Final in honour of the goal which won the Scottish Cup, but my vivid recall of a spine-chilling night was that Jimmy Millar produced what was probably his best ever game for Rangers. He found the legs to be everywhere. Dropping deep to take a short pass from defenders, moving close to any Rangers player, in possession and under pressure, to take a pass and create calm. And always looking to make the diagonal pass which could free Willie Henderson on the right, or the slide rule ball down the line to release left-winger Willie Johnston.

It was from one such pass that Johnston started an attack, used his amazing speed to get to the by-line and cut the ball back, right into the path of McLean. There was nothing of the big Dandy about his efforts. He was Mince McLean as he took a wild swipe which missed making contact completely. A fresh-air shot. The chance looked to have gone.

But the Celtic defenders, never expecting McLean to make such a hash of things, were on their heels and allowed the ball to carry on to the right wing where Willie Henderson, perhaps half-expecting McLean's mess, pounced with a shot which was hacked away by Murdoch. And Kai Johansen's moment arrived. He had broken forward in that hunched and strange running style which was his trademark, and although the angle was tight, he aimed for the near corner of Ronnie Simpson's goal. Simpson, anticipating that Johansen would go across him, had left enough room for the shot to blur beyond his dive.

There were twenty minutes left and Celtic threw everything but the kitchen sink at Rangers. Strangely though, especially for a man history tells us was Symon's superior in the field of tactics, Jock Stein had no master-plan to change things. Of course there were hair-raising moments. There always are in the white-hot heat of any Old Firm game, never mind a Scottish Cup final replay when one team is hanging on to a single-goal lead. Ritchie performed heroics and carried luck when he went one way for one effort, only for the ball to go in the opposite direction, but strike his leg. Celtic also struck both posts.

But it was Rangers' night. Rangers' Scottish Cup. And a triumph and vindication for Scot Symon's belief in his ability to summon extra effort from his players and to deploy them to maximum effect. As ever, however, Symon did not take any bow. He slipped into the background as the team celebrated.

This self-effacing aspect, which was possibly Symon's most dominant characteristic, was at once his greatest strength and biggest weakness, especially in the public battle with Jock Stein, an arch-manipulator who was never afraid to blow his own trumpet.

37

SYMON'S SIGNING SPLURGE

THE idea that the comparatively recent introduction of the opening and closing of the transfer window has meant last-minute signings are a new phenomenen can be put to bed by examining what Scot Symon did on the eve of season 1966-67. The campaign, as it did in those days, started with the League Cup, though even by the standards of the time, the League Championship kick-off date of 10 September that season was unusually late. Despite out-thinking and outmanoeuvring Jock Stein twice in four days at Hampden in April to win the Scottish Cup for Rangers, Symon knew his team needed strengthening and spent the summer pondering on how best to do this. In the end, he chose two players called Smith who had both operated at wing-half for their clubs. Alex Smith was signed from Dunfermline for another Rangers record fee, this time £35,000 on 9 August, with Dave Smith arriving from Aberdeen three days later, a mere twenty-four hours before the season started, with the record upped again, this time to £45,000.

Of the two signings, Alex never really looked convincing, possibly because he was never accommodated in his favourite right-half role, operating as either an inside-right or even at centre-forward. Despite that though, he was the top Rangers scorer in his first season at Ibrox, netting twenty-three times. Dave Smith, an elegant playmaker of a left-half, also suffered from being pushed upfield to an inside-forward role to which he was not best suited, but there was no denying Symon's eye for a player, as Dave's career at Ibrox saw him become part of the team which won the European Cup Winners' Cup in 1972, with Willie Waddell managing and Jock Wallace coaching.

The opening salvos of the season pointed to another campaign during which Symon was clearly going to struggle to find a settled side, blending in the way so many of the teams he had put together and sent on their way to glory had merged. There were times in the months ahead when John Greig filled in as left-back. When Jimmy Millar operated as a sweeper, wearing the number four shirt, at inside-right as a playmaker and even sometimes wearing his old number nine, though in a more with-drawn role from when he was in his heyday.

And there were further changes halfway through the season when Rangers suffered what Symon described as the club's blackest-ever day, going out of the Scottish Cup away to Berwick Rangers. One of those changes introduced a name which was to go on to become a Rangers legend and which is still associated with the club, Sandy Jardine. But back in August 1966 there was nobody who could have predicted the turmoil of Berwick lay ahead, though there were hopes of a good run in Europe, which were justified as Symon guided Rangers to a second European final.

The League Cup campaign, which was to end at Hampden in such controversy, began with a George McLean goal five minutes from time, giving Rangers a 1-0 Ibrox win over Hibernian, which was followed by the 8-0 thrashing of Stirling Albion at Annfield. But a goalless draw against Kilmarnock at Ibrox, a 3-2 defeat away to Hibs and a 1-1 draw at home to Stirling Albion meant Rangers needed to win the last game of the section away to

Kilmarnock to be sure of qualifying ahead of Hibs on goal differ-ence, thanks to those eight goals in Stirling.

They managed that win, Jim Forrest netting the game's only goal in seventy-four minutes, and followed a 1-1 draw against Ayr at Somerset in the quarter-final first leg with a 3-0 Ibrox win. The semi was a repeat of the one in the previous season's Scottish Cup, with Aberdeen the opposition and just as they had in that tie, Rangers struggled, needing a replay after a 2-2 draw. However, that first game was significant in that it signalled the end of Billy Ritchie's long run as the undisputed Rangers goal-keeper. Ritchie was uncharacteristically out of form and misjudged the two shots that led to the Aberdeen goals. There had been nothing in Ritchie's play in previous games that season to suggest he had lost any of his steady style, and as he had just turned thirty, age was not a consideration.

Ritchie had been the quiet man of the all-conquering Sixties side, a sure-handling last-line who inspired confidence in those who stood in front of him. Solid and dependable just about summed up Billy Ritchie. Rangers did not have a goalkeeper of real stature after Ritchie until Peter McCloy's long reign, though there are those – and count me among them – who firmly believe Billy Ritchie was never properly replaced until Chris Woods arrived twenty years later. In his own defence, although a quiet man, Ritchie never spoke about it, he could point to a successful spell at Partick Thistle after he left Ibrox, followed by a superb Indian summer for Motherwell, during which his superb fitness saw him carry on until he was close to forty years old.

The man Scot Symon chose to replace Ritchie was the taller Norrie Martin, who had been at Ibrox since 1958, first as George Niven's understudy and then as cover for Ritchie. Martin was in goal when Rangers had a comfortable 2-0 semi-final replay win over Aberdeen to earn another trip to Hampden for the third successive Old Firm League Cup final. But the final that took place at the grand old lady of Mount Florida, in front of a near 95,000 crowd on 29 October, was by far the most controversial of the trio. Indeed, of the seven Cup finals – including replays – which had featured the two great rivals since the 1963 Scottish Cup final became the first such meeting for thirty-five years, this was the one which provoked arguments that echo down to the present day, with legendary giant referee, Tom 'Tiny' Wharton at the centre of the rumpus.

Once again Scot Symon, as he had done so successfully in the two Scottish Cup final matches, decided to deploy Bobby Watson, who had turned twenty in the summer, in midfield, allying his strength to the subtle passing of Dave Smith, with Alex Smith asked to partner George McLean through the middle and the two Willies, Henderson and Johnston on the wings. This time there was no pre-final talk of what John Hughes was going to do to Kai Johansen, but despite that Scottish Cup final mastering of Jock Stein by Symon, Rangers were outsiders again, this time at the unheard of price of five to two against, with Celtic an unprecedented seven to four on. Stein's silver tongue had once again convinced everyone his team were years ahead of Symon's in the tactical stakes. Johansen said, 'Scot Symon would never talk us up in the papers, but Jock Stein never did anything else than tell everyone how good Celtic were, though we had shown we could cope with them, and if we had not suffered a terrible decision that day, I believe we would have dealt with them again. Had we won that League Cup I do not think people would have kept swallowing the Celtic propaganda, even from Stein.'

Rangers had started the game in much the same way as they had the first Scottish Cup final the previous season, but suffered a blow to their plans when Bobby Lennox gave Celtic a nineteenth-minute lead. But the truth was that once again Symon's tactics were working and Bobby Murdoch, the piston that drove the Celtic engine, was forced into a defensive role which did not suit him. An equaliser seemed certain to come and everyone – with one notable exception – thought it had a mere twelve minutes after Lennox netted.

Johansen, who snuffed out Hughes yet again, floated a free-kick into the box, which Ronnie Simpson, the son of the legendary 1930s Rangers centre-half Jimmy Simpson, left his goal to attack it. Simpson, a brilliant shot-stopper, was as agile as a cat, but on the small side for a keeper. When he came out to attempt to deal with Johansen's free-kick, he was stretching to try and reach it and, although he got a fist to the ball, his punch was not good. The ball fell to the feet of Bobby Watson who smacked it into the net.

Amazingly, referee Wharton disallowed it. I say amazingly because there had been no clear foul on Simpson and, in those more robust days, every half-challenge on a keeper in the air was not penalised the way it is now. Keepers were not the protected species they are nowadays. Except Celtic goalie Simpson that day against Rangers. Johansen recalled, 'We were all very surprised, as there had been nobody going in on Simpson, and it seemed as though he could just not jump high enough to reach my cross and get a good punch on it. But we tried to get on with things and even after that blow we were the better team for the rest of the game and should have scored.'

George McLean, as he had been doing for years, missed a golden chance, and then Alex Smith seemed certain to score, but stumbled and could only make poor contact, and even though his effort headed goalwards with Simpson beaten, the ball trickled slowly and Willie O'Neill got back to clear off the line. Of such moments Old Firm legends are born. Davie Meiklejohn's nerve-shredding penalty to put Rangers on the way to their 4-0 1928

Scottish Cup final win over Celtic, smashing a quarter-of-a-century hoodoo in the competition, Kai Johansen's brilliant blur of a Scottish Cup winner in April 1966 and sixteen-year-old Derek Johnstone's still-to-come heroic header for the only goal of the 1970 Old Firm League Cup final. All three enjoyed long careers at Ibrox after and who knows what Alex Smith would have gone on to do as a Ranger had, with just a quarter of an hour's play remaining on the afternoon of 29 October 1966, he kept his balance and struck a firm shot into the net. Who knows also what would have happened in the Symon–Stein stakes had referee Tom Wharton not ruled out what looked like a perfectly good Rangers goal and had Symon gone on to eclipse Stein in a major final for the second time in six months. Or how things would have turned out for Symon had he not kept faith with McLean after big Mince missed another sitter, with twenty minutes left and Rangers well on top. Would, for instance, Symon have had to suffer the indignity of Berwick had he got rid of McLean after his appalling miss of a sitter in the 1966 League Cup final?

Of course, we shall never know. But I firmly believe Jock Stein and Celtic's controversial and totally undeserved win over Scot Symon and Rangers on that October afternoon at Hampden was a turning point in Stein's favour, and that had Rangers lifted the Cup, as they deserved to, much of what followed in the next year would not have unfolded as it did. One thing, though, that what happened at Hampden that day proves is that all the Celtic talk about how referees favoured Rangers over them has no basis in historical fact.

38

BERWICK

THE night before Rangers were due to play little Berwick Rangers in the Scottish Cup, a group of Rangers players gathered in the team hotel for a card school which lasted into the wee small hours of the day of the game. This little-known fact was revealed to me by someone few even recall was in the travelling party, defender Colin Jackson, then a twenty-one-year-old reserve, who was to be pitchforked into European action a few weeks later against Real Zaragoza in Spain, but who went to Berwick as the travelling reserve, as was the custom back then.

Jackson first revealed this startling revelation when he and I spoke to a group of football fans in a question-and-answer night in an east end of Glasgow pub in the summer of 2011. Jackson, who served Rangers well and with honour and distinction for twenty seasons, said, 'I was very much the young outsider and kept quiet, but I was shocked by what I saw. There they were, some of the biggest names in the Rangers team, staying up late to play cards. It was all lighthearted and it seemed to me that they were not taking Berwick Rangers seriously enough.' Even after close to forty years, Jackson refused to name names, but many believed that their actions were a betrayal of Scot Symon.

Whatever the real story was that night and whoever was involved, it is a matter of record that one player who left the club shortly after was George McLean, which led some people to speculate about his involvement. He was a player who always gave the impression that he took nothing too seriously and, following his Ibrox exit after Berwick, his career suffered.

That 1-0 defeat inflicted by Berwick Rangers on *the* Rangers, courtesy of a Sammy Reid goal and an outstanding display of goalkeeping from player-manager Jock Wallace, meant that 28 January 1967 was a day that will live in infamy for Rangers. Symon summed it up perfectly when he said, 'This has been the darkest day in Rangers' history and the players who were in team will have to carry that fact with them for the remainder of their careers and the rest of their lives.'

Jackson recalled the coach journey home, saying, 'Symon said nothing on the coach, but his face was like thunder and nobody spoke. I know I was just glad to get back to Ibrox and get off the bus and get away.'

Veteran sportswriter Brian Scott, for so long an elegant writing presence in the *Scottish Daily Mail*, was then a young DC Thomson reporter, sent to cover the game for the *Sunday Post*. Scott told me, 'Back then, only chief sportswriter Jack Harkness got his name on a match report, but this was such a big story that my by-line was used and that was a first in the *Sunday Post*. There were no quotes from Symon as there was no press conference after. I got back to Glasgow and was heading for the bus station in Buchanan Street when I met Alex Willoughby, who had been playing for the reserves that afternoon, and he insisted I told him everything that had gone on. Wee Willoughby was a great Rangers man and his face was serious and he kept shaking his head in disbelief.'

During the weeks and months before Berwick, Symon had acknowledged that the changing face of football meant he needed more help with the team than could be provided by trainer/physio Davie Kinnear. So Symon started a search for a coach, with even Real Madrid's legendary Ferenc Puskás being tipped for the job. Symon's choice was a member of the great Hibernian Famous Five forward line, Eddie Turnbull, who was making a name for himself as Aberdeen manager. He was offered the post of assistant manager to Symon, but could not agree terms and turned it down on 1 November. Just over a fortnight later, former Dundee title-winning wing-half Bobby Seith arrived to help Symon, but as a coach and not assistant manager.

Once again this puts to bed a Symon myth, the one about him not wanting to change with the times and insisting on ruling the roost at Ibrox on his own. The way the first half of the season had been going, Symon, always mindful of what would be best for Rangers, knew he needed help and that an injection of fresh ideas from a younger man was his solution. Symon putting his faith in youth yet again.

A 2-0 defeat to Celtic at Parkhead in September, a draw away to Hearts in October, another point dropped when his team went to meet St Johnstone, plus a 3-2 defeat by Dunfermline at East End Park in December, when two of the Fifers' goals were scored by Alex Ferguson, meant that a week before Christmas Rangers trailed Celtic by four points and lost the chance to gain a morale-boosting Ibrox win against them when the January game was called off.

The fall-out from Berwick meant that Symon was put under the sort of pressure chairman John Lawrence should actually and actively have protected him from. But Lawrence, egged on by the sinister figure of Willie Allison, actually poured oil on the fire by demanding that McLean and Jim Forrest should never again play for Rangers. His hand weakened by the Berwick disaster, Symon was in no position to argue, even though of the two he would dearly have liked to hold on to Forrest, and as events in Nuremberg proved, Lawrence's intransigence cost Rangers a European trophy and denied the increasingly doddery Ibrox chairman the knighthood he so craved.

In the weeks that followed, Forrest was shipped out to Preston North End for £38,000 and McLean moved to Dundee, along with £25,000 for the ball-playing inside-forward Andy Penman, whose arrival at Ibrox was too late for him to be registered to play in the European Cup Winners' Cup or in the league. Symon was planning for the future and saw Penman as a new Ian McMillan.

There was only one good thing to come out of the Berwick disaster for Rangers and this was once again Symon at his managerial best, believing the club could be regenerated from within and revitalised by the promotion of young talent. This time the youngster who stepped up, was promoted by Symon and who went on to become one of the greatest-ever Rangers of all time, was a then eighteen-year-old Sandy Jardine. Jardine made his debut against Hearts at Ibrox, with Symon again turning to Alex Willoughby, by then twenty-two.

The strange relationship between Symon and Willoughby was to take another twist in the closing weeks of the campaign, one I believe cost Symon the European prize he deserved. It was a mystery which, as we shall learn later, Willoughby went to his tragically early grave without resolving.

Things almost went horribly wrong just seven days after Berwick when, with McLean and Forrest in permanent exile and Jardine and Willoughby in, Hearts opened the scoring in thirty-eight minutes. The boos which were starting to echo round Ibrox were silenced by a Willoughby equaliser on the half-time whistle. He got another two for his hat-trick as Rangers regained their confidence and Willie Henderson and Davie Wilson chipped in for a 5-1 win. Symon had bought himself time and in midweek

Willoughby hit another threesome in another 5-1 win, this time Clyde at Shawfield being the victims.

By the time March dawned, with the on-fire Willoughby grabbing four in a 5-1 win over Motherwell at Fir Park, Symon's reinvented and reinvigorated Rangers had closed the gap on Celtic to just two points. Willoughby was missing when a 1-0 Ibrox defeat to Dunfermline put the Parkhead outfit firmly in control in the title tussle, while a 1-1 draw with Dundee at Dens Park, Willoughby scoring, meant the title was almost over the horizon.

The championship chase ended on the last day of the season when Celtic visited a muddy and rain-lashed Ibrox on 6 May, needing just a point to take the title. Symon once again lost faith with Willoughby's wiles, the game ended 2-2 and the title went to the east end of Glasgow. Perhaps more significantly, though, was that was the day when Symon, almost certainly with one eye on the looming European Cup Winners' Cup final, played the Smiths – both wing-halves – as inside-forwards and called in burly full-back-cum-centre-half-cum-wing-half, Roger Hynd, at centre-forward as a prelude to igniting a pre-Euro final row with chairman Lawrence, which almost certainly started the countdown to the manager's sacking a few months later.

39

NUREMBERG

CHAIRMAN John Lawrence's behaviour on the very eve of Scot Symon preparing Rangers to face Bayern Munich in Nuremberg in the European Cup Winners' Cup final in May 1967 was nothing short of disgraceful. He and his coterie of vice chairman Matt Taylor and the shadowy Willie Allison were only to surpass what they did in Germany by the way they went about sacking Symon a mere five months later. But what they did in May 1967 was a stab in the back for Symon that undermined his authority and most certainly upset the frame of mind of the Rangers players who were getting ready for the biggest night of their careers.

There are conflicting stories and reports about how Lawrence made his displeasure at Symon's team selection known, with the main thrust being that the chairman held a press conference at which he announced that never again would Rangers go into a major match with three half-backs in the forward line. Symon had announced that Alex Smith and Dave Smith would be inside-right and left respectively, with Roger Hynd – and this was the most controversial aspect of the manager's team selection – at centre-forward. Yet veteran reporter Rodger Baillie, famous for his recall and ability to accurately recount events even from long ago, told me he had no recollection of Lawrence calling a press conference. Baillie, then with the *Sunday Mirror*, added that as a Sunday newspaper reporter, he would have had no need to attend and that is why, he says, he can't be sure if one was held. My view is that, despite not needing to attend such a briefing, the unusual nature of John Lawrence holding a press conference would have attracted the curiosity of one of the most professional and diligent sports reporters I have ever known. There is also another aspect. Even if Baillie had not attended, a John Lawrence press conference would have been a hot topic for gossip among the press pack. For those reasons my belief is that it is more likely a series of private briefings, not by John Lawrence himself, but on his behalf, conducted by that shady figure Willie Allison, took place and undermined the chances of Rangers winning the European Cup Winners' Cup.

The reasons why Symon chose the burly Hynd – whose normal roles were in either full-back slot, at centre-half or wing-half – have never been properly examined. It has become common practice to just dismiss the Symon choice as an example of his tactical naivety. But once again a closer inspection of what actually happened and why tells a different story. Symon was fond of returning to any tactical ploy which had worked for him in the past, as was common with all managers through the ages. And when Rangers met a very strong Wolves side in the Cup Winners' Cup semi-final of 1961, Symon threw Doug Baillie, a big, burly centre-half who was good in the air, in at centre-forward. Rangers won 2-0 and Baillie did well.

By the time Nuremberg came around in 1967, West German sides were viewed as being the most British in their style of any continental country. Symon, therefore, had good cause to believe that what worked against an English side would also be effective against a West German team. Particularly as, he reasoned, Hynd's power in the air would be serviced by crosses from the two Willies, Henderson and Johnston. As it had worked, Symon gave his tested theory another try in the second leg of the semi-final against Slavia Sofia and it provided enough success to see Slavia Sofia beaten 1-0 at Ibrox. I was at Ibrox that night and recall that Hynd produced a decent enough performance, causing panic in the opposition defence as he got on the end of crosses. Unfortunately in Nuremberg both wingers were closed out. If there is a criticism to be levelled at Symon's selection it centres on Alex Willoughby, who had been recalled to the colours immediately after Berwick and whose form had been fabulous with a goal haul of sixteen from twelve League and three Cup Winners' Cup appearances. Willoughby had been left out after the first leg of the semi, won 1-0 in Sofia.

Against that, Alex Smith boasted a nineteen-goal haul and was a better than decent player. Symon's dilemma was to keep his top scorer in the team and find a place for Willoughby, and he could not leave Dave Smith out, as his passing was crucial to the way Rangers played, while at right-half, Sandy Jardine, though still a teenager, was an outstanding talent who gave the team drive, pace and power. Once again, as had so often been the case in Europe when he was the manager, Dame Fortune did not smile on Scot Symon. After a straightforward 5-1 aggregate win over Glentoran in the opening round, Rangers were drawn to meet the holders, West Germany's finest at the time, Borussia Dortmund. The previous year Liverpool had beaten Celtic in the Cup Winners' Cup semi-final, but on a rainy night at Hampden found Dortmund too much for them, losing 2-1 in extra time.

It looked as though Rangers' run was over before it had got into its stride. Kai Johansen gave Rangers the lead at Ibrox before the Germans scored a controversial equaliser. Alex Smith gave Rangers a slender advantage to take to West Germany, but few fancied their chances. Symon stiffened his side by resorting to the trick that had outfoxed Jock Stein in the previous year's

Scottish Cup final, with Bobby Watson picked, but five minutes before half time Watson was carried off and Rangers were reduced to ten men.

Johansen recalled, 'They were a terrific team and we could hardly get out of our own half, but Ronnie McKinnon was outstanding and Norrie Martin had one of those nights keepers often have. Dortmund could not get past him and the game ended goalless. After that we started fancying ourselves to go all the way. It was unlikely we would meet a better team than Dortmund, who had Siggi Held, Stan Libuda and the great Lothar Emmerich playing for them. But we knocked them out.'

A more subtle approach was needed when Real Zaragoza arrived at Ibrox from Spain and Symon turned to Willoughby, whose goal added to one scored by Alex Smith for a 2-0 lead. And what a night of drama it was in Spain! Rangers were hit by the loss of Ronnie McKinnon, who suffered a broken nose at Ayr the previous weekend, but had a dogged and determined Colin Jackson in for the first of many brilliant European perform-ances in his long Rangers career. But Symon's side were a goal down halfway through the second half. Then Dave Smith missed a penalty and Real were awarded a dodgy spot kick four minutes from time, when the ref saw a handball after the ball hit John Greig on his chest. Zaragoza equalised.

Rangers hung on through an extra half hour, with the young Jackson outstanding. And so, in the days before away goals and then penalties, it was down to the toss of a coin. John Greig guessed correctly and Rangers were through to the semi-finals where they saw off a dour and difficult Slavia Sofia outfit 2-0 on aggregate for Scot Symon's side reach the club's second European final in six years. A remarkable achievement.

But then the infamous bad luck which dogged Symon struck again. Not because Rangers were to face a brilliant Bayern Munich side which contained the magnificent Franz Beckenbauer, goalscorer supreme; Gerd Muller, the outstanding; Franz Roth; and the only goalie in the world to rival Gordon Banks at the time, Sepp Maier. But because the venue, chosen by UEFA for the 1967 European Cup final, was Nuremberg, a mere ninety-minute drive from Munich.

Sandy Jardine, who had such a superb game that night, particularly when you remember how young he was and who he was up against, remembered going out onto the pitch about an hour before kick-off. He said, 'There were around eight thousand Rangers supporters in the ground, singing and cheering and making plenty of noise, and I remember thinking that we were going to have a great support to help us. But by the time we came out for the game and the ground was full, there were 55,000 Bayern supporters making even more noise and drowning them out.'

Among the many things forgotten about events during the next one hundred and twenty minutes is the fact that Rangers were denied a perfectly good goal. Roger Hynd, seemingly justifying Symon's faith, scored only for a wrongly raised offside flag to deny him and Rangers. And another thing: Hynd, as is often wrongly written, did not miss the chance which was carved for him by a Dave Smith pass in the thirty-third minute. Hynd did not balloon the ball over the bar. Nor did he pull it wide or mis-hit the ball. Instead, Hynd tried to place the ball. Years later, as we shared a drink in the Walsall FC social club where Hynd was winding down his playing career, he told me, 'It was a great pass from Dave Smith and I knew that I was slightly off balance, so any attempt by me to hammer a shot would have seen the ball go anywhere. I had a split second to think and knew I had to control my effort.'

That is just what big Roger did. He was unlucky in that he faced one of only two goalies in the world at the time who possessed the brilliance to stop it. That's what Maier managed as he somehow managed to stretch back and claw the ball away. I watched a re-run of the match recently on ESPN Classic, and was reminded of something which has been forgotten with the passing of time. That is, just how well Rangers performed against such formidable opposition. But, when the game moved into injury time they were finally undone when Beckenbauer produced a trademark pass and Roth hooked a shot on the run which beat Norrie Martin.

The truth is that Rangers did not lose to Bayern Munich because Scot Symon chose Roger Hynd at centre-forward and flanked him with Alex and Dave Smith. The truth is that he was within a bad linesman's flag and a brilliant save of being proved right. But, given what had been reported as to what John Lawrence said on the eve of the game, Scot Symon must have known that, with Willie Allison, dagger in hand, working in such a rancid way behind his back, his time as Rangers manager was running out. Symon, as was so often the case, was right. But even he could not have predicted how low Lawrence and Allison would stoop in getting rid of him.

40

SYMON SACKED

WHEN the still then plain old Alex Ferguson heard on 1 November 1967 that Scot Symon had been sacked by Rangers, he was so enraged that he had to be physically stopped from demanding a transfer. It is often forgotten that Ferguson was Symon's last major signing and the £65,000 he paid Dunfermline for him was a Scottish transfer record fee. Ferguson made his distaste for the way Symon was stabbed in the back known in his autobiography *Managing My Life*. That was even before he was made aware of the sly and cowardly way Rangers had gone about getting rid of Symon. No wonder Fergie was in a fury.

Bobby Seith, taken on by Symon the previous season as a coach, was all that stood between Ferguson and the Ibrox exit door on that fateful day. Seith said, 'When Alex heard the news, he didn't want to be associated with a club that would do such a thing. He came to me so angry he was about to demand a transfer. So, I took him to the gymnasium and gave him a bit of a talking-to. It wasn't a bollocking as such. I was just trying to make Alex see that it made no sense, at least from his point of view. "Look," I said, "if you want to do something for Scot Symon, go out there and show the people – the directors who have sacked him, the fans who have lost faith in him – that he did the right thing in signing you, that he knew a player when he saw one." Alex went out and scored twice in the next match – a 3-0 win over Cologne in a Fairs Cup tie.'

It is a measure of the respect and affection the now universally lauded Manchester United manager retains for Scot Symon that when I approached Sir Alex Ferguson and explained the purpose of this book, he was keen to co-operate and take time from his busy schedule to recall the Symon he knew and why he was such an angry young man when the Ibrox manager was sacked. Sir Alex said, 'When the players were at training I had no idea Symon had been sacked and it was only when we came out of the Albion training ground that I realised something was going on, as the road outside Ibrox was full of cars and television crews. There was genuine shock and disappointment among the players, particularly those who had grown up under Mr Symon's management. It was one of the darkest days in Rangers' history and the way it was done was shameful. Rangers sent an accountant, an old man called Alex McBain who had no connection with the club, to Mr Symon's house.

'It was a pretty poor way for a club with such an illustrious history as Rangers to treat their manager, who had been a player with them and who had managed the club for thirteen years. As players, as a group, we did not get the chance to say goodbye to him. He was not even given the chance to speak to us one last time, though he may have spoken to some of the long-serving players, but I have no idea if he even managed to do that.'

As Rangers coach and Symon's right-hand man, Bobby Seith was closer to what went on and he is able to paint a more detailed picture which serves to underline how duplicitous and disgraceful the actions of chairman John Lawrence and his bowler-hatted puppet, Willie Allison, were. Seith said, 'Mr Symon was not even allowed to return to Ibrox to clear out his desk and office of personal possessions. It was shabby. I had to do that for him and take things out to him at his house.'

Seith, despite talking Alex Ferguson out of quitting Rangers, had different thoughts about his own future and he recalled, 'I spoke to my wife about it and decided to follow my conscience. I know I had talked Alex out of it, but there was a difference in that Alex was at the peak of his playing career. I'd been Scot's coach and wanted no part in a club that could treat such a loyal servant in this way.

'Okay, he might never have got into a tracksuit – and in the end that might have been held against him – but he dedicated his life to the football club, helping them to win a lot of trophies. He was a man to be admired, as straight as a die.'

Seith resigned the next day, the same day Davie White was appointed as Symon's successor. Typically, despite his anger and deep hurt at the way he had been treated, Symon said, 'Davie is a very fine man and I wish him all the best. He is with a wonderful club.'

Looking back on how he, as a young player, viewed Symon, Sir Alex Ferguson said, 'He stood by his players and he never went out and publicly criticised them, and another thing which certainly came across was that he had a great inner strength.' And, as a young manager, the man who was to go on to rule in England for two decades, winning two Champions Leagues with Manchester United, Ferguson often listened to Symon when their paths crossed during the years Fergie was in charge at St Mirren and Aberdeen. He said, 'I often enjoyed his company when he was at Partick Thistle and, looking back, I rated him a truly very good manager.'

One thing Ferguson did seem to learn from Symon was the importance of an early start to the day, something for which the Manchester United supremo is well known in football and journalistic circles. Sir Alex said, 'He was in at his office every day at eight in the morning and did not leave until six at night. He only had one secretary, Isobel, to run Rangers. I know there is criticism that he was behind the times and was not a track-suit manager, but he did watch training every day and his presence was powerful. Also, he had taken on Bobby Seith as a coach the previous year, and he was a top coach and had a nice way with him. So, Mr Symon had actually placed Rangers in a good position to deal with the emergence of Jock Stein and the way the game was changing in the 1960s.

'Certainly there was very little in the way of team talks or tactics, but Mr Symon would remind us of our responsibility in wearing the Rangers jersey and also mention any opponent we should be aware of.'

The sacking of Scot Symon was the first major football story I was involved in as a teenager working on the editorial floor of the Glasgow *Evening Times*. My pal Neil and I had been at Ibrox on Saturday 28 October and we had both been disappointed at the way Rangers played in a 0-0 draw against Dunfermline. There had been criticism of a lack of goals from the team, though Ferguson, the big summer signing, had managed half a dozen during the time it takes every new arrival at Ibrox carrying heavy expectations to settle in. Certainly, there had been some booing directed at Symon when he took off one of their favourites, Alex Willoughby, and sent on Andy Penman, but the bulk of the jeers were aimed at the directors. Directors hated that just as much then as they do now. When supporters attack the board, it is usually the manager who suffers. But there had been no hint that Symon was under pressure. The team had gone out of the League Cup in the section stage, drawing with Celtic at Ibrox and losing unluckily 3-1 at Parkhead after taking an early lead and then missing a penalty before Celtic equalised.

In the league, though, an amazing goal from another Symon summer signing, Örjan Persson from Dundee United, had beaten Celtic at Ibrox and even after that 0-0 home draw against Dunfermline, Rangers were still at the top of the table and were undefeated with six wins and two draws from eight matches. If there was a problem getting goals, there was none keeping the back door shut – two goals conceded from eight outings.

The first hint I got that a bombshell was about to break came when I was hanging around the *Evening Times* sports desk talking to chief sports writer Gair Henderson. If memory serves me well, it was around nine in the morning. Gair's phone rang and when he picked it up it was clear to me something big was happening. Gair then signalled for me to keep quiet but to stay there, and I heard him say, 'Yes, Scot. Oh. Okay, right away.' He was almost off his chair before the phone was back on its cradle and was shouting across to sports editor Bill Stewart, 'That was Symon on the phone. He's just been sacked. I've got to go to his house. We'd better sort a photographer.'

My part in the story as a sixteen-year-old was small, helping to sift through pictures to illustrate Symon's career as a player and manager and sorting out the cuttings of stories printed about him down through the years so that dates and facts could be checked. One thing I can recall as though it were yesterday is that even in the hubbub of a busy big city evening newspaper, selling around 200,000 copies daily and printing anything between five and seven different editions every day, there was a sense of not merely shock, but unreality. The editor, S.L. 'Sam' McKinlay was not a football fan, but a golf man and he was old school, someone who, when I reflect, was cut from the same cloth as Symon. He shook his head and made some sort of comment about Rangers losing something more than a manager. As the full details of what exactly took place and as the world at large learned of how Rangers had gone about sacking Symon, the wisdom of those words became clear.

Alex McBain, an accountant who was friendly with chairman Lawrence but who had no connection with Rangers, was sent to Symon's house on the Tuesday night, just seventy-two hours after the goalless draw with Dunfermline. He offered Symon terms to resign. Symon had been ill in bed, suffering from a heavy cold. He was shocked at seeing McBain, who he recognised but did not know, and refused to take part in any subterfuge, probably plotted by Allison. Symon's reply was that he would not resign and that Rangers would have to sack him. He then slept on it – if, in fact, he could sleep. It must have become clear to him that he had to get his side of the story in first. That's why he chose to summon Gair Henderson from the *Evening Times* and George Aitken, of the *Evening Citizen*, to his house the next morning. Both were seasoned journalists, and although Symon did not have a close relationship with either, he had known them for many years and recognised they could be trusted. The story which broke in both evening newspapers was quite simply: SCOT SYMON SACKED BY RANGERS!

John Lawrence was now left looking both foolish and duplicitous. After trying to claim Symon had resigned, the Rangers chairman then tried to push the line that Symon had been offered a new contract and turned it down, thus effectively quitting. Nobody bought into it and all Lawrence succeeded in doing was increasing the criticism of him and Rangers and also the sympathy for Symon. Even those who felt it was time for Rangers to look for a younger man were angry at the club's behaviour and felt things should have been handled in a more dignified and proper fashion.

For a start, Lawrence should have met Symon privately, face to face. He could have offered Symon another position, even a seat on the board. Symon had certainly shown that he knew the changing times demanded that he move with them. Seith had been brought in as his coach a year before and in the summer of 1967 the young Davie White was Symon's choice as his assistant manager.

White had managed Clyde to third place in the top flight in season 1966-67 and, after having gone with Celtic to Lisbon to observe them and learn, he had travelled with Rangers to Nuremberg for the same purpose. Symon had been impressed and, despite White's only Ibrox credentials being that he supported the club, championed his appointment as assistant manager. It is also worth noting as further ammunition against those who unjustly claim that Symon was hidebound by Ibrox tradition, that coach Seith was another with no Rangers background. Clearly, Symon wanted White to work with him, learn from him, learn about Rangers and grow into the mammoth task of succeeding him as only the fourth manager in the club's then near one hundred year history. But White had only been at Symon's side for four months and was clearly – as subsequent events were to prove – a long way short of being ready to cope with Jock Stein's crafty ways.

While the history of Rangers is celebrated by glory upon glory at home and abroad, there have been some dark days and bleak periods for the club – especially recently. However, as far as football matters are concerned, the sacking of James Scotland Symon and the manner in which the club conducted itself, dealing with one of its own, was by far the most utterly shameful episode. In that context, it remains so.

41

DAVIE WHITE

WHATEVER John Lawrence and his cronies thought about Scot Symon's team, it was clear that the man they chose to replace him, Davie White, looked around the dressing room and liked what he saw. It was also clear there were others who liked what Symon left behind, for in April Portuguese giants Benfica tried to sign Andy Penman, a Symon capture, and Willie Johnston, another the manager had promoted when the winger was still a teenager. Rangers turned the Benfica bids down.

There is also little evidence to suggest the season which continued after Symon's shocking sacking played out any differently than it would have had he remained. Celtic were marginally better than Rangers. That is a fact. They were not streets ahead of their rivals, as Rangers had been in Symon's first ten years. Rangers, under Symon, had lost one and drawn one against Celtic in the League Cup and beaten Jock Stein's team in the league, with White drawing the return championship encounter at Parkhead. That fine margin was once again reflected and, indeed, underlined by the final league placings, Celtic on top with sixty-three points and Rangers just behind on sixty-one points.

Both sides had lost only once, the Rangers defeat coming at home to Aberdeen on the last day of the season. But the margin in Celtic's favour was created by the five matches Rangers drew, as opposed to the three drawn by Celtic. That is where the two-point difference came from. In the Scottish Cup, the best White could manage were wins over Hamilton Accies and Dundee, after a draw at Dens Park, followed by a third-round exit to Hearts, who held Rangers at Ibrox before winning at Tynecastle.

In Europe, competing for the first time in the now-defunct Inter-Cities Fairs Cup, Symon's side had a 3-2 aggregate win over Dinamo Dresden, then White took over and Rangers beat Cologne 4-3, after extra time, over two legs to set up an attractive quarter-final with Leeds United, who had emerged in the mid-1960s under Don Revie as a real force in England, boasting such outstanding stars as Scots Billy Bremner and Peter Lorimer, plus Jack Charlton, Terry Cooper, Norman Hunter and Johnny Giles.

Rangers rose to meet the challenge and more than matched Leeds in the first leg at Ibrox, but when Andy Penman missed a penalty kick the writing was on the wall and Leeds won 2-0 at Elland Road. But Symon's legacy included twenty-five goals from his last signing, Alex Ferguson, twenty from Willie Johnston, seventeen from another of his summer of '67 signing, Örjan Persson, plus fourteen from his captain, John Greig.

While all this was going on, Scot Symon was struggling to come to terms with what had happened to him and, amazingly, there was no stampede to batter down his door and offer him a job. The only offer came from lowly Dumbarton and he accepted the newly-created post of director of football. But it was clear Symon still had more to offer football and, perhaps deep inside this intensely private and ultimately extremely shy man, there burned a passion to prove wrong those who said he was too old.

For the record – and I have deliberately left this until now to highlight – when Rangers unceremoniously dumped him, Scot

Symon was a mere fifty-six years old. Contrast and compare. In January 2007, after the farcical fiasco of Sir David Murray's so-called French moonbeam, Paul le Guen, when Rangers turned to Walter Smith and begged him to return and save them, he was fifty-nine. Smith, when he arrived again, was three years older than Symon was when he left. At the other end of the scale, White was a mere thirty-six and, as a player with Clyde and then the Shawfield club's manager, had never had to cope with the pressures and demands of being involved with a club as big as Rangers, never mind managing it. After White had failed against Celtic in the opening weeks of season 1968-69, in the League Cup section, losing 2-0 at Ibrox on the opening day of the campaign and then 1-0 at Parkhead, it became obvious, even to chairman Lawrence and the powerful Willie Allison, that White needed help. He required wise counsel. A steadying hand. And a Rangers man.

Rangers turned to one of the greatest names in their history, Willie Thornton. Thornton had built the great Dundee team that emerged in the early 1960s, leaving Dens Park just before they won the title to take over as manager of Partick Thistle after the tragically early death of another great Ranger who was in charge at Firhill, Davie Meiklejohn. At Partick Thistle, Thornton had again displayed his aptitude at team building and his side were great entertainers whose high spot had been in season 1962-63 when the Jags finished third. When the call came from Ibrox, Thornton could not resist the lure of Rangers and he returned as assistant manager on 7 September 1968.

Partick Thistle had a long tradition of being able to squeeze an extra drop of talent out of Rangers men who were deemed past their sell-by date at Ibrox. At the time they were doing it with goalkeeper Billy Ritchie, allowed to leave Ibrox by Symon, just as they had with the man Ritchie had replaced at Ibrox,

George Niven. There was also a tradition of men who had played for Rangers managing the Maryhill men, with Thornton, an Ibrox post-war legend taking over from 1920s and '30s icon Meiklejohn. The way was open and obvious for Thistle, and within days of Willie Thornton heading off across the Clyde to return to his spiritual home, James Scotland Symon was back in full-time employment as a manager, in charge of Partick Thistle. By this time he was still only fifty-seven years of age, but he was a changed Symon. The trauma of being so brutally treated by Rangers stayed with him and, according to someone who was close to him during his Firhill years, Symon had lost his confidence as a manager.

Robert Reid is the venerable sage of Firhill, a man who bleeds red and yellow. He has been in and around the Jags for over half a century as a fan, programme editor, associate director and official historian, and can still be found in the old ground a couple of mornings a week keeping the records to pass on for posterity to examine. A combination of Reid's records, his memory and his judgment formed over a lifetime watching football and gaining a feel for Thistle greater than any other person has been invaluable in putting these often-neglected Symon years under the microscope and into context. It is all too easy to merely glance at Thistle's league positions during Symon's two seasons as manager – in the bottom half in his first campaign and relegated at the end of his second – and dismiss his time there as unsuccessful and a justification of Rangers unseating him, though not, of course, the way Lawrence and Allison went about that dismissal.

However, other facts emerged and, added to Reid's observations, the truth of Symon's last job as a football manager is much more complex. Reid said, 'The truth is we were on the slide before Symon arrived. The team was growing old and needed rebuilding, and there was not a great deal he could do. Having said that, I do believe he was too old for the job when he came to Thistle.'

But perhaps it was not the actual birth date that made Symon seem older than he actually was. Perhaps that illusion was created by his quiet, shy and gentlemanly demeanour at a time in the Swinging Sixties when respect and good manners were going out of fashion. Perhaps, too, Symon never recovered from the blow, the stab in the back, from Rangers.

Reid recalled, 'He would be in and around the ground, still wearing his soft hat, but I spoke to Davie McParland and he said that, although he did not wear a tracksuit, Symon watched training every day. But once, when we were sitting together on the team bus, he [Symon] asked me how I thought he was doing and what the Thistle supporters were saying about him. I found that curious, and it is the only time any Thistle manager has ever asked me such a question. I think he had lost his confidence as a manager.'

One thing, though, which Symon had not lost confidence in was young players. And the evidence of that belief in youth and in giving young talent its chance is there from the two years Symon spent as Partick Thistle manager. In fact, according to Robert Reid, the players Symon often picked in his second season were too young to cope with the rigours of a relegation fight. Though, again according to Reid, the fledgling Thistle team which found itself in the old Second Division just breezed through the campaign and were miles better than any other team, winning the title and bouncing straight back to the top flight.

Symon was replaced as manager by Thistle old boy Davie McParland in the summer of 1970, following relegation, and it was McParland who reaped the rewards of Symon's far-seeing policy. And not just by winning the Second Division. There was an even more tangible reward and even greater glory lying in wait for Symon's striplings, and it came at Hampden Park on an October afternoon in 1971. By that time Scot Symon was the general manager of Partick Thistle and, although he had no more direct contact with the players or the playing side, he was still available to provide help and advice, or even just to listen, and it is hard to imagine a young manager such as McParland would not have availed himself of Symon's shrewd wisdom. One thing McParland certainly did was avail himself of the players who Symon had promoted to the first team during his two seasons as Thistle manager and, in doing so, he gave Symon one last victory over Jock Stein and Celtic.

The part Symon played on the afternoon when Jock Stein and Celtic rolled up at Hampden, full of themselves and expecting to simply roll over the newly-promoted Thistle team, is either forgotten or perhaps even conveniently overlooked by those who may seek to venerate Stein and ignore Symon. For, of the eleven Partick Thistle players who took Stein's Celtic apart and won the Scottish League Cup 4-1 in what is the biggest Cup final shock in British football history, an amazing six were given their first team debuts by Symon. He spotted the potential of Alan Rough, Alex Forsyth, Ronnie Glavin, Dennis McQuade, Jimmy Bone and Bobby Lawrie and, just as he had through his thirteen years at Ibrox, he gave those six youngsters their head, trusting in their natural talent to shine through, and for it to be honed by the experience he was willing to let them gain at the top level. The substitute on that never-to-be-forgotten day in Partick Thistle's history was Johnny Gibson, a seventh who had been given his debut by Symon.

It is interesting to speculate on just what the Partick Thistle general manager with no more direct football involvement thought that October day in 1971, four years after he had been sacked by Rangers. Here was the Celtic team and manager, Jock Stein, who had caused panic in the Ibrox boardroom and stampeded the Rangers directors into getting rid of Symon. And here was a Partick Thistle team, more than half of whose players had been promoted by Symon, giving Celtic the sort of hammering his Rangers teams had handed them so often.

It must have indeed been a sweet moment for Scot Symon, though, in keeping with his low-key approach, there was no sign of Symon when everyone connected with the triumphant Jags partied as they had never partied before, or have done since. He was no doubt back in the family home, door closed and curtains drawn. And, of course, the after-match coverage in the media focused on the shock of the result, on young Thistle manager McParland, plus Jock Stein. Symon's contribution was completely overlooked and it is only now, thanks to my research and Robert Reid's records and kind co-operation, that the part Scot Symon played in Partick Thistle beating Celtic in the 1971 Scottish League Cup final can be fully recognised.

Symon continued in his behind-the-scenes role in administration as Partick Thistle general manager right up to 1984, by which time he was seventy-three and starting to suffer from failing health. The reason why he continued to work in a job which was unlikely to have fulfilled him can surely only have been that he did so out of financial necessity. Nobody knows for certain how much Symon earned as Rangers manager. Veteran sportswriter Rodger Baillie did get a close-up view of the Symon family lifestyle and compared it to that of a bank manager or headmaster, though not with the sort of pension such a profession would provide. That would put Symon in the £4,000 to £6,0000-a-year salary bracket at Ibrox. That's around £80 to £120 a week, at a time when, even with overtime, a skilled engineer could expect a weekly wage of £25 a week. However, despite being well enough paid, Symon never amassed the sort of fortune which leaves modern managers inured from the need to work if they are sacked. There was also no question of a big pay-off from Rangers. At best, Symon would have got a year's worth of money. It is also strange to realise that the time Symon spent at Firhill, first as manager and then general manager, was longer than his period as team boss at Ibrox. He sat in the office at the top of the marble stairs at Ibrox for thirteen years, but was with Partick Thistle for sixteen seasons.

Brian Scott, who by the late 1970s was the *Scottish Daily Mail's* chief sportswriter, recalled, 'When you went to Firhill during the week to see the manager, to get into the ground you had to ring the bell at a wee window and it was often Symon who opened it and let you in. It seemed strange seeing a man who had been such a successful manager of Rangers doing this.'

Robert Reid said, 'Molly Stallon, who was the Thistle secretary and a Jags legend herself, used to get fed up with Scot just hanging about the office, for there was not really enough work for him to do.' This reinforces my view that Symon, although by then in his seventies, still needed the job and that Thistle owner and chairman, that wonderfully colourful character, Tom Reid, had more regard for Symon than those at Ibrox who treated him so shabbily. For all of the hurt in his heart about that, Symon, according to Robert Reid, could never be either goaded or tempted into saying a bad word about Rangers, despite being given ample opportunity to do so.

Said Reid, 'There were plenty of people around Firhill then who had no great love for Rangers and who often tried to get him to talk about Rangers, but he never would. He was a gentleman and, as a man, I had great admiration for him. We got to know each other better when he was the official head of the Partick Thistle party when our youth team competed in a tournament in France.

Even though we sat together on the bus and talked, I always called him Mr Symon. He was just that sort of man, Very formal. I know he was a great family man, though he didn't discuss either his wife or his son or daughter much, but when he mentioned his wife he always referred to her as Mrs Symon.

'Which isn't to say he didn't have a sense of humour. Once, in France, we had to share a bus with the Celtic youth team, dropping them off for their game and then picking them up on the way back from our match. He asked me if we had to go to collect them, as he was tired. Could they not just make their own way? I thought he was serious and replied that it was out of the question, but then he smiled and said something about it being quite a story if we did leave them behind.

'He was not joking, though, when we were held up because Mo Johnston, then still a youth player, had mislaid his bag and was in the hotel trying to find it and Symon wanted us to leave him behind. That was probably because he hadn't been used to that sort of thing happening when he was with Rangers.'

Much of what Robert Reid has recalled gives a good picture of Symon in his latter years. But still, the image of him as dour, perhaps even snobbish, far removed from the man-of-the-people image Jock Stein cultivated, continues. Someone who was close to Stein at Parkhead during Celtic's great years is therefore better equipped to dispel this illusion about Symon more than anyone who played with him or for him at Rangers. Bertie Auld is the man, and he admitted that when he was appointed Partick Thistle manager in 1974, he arrived at Firhill with the idea of getting rid of Symon as his top priority. It was a view of Symon which was wrong and a perception Auld, after getting to know Symon, soon changed, as the former Rangers manager not only became a trusted friend and confidant of the rookie boss, but also offered Auld sage advice.

Auld said, 'One of the first things I wanted to do at Thistle was sack Scot Symon! The former Rangers manager was in a backroom capacity and I didn't want him looking over my shoulder. He had blanked me one day and I kept that in mind. I didn't think we would get on, but I am glad he stayed around. He became invaluable to me and was a superb confidant. Shortly after I had taken over, he pulled me aside and gave me a great bit of advice. He said, "Always tell the players what you think of them – no matter how harsh. Be truthful because these guys can get you the sack. They'll knife you in the back without any hesitation." I knew what he was saying, after the awful way he had been treated by Rangers.

'I enjoyed my talks with Scot in the manager's office at Firhill. He would tell me things about Rangers and I would exchange stories about Celtic. There was always a lot to talk about and I always found it fascinating. One thing that always came over was the fact he was a gentleman. However, it was obvious he was very hurt at the way he had been treated by Rangers.'

Thanks to a curious quirk, Symon only returned to Ibrox once as Partick Thistle manager. By the time he took over Thistle had been there in both the league and League Cup. His only return as manager came on New Year's Day 1970, always a thought-provoking time for Scots of Symon's generation and background, with the visit to Ibrox adding poignancy. Robert McElroy, whose book *Rangers: The Complete Record* has been an invaluable tool in my Symon research, who also publishes the *Rangers Historian* magazine, who has written many books on Rangers and who has been constantly pestered by me for help (which he has kindly given), remembered the occasion. McElroy said, 'Symon came out of the tunnel about fifteen minutes before the kick-off. This was not something he had done when he was Rangers manager. He stopped and looked around him, paying particular attention to the home dugout. I remember thinking that he had a wistful look in his eyes.'

Rangers beat Partick Thistle 3-1 that day, the opening goal coming after half an hour, being scored by one of the many young players given their chance by Symon, Willie Johnston. He did not put himself through the torment of visiting Ibrox with Thistle during his time as general manager, but there was to be one final homecoming for James Scotland Symon, just weeks before his death.

42

BACK AT IBROX

WILLIE WADDELL, another great Ranger and Scot Symon's closest friend in football, was the man who brokered a peace deal between Symon and Rangers. It was sealed on the night of 13 February 1985 at Ibrox Stadium. Rangers played a friendly against their oldest friendly foes, Dynamo Moscow. It was a friendship which stretched back to 1945 when Dynamo enjoyed what had been an all-conquering tour of Britain which, for their fitness and football, had them being talked about as the best team in the world.

It looked as though they were going to prove that they were when they streaked to a 2-0 lead over Rangers before 90,000 at Ibrox in a match during that immediate post-way era which is still talked of with awe by the few left alive who saw it and those who grew up listening to tales of it. It was the day when Dynamo tried to pull a fast one. As it was ostensibly a friendly, substitutes were allowed and the visitors attempted to get away with sending on a fresh player without withdrawing one. Legend has it that the joker in the Ibrox pack, Torry Gillick, having beaten an opponent he didn't recognise, stopped and counted twelve Dynamo Moscow men. Legend again has it that the biggest surprise to all was that Gillick could count to twelve without taking off his boots.

Rangers, inspired by Symon, fought back for a 2-2 draw and many, including Waddell, who played in the game and had a penalty saved by the great Tiger Khomich, insisted that it was Symon's finest performance in a Rangers jersey. Therefore, as Waddell, who had by 1985 returned to Ibrox, first as manager, then general manager, managing director and director, arranged for the heroes of 1945 to be present and parade in front of the crowd. Clearly, he wanted Symon there, and just as obviously the intensely private and proud Symon wanted nothing to do with it.

However, by this time, Symon, who was seventy-four, was in poor health and probably knew he had not long left. Even when he spoke to me about his old friend, Waddell never mentioned Symon's return to Ibrox and the part he played in it. In fact, it was only thanks to the computer-like memory of Rodger Baillie, who told me about Waddell's role, that the whole affair came to be put into context. Those who have ever been in Waddell's company will need to use no great imagination to conjure the conversation, as Deedle had a gruff, straight-to-the-point way of talking. Symon agreed to join his old comrades from 1945 and take a bow, but insisted he be introduced only as a former player and not an ex-manager. His pride and integrity, even as he battled against cancer, remained intact.

I was at that match against Dynamo Moscow in February 1985 and, even from my high vantage point in the old Ibrox press box, perched on the roof of the main stand, it was clear that Symon, wearing his trademark soft hat, was frail and ailing. The crowd gave him a rousing cheer, though there were perhaps some cheering that night who had booed him in October 1967 during his last match as manager. The game against Dynamo Moscow had come at a particularly low point in Rangers' fortunes, around eighteen months before the arrival of Graeme Souness, who sparked the Rangers revolution. For that reason there were only around 13,000 in the ground to see Symon take a final bow.

And Symon, who had been suffering from cancer, died two and a half months later, aged seventy-four, on 30 April 1985. His managerial record with Rangers is impressive, even when reduced to cold statistics: Six League Championships, five Scottish Cups and four Scottish League Cups – fifteen major domestic trophies in all, including the Treble of season 1963-64. In Europe, he took Rangers to the semi-final of the 1959-60 European Cup, plus blazed a trail that saw Rangers become the first British club to reach a European final when the Ibrox side made it to the 1960-61 European Cup Winners' Cup final. They reached the final of the same tournament again in 1967. His total tally of matches in charge of Rangers was 681, with 446 won, 114 drawn and 121 lost, with twenty-one of those defeats in Europe. Therefore, from the summer of 1954 until the autumn of 1967, Rangers lost only one hundred times to Scottish opposition.

But those are just bare facts. They don't add the glitz and the glamour of Symon's sides. They don't tell of the pounding on the wing of Alex Scott, the zest of Willie Henderson, the craft of Ian McMillan, the all-round brilliance of Jimmy Millar, the darts of Ralph Brand, the blond bombshell that was Davie Wilson or the blur of speed that was Willie Johnston. Nor do the cold statistics show the class of Eric Caldow, the excitement of Scottish football's first attacking full-back, Kai Johansen, the smoothness of Ronnie McKinnon, the outstanding skill and leadership of John Greig, to name just a few of the men Symon either bought, or in the case of so many, handed their chance by a manager who loved to throw young players in at the deep end.

And, of course, no amount of statistics, however impressive, could ever conjure the gold dust Scot Symon sprinkled on Rangers and Scotland when he bought Jim Baxter. Of all the players and all the opponents Symon picked and faced during thirteen years as the manager of Rangers, two names stand out: One is Baxter, and the other is Jock Stein.

The first was the apple of Symon's eye and showed just how the manager wanted Rangers to play, as if there could ever be any doubt about the football philosophy of a man who had signed Ian McMillan two years earlier. Baxter may have been a divisive figure in the dressing room, with Harold Davis, as honest and brave a man as Scottish football as has ever seen, believing Symon let Baxter get away with too much. But Symon himself once said, 'If Jim had actually done half the things even Jim said he did, never mind all the other stories which went around about him, he would never have been able to play for Rangers the way he did. Jim Baxter never let me down.'

And Baxter, whose respect and admiration for Symon were sincere, insisted, 'Scot Symon was a gentleman and, although he and I had a different outlook on life, I respected him. He would never do anything that was not for the good of Rangers and he cared very deeply for the club. He did not need to shout the odds, for all the players – me included – knew how much he cared, and I would never have done anything to let him down or cause him hurt.'

He also held sway over players long after both he and they had left Rangers. Alex Willoughby told the story of how, when he was playing for Hong Kong Rangers and was back in Glasgow on a visit, Symon, then at Partick Thistle, heard he was in town and sent word for Willoughby to call in at Firhill. Willoughby said, 'I had always wondered why he left me out for the European Cup Winners' Cup final in Nuremberg in 1967. I had come into the team the week after the Scottish Cup defeat at Berwick and not only scored a lot of goals, but I knew I had been playing well. Then, with the European final coming, he dropped me. I was so angry I asked for a transfer, and it was not long after that I left, though I never wanted to leave Ibrox. Rangers were always my club.

'So I went to see him, and I still called him Mr Symon, but I was determined to ask him about why he dropped me. We sat together for an hour or so talking about this and that, and as I left he wished me well for my career. But I still had not asked him. I just could not bring myself to. He was that kind of man.'

Perhaps more than any other aspect of his management, Symon's apparent lack of faith in trusting Alex Willoughby as a regular was his biggest mistake. The inside-forward was a craftsman of the old school, who also weighed in with goals, and for those who never saw him play, think Steve Davies.

And so to Jock Stein, a man about whom so much more has been written since his death, which came a mere five months after Symon passed away. A classic example of this is veteran commentator Archie Macpherson's 1991 autobiography *Action Replays*. As well as a whole chapter entitled 'Taking on Mr Stein', the Celtic manager features over and over again in Big Archie's otherwise excellent book. I say otherwise, for there is only one mention in the book of Scot Symon.

Macpherson recounts being in a Perth restaurant just after Symon had been sacked and just after the reporter had gone on television and declared that Symon did not fit the future. At that point, what is every journalist's nightmare – someone you recently rubbished appearing – became a reality. For approaching Macpherson's table was James Scotland Symon.

It is what big Archie describes next which tells us a great deal about Symon. Macpherson said, 'Symon told me that if his wife had got hold of me the previous Saturday she would have torn the eyes out of my head. He then added that, for himself, he accepted that I was entitled to my opinion.'

What Macpherson did not speculate on, despite a seeming obsession with Stein stories, is how Stein would have reacted in similar circumstances. My view is that the courtesy and dignity, even at a time of such extreme personal hurt, which Symon showed, would not have been forthcoming from Stein.

I have already gone through why, as a tactician, Symon's reputation has suffered unfairly in comparison to Stein's, citing the way the Ibrox manager outfoxed him over the one hundred and eighty minutes of the 1966 Scottish Cup final. There are other examples of how Stein fell far short of being the tactical genius many of his biographers and others, such as Archie Macpherson, would have us believe he was. The 1970 European Cup final is a good example. Stein told his players that Feyenoord playmaker, Wim van Hanegem, was no more than a poor man's Jim Baxter. The elegant left-footed Dutchman then proceeded to unpick all of Stein's plans and the so-called tactical genius could not come up with a solution as Celtic lost a match we were all told they would win with ease.

Stein had been lucky in not having had to deal with a similar problem three years earlier, as Inter Milan's world-class playmaker Luis Suarez missed the match with an injury, as did brilliant Brazilian winger Jair. To put that into context, imagine Celtic in their first final without Bertie Auld and Jimmy Johnstone. There was also the curious spell of Stein's forty-four days as manager of Leeds in 1978 after he was sacked by Celtic. Whichever way the Parkhead club sought to spin the story and however much they continue to attempt to dress up his departure, every picture tells a story. And the look on Stein's face as his old captain Billy McNeill was presented by chairman Desmond White as his successor told all.

Stein had been fired, just as Scot Symon had been eleven years before, though unlike Rangers, Celtic at least plunged the dagger into his chest. I was part of the press pack interviewing Stein at Highfield Road after a Leeds visit there to play Coventry, and he looked like a man struggling out of his own wee backyard. It was as if he knew, looking round the unfamiliar faces, that there were none there who he could intimidate in the way he bullied so many Scottish newspapermen. Stein leapt at the chance to get out of the shark-infested waters of English football and return to Scotland on 25 October 1978 to take over as Scotland manager.

According to every newspaper, Scotland was about to experience the second coming. It didn't work out that way, as Scotland failed to reach the finals of the 1980 European Championships but did get to the World Cup in Spain in 1982. Stein took to Spain what many believe was the best Scottish squad to leave these shores. It included eleven players who either had already won or would win winner's medals in either the European Cup, Cup Winners' Cup or UEFA Cup: Jim Leighton, Allan Evans, Gordon Strachan, Graeme Souness, John Wark, John Roberston, Kenny Dalglish, Steve Archibald, Alan Brazil, Willie Miller and Alex McLeish. Others of an impeccable pedigree who Stein had available were Joe Jordan, playing in his third World Cup finals, and Celtic's Danny McGrain, who was performing in his second finals.

Yet Stein's record was exactly the same as Ally MacLeod's had been in Argentina: played three, won one, drawn one and lost one. Unlike MacLeod, though, Stein, who manipulated the press as puppets, escaped without any censure. I dealt with him during the last eighteen months of his life and found him a bully, but shrewd and well informed. At least, that is to say, he knew all about my background, where I grew up, where my dad came from, who my particular press pals were and the pubs I preferred. When you climbed the stairs to the attic dookit that was his office at the Scottish Football Association's headquarters at Park Gardens on a Friday morning, you knew that Stein knew where you had been and who you had been with in the week which had passed since you last saw him.

It was often uncanny and intimidating, and I always pondered on just why the Scotland manager was interested in where a still relatively young reporter chose to go for a drink. There is no evidence to suggest Scot Symon ever took such an unhealthy and, indeed, perhaps sinister interest in the private lives of reporters.

And then we come to comparisons between James Scotland Symon and John 'Jock' Stein as men. Symon's reputation is unblemished, without even the hint of scandal. He was, as everyone who spoke about him, from Sir Alex Ferguson to Jim Baxter, Celtic's Bertie Auld and Partick Thistle's Robert Reid, a gentleman. He was also a family man. Stein's reputation as a man is more complex, though you would never think so by reading the many biographies about him and other books in which he looms large. For a start, there was the gambling, which has been touched upon in some books, and his best friend outside of football was well-known Glasgow bookie Tony Queen. Symon's closest friend outside the game was his old cricketing team-mate, Alma Hunt. There has also been talk of Celtic having to pay off a Stein gambling debt of the then considerable sum of £40,000. It is doubtful if Symon was ever in a bookmaker's shop or even knew how to write a line. Stein also had a reputation as a womaniser, including an affair with one now-deceased newspaperman's first wife. And, according to one of Scotland's most experienced news reporters, who told me this in the 1980s, Stein had a long-standing affair with a professional dancer. He knew this, he told me, because he had courted another member of the same dance troupe.

Finally, when comparing Stein the man with Symon the man, there is one aspect that must be mentioned. That is the sexual abuse of young boys that existed on the Parkhead doorstep for a decade or more and which led to the pervert who ran Celtic Boys' Club, James Torbett, being jailed. Among those who testified about what had gone on when Stein was manager was one of the players he took to the 1982 World Cup finals, Alan Brazil.

During Torbett's trial, evidence was given that it was unlikely such a thing could have gone on right under Stein's nose without Stein having at least got wind of it. Celtic directors gave evidence that they could not believe Stein would have known about Torbett's grooming and molestation of young boys and not taken action. Of course, Celtic Boys' Club formed no official part of Celtic Football Club. Against that was my own experience of Stein's vast store of personal knowledge about my background and movements, plus the many books by those who played for him, and others who were around at the time, who love recounting how Stein knew just what everybody at Celtic Park and beyond got up to.

When researching Scot Symon, one story about a Stein book-which-never-was was told to me by a well-known football writer. He claimed he had been told it by someone with a pedigree about writing on Celtic matters. This writer mentioned to an extremely famous broadcaster and writer that he was considering writing a warts-and-all biography on Stein, only to be advised that such a book would probably not be in his interests. And so, the Stein myth continues, and until now the pride of place Scot Symon should have, not just in the history of Rangers, but in the annals of Scottish football has not been afforded him.

Scot Symon was a giant of a figure in Scottish football. Remember, he won two League Cups with East Fife and took Preston North End to a Wembley FA Cup final, all while he was still learning the managerial ropes. But of course, he reached his pinnacle of power during those thirteen years in charge at Ibrox, during which time Rangers were league champions six times, Scottish Cup winners five times, League Cup winners four times, European Cup semi-finalists once and European Cup Winners' Cup finalists twice. He even managed to blood more than half the Partick Thistle team that won the Scottish League Cup, beating Jock Stein's Celtic in 1971. Towering achievements. Yet in the landscape of Scottish football they appear to have been pushed aside and forgotten.

I knew he deserved greater recognition than he has had when I started researching and writing this book, but it was only as the project moved along and previously unknown facts were unearthed, previously unregaled memories unlocked and other aspects pored over, that I grew to realise that Symon was an even better manager, larger figure and greater man than I had previously believed him to be.

Now, it is my earnest wish and hope that I have done some sort of justice in placing him more firmly in the public consciousness and giving him his historical position in Scottish football. A position denied him for so long, but one he most surely deserves to have.

Rangers should acknowledge this and put right a great wrong by naming something other than a small room at the back of the Govan Stand after this giant from the club's history. It would go some way to making amends for the dastardly way such a fine servant was sacked. For if there is one name which is not properly celebrated at Ibrox and in the wider circles of Scottish football, it is that of James Scotland Symon. Scot Symon.

SCOT SYMON'S
MANAGERIAL RECORD

East Fife
League Cup Winners 1947–48, 1949–50.

Preston North End
FA Cup finalists 1953–54.

Rangers
League Champions 1955–56, 1956–57, 1958–59, 1960–61, 1962–63, 1963-64.
Scottish Cup Winners 1959–60, 1961–62, 1962–63, 1963–64, 1965–66
League Cup Winners 1960–61, 1961–62, 1963–64, 1964–65.
European Cup semi-finalists 1959–60
European Cup Winners' Cup finalists 1960–61, 1966–67.

Partick Thistle
League Cup 1971–72 (as general manager)

BIBLIOGRAPHY

Docherty, David. *The Rangers Football Companion*. John Donald.

Esplin, Ronnie (ed.). *Ten Days That Shook Rangers*. Fort Publishing.

Esplin, Ronnie R. and Graham Walker. *The Official Biography of Rangers*. Hachette.

Gallacher, Ken. *Slim Jim Baxter: The Definitive Biography*. Virgin Books.

Greig, John with Jim Black. *John Greig: My Story*. Headline.

Macpherson, Archie. *Action Replays*. Chapmans.

McElroy, Robert. *The Enduring Dream*. Tempus.

McElroy, Robert and Bob Ferrier. *Rangers: Player By Player*. Crowood Press.

McElroy, Robert and Bob Ferrier. *Rangers: The Complete Record*. Breedon Books.

McPhail, Bob with Allan Herron. *Legend: Sixty Years At Ibrox*. Mainstream.

Peebles, Ian. *Growing with Glory: The 100 Year Story of Rangers FC*. Rangers FC.

Taylor, Hugh. *The Scottish Football Book*, nos. 4 to 13. Stanley Paul.

Taylor, Hugh. *We Will Follow Rangers*. Stanley Paul.